Praise for
Think and Grow Rich for Women

"*This book is going to impact the lives of millions of women all over the world, and rightly so, as the principles that both Napoleon Hill and Sharon write about are universal and will work for everyone everywhere. Any woman who makes the content of this book a part of her way of thinking, a part of her way of life, will accomplish every objective that comes to her mind.*"

—**Bob Proctor**, chairman, The Proctor Gallagher Institute,
and author of *You Were Born Rich* and featured in *The Secret*

"*Move over gents, Sharon has become the new voice of modern inspiration.*"

—**Greg Reid**, best-selling author of *Stickability* and
coauthor of *Think and Grow Rich: Three Feet from Gold*

"*If you are looking for a book to read that will inspire your being and move you to achieve your biggest goals,* Think and Grow Rich for Women *is the answer! The world of business is a much better place as even more women have become wildly successful entrepreneurs and business owners. Sharon has a gift to bring out the best in everyone around her through her words, thoughts, and actions. The insight and wisdom that is shared in this book is exactly what every aspiring entrepreneur needs to read to understand specifically what it takes to succeed in life and business!*"

—**Bill Walsh**, America's small business expert

"*Sharon Lechter goes about her work with passion.* Think and Grow Rich for Women *is simply a book that needed to be written for today's woman to help her grow and serve others.*"

—**Don Green**, CEO, the Napoleon Hill Foundation

"*I believe that* Think and Grow Rich for Women *is the right book and written at the right time to bring Napoleon Hill's science of personal achievement to millions of women. It is destined to become a classic for all women with desire to realize their potential.*"

—**James Blair Hill, M.D.**, Napoleon Hill's grandson

"*Napoleon Hill was a man of great vision and remarkable perception. He had an amazing ability to take massive concepts and mold them into facts that we all could understand and utilize for our betterment. It seems fitting that Sharon Lechter can now lend her well-defined knowledge and understanding of Napoleon's success principles to help women shatter any vestiges of the glass ceiling.*"

—**Charles Johnson, M.D.**, Napoleon Hill's nephew

Think and Grow Rich for Women

Using Your Power to Create Success and Significance

SHARON LECHTER

Authorized by the Napoleon Hill Foundation

JEREMY P. TARCHER/PENGUIN
a member of Penguin Group (USA)
New York

JEREMY P. TARCHER/PENGUIN
Published by the Penguin Group
Penguin Group (USA) LLC
375 Hudson Street
New York, New York 10014

USA • Canada • UK • Ireland • Australia
New Zealand • India • South Africa • China

penguin.com
A Penguin Random House Company

Earnings and unemployment rates by education attainment chart on p. 68 courtesy
Bureau of Labor Statistics, Current Population Survey.

Fortune 500 Women CEOs chart on p. 97 courtesy Catalyst, *Historical List of Women CEOs of the Fortune Lists:
1972–2013* (2013). Based on the percentage of women CEOs at the time of the annual published Fortune 500 list.

Opposing Force Paradox illustration on p. 211 copyright © Donna Root.

Supply and demand illustration on p. 212 copyright © Donna Root.

The Six Rs of Transformation illustrations on pp. 213 and 214 copyright © Donna Root.

Most Tarcher/Penguin books are available at special quantity discounts for
bulk purchase for sales promotions, premiums, fund-raising, and educational needs.
Special books or book excerpts also can be created to fit specific needs.
For details, write: Special.Markets@us.penguingroup.com.

Library of Congress Cataloging-in-Publication Data

Lechter, Sharon L.
Think and grow rich for women : using your power to create success and significance / Sharon Lechter.
p.   cm.
ISBN 978-0-399-17082-9
1. Businesswomen.   2. Success in business.   3. Success.   4. Businesswomen—Case studies.
5. Success in business—Case studies.   6. Success—Case studies.
I. Hill, Napoleon, 1883–1970. Think and grow rich.   II. Title.
HD6053.L3495   2014   2014006260
650.1082—dc23

Printed in the United States of America
1   3   5   7   9   10   8   6   4   2

BOOK DESIGN BY TANYA MAIBORODA

This publication is designed to provide accurate and authoritative information in regard to the subject matter
covered. It is sold with the understanding that the publisher is not engaged in rendering legal, accounting, or other
professional services. If you require legal advice or other expert assistance, you should seek the services of a
competent professional.

While the author has made every effort to provide accurate telephone numbers, Internet addresses, and other
contact information at the time of publication, neither the publisher nor the author assumes any responsibility for
errors, or for changes that occur after publication. Further, the publisher does not have any control over and does not
assume any responsibility for author or third-party websites or their content.

Contents

Foreword
from Women Who Know

WHEN I WAS GROWING UP IN SOUTHWEST VIRGINIA, I WAS encouraged to read Napoleon Hill, a local boy who grew up in our hills and "made good." It wasn't enough for Mr. Hill to become a star in our heavens . . . he was determined to bring us all along with him. He wanted success for everyone, and encouraged us to believe that there was no obstacle we could not overcome on the way there.

Sharon Lechter not only honors Napoleon Hill's work, but she is the walking embodiment of his philosophy.

She takes his philosophy and applies it to women, our specific needs and our particular paths to success. Of course, Ms. Lechter addresses the themes of juggling life and work with such wisdom and practical advice that you will feel a sense of empowerment and relief (!) as you read the pages. Ms. Lechter takes the stand that you can have it all, because in your heart and soul you already possess all you need to make it on your own terms. I will give this book to every young woman I know who is looking for help on the path to success.

Adriana Trigiani
New York Times *best-selling author*
from Napoleon Hill's hometown

The philosophy of my grandfather Napoleon Hill permeates everything that I do as a woman, wife, and mother. I am delighted that Sharon Lechter has brought to the public *Think and Grow Rich for Women*, a book that can help all women to achieve success in anything to which they aspire.

There were books by Napoleon Hill scattered about our home well before I went off to college. I earned my degree in pharmacy and chemistry and became a registered pharmacist. Within a few short years, I found myself very busy with four sons. I made up my mind that raising my boys would be my primary profession.

For the next twenty years, I adapted Napoleon Hill's principles of success to help me build character in my sons while giving them the tools needed to succeed in life, including setting goals so that they were never without a purpose.

My sons responded well to this approach and each has done well. Three of our sons are medical doctors and another is a top-tier corporate employee. My brother, James Blair Hill, once told me that he thought the book was the key to everything—financial security, personal relationships, and happiness, and that it could be used to achieve anything of value. The Hill family has made good use of Napoleon Hill's legacy.

I know that every woman who reads *Think and Grow Rich for Women* will gain insight that will help her in the many aspects of a woman's life, whether inside or outside the home.

Terry Hill Gocke
Napoleon Hill's granddaughter

Introduction

SO WHY WRITE *THINK AND GROW RICH FOR WOMEN*?

The rules of success are the same for everyone. Why mess with the brilliance of Napoleon Hill's original book, *Think and Grow Rich*? Why write something special just for women?

These questions, and many more, are sure to be asked. In fact, for most of my career, I have felt the same way. I originally read *Think and Grow Rich* when I was nineteen and have read it many times during my career, and it has had a huge, positive impact on my life.

My parents taught me that I could be anyone or do anything I wanted as long as I worked hard and focused on my goals. They had worked hard all their lives and were fabulous role models. It wasn't until I started my career, all alone in a different city, that reality started to set in. It was in the late 1970s and I was one of only a few women in my field. I quickly learned that I definitely had to work harder than my male counterparts if I wanted to get ahead. So I did.

No one said it would be easy—and it wasn't. No one said it would be a smooth ride—and it hasn't been. But the resilience and lessons I learned from facing and surviving the tough times were essential contributors to my success today.

Now, more than thirty-five years later, I continue to be amazed by the stories of the incredible businesswomen I meet and how they too, in the face of the glass ceiling or sexual bias, found ways to forge ahead. Many of them had read and followed the teachings of *Think and Grow Rich* and created great success in their lives, but they have gone even further. They have each taken their success in stride and continued on to open new paths for the women who follow them, evolving their lives of success into lives of significance.

Think and Grow Rich for Women is a celebration of these women and every woman who has succeeded in spite of the obstacles she has encountered—women who have changed history, created great business success, and provided great opportunities for others.

In addition, there have been some incredible economic developments that have brought greater attention to successful women, and in doing so, have revealed that while the rules may be the same, women approach those rules differently, and they apply them differently than men do. While there is still much progress to be made, there has been a "quiet revolution" as women have gained momentum in every aspect of life. The following statistics showing the increasing power of women are the most recent available at the time of this writing.

IN THE ECONOMY

These financial statistics prove, without a doubt, that women have tremendous power and influence globally. Can you imagine what would happen if women came together and used their economic power to create positive change?

- 60 percent of all personal wealth in the United States is held by women.[1]

- 85 percent of all consumer purchases in the United States are made by women.[2]
- Women over the age of fifty have a combined net worth of $19 trillion.[3]
- Two-thirds of consumer wealth in the United States will belong to women in the next decade.[4]
- $7 trillion is spent by women in the United States in consumer and business spending.[5]
- Globally, women are responsible for $20 trillion in spending, and that number is expected to rise to $28 trillion by the end of 2014.[6]
- Globally, women stand to inherit 70 percent of the $41 trillion in intergenerational wealth transfer expected over the next forty years.[7]

IN EDUCATION

The United States Department of Education estimated that in 2013 women earned:

- 61.6 percent of all associate degrees;
- 56.7 percent of all bachelor's degrees;
- 59.9 percent of all master's degrees;
- 51.6 percent of all doctorate degrees.

In summary, in 2013, 140 women graduated with a college degree at some level for every hundred men.

IN THE CORPORATE WORLD

While tremendous progress has been made in the lower ranks of management, there is still a great need for women to advance to the higher levels of leadership in corporations, which is evidence that the glass ceiling still needs to be shattered:

- There are twenty-three, or 4.6 percent, women CEOs of Fortune 500 companies.[8]
- Women hold 14.6 percent of executive officer positions.[9]
  - According to a report by *Catalyst* titled "The Bottom Line: Corporate Performance and Women's Representation on Boards," Fortune 500 companies with the highest representation of women board directors attained significantly higher financial performance, on average, than those with the lowest representation of women board directors. In addition, the report highlights that boards with three or more women directors show notably stronger-than-average performance. It shared three key measurements:
    - ◊ **Return on Equity:** On average, companies with the highest percentages of women board directors outperformed those with the least by **53 percent**.
    - ◊ **Return on Sales:** On average, companies with the highest percentages of women board directors outperformed those with the least by **42 percent**.
    - ◊ **Return on Invested Capital:** On average, companies with the highest percentages of women board directors outperformed those with the least by **66 percent**.[10]
- Women hold 16.9 percent of board seats in the United States, as compared to 40.9 percent in Norway, and 6 percent in Asia.
  - It is important to note that Norway passed a law in 2003 requiring companies to appoint women to 40 percent of board posts.[11]
  - A study of companies in the MSCI AC World index, which is an index designed to measure the equity market performance of developed markets in twenty-four countries, found that companies with a gender-diverse board outperformed those with only men by 26 percent over six years.

IN EARNINGS

While the overall statistics are still disturbing, when you dig into the detail, a positive trend emerges:

- Women are paid an average of 77 cents for every dollar men make. In 1970, it was 59 cents.[12]
- While the 77 cents statistic has remained constant over the last few years, a total of sixteen states report that their women are earning 80 cents or more for every dollar men make.[13]
- When you exclude self-employed and workers who work only part of the year, in 2012 women earned 80.9 percent as much as men.[14]

And a review by age group shows significant improvement for younger women. According to the Bureau of Labor Statistics:

PAY EQUITY BY AGE

Age Groups	Women's Percentage of Men's Earnings
20–24	93.2 percent
25–34	92.3 percent
35–44	78.5 percent
45–54	76.0 percent
55–64	75.1 percent
65+	80.9 percent

- Globally, men's median full-time earnings were 17.6 percent higher than women's in developing countries. The biggest gender wage gap was in Korea and Japan.[15]
- Globally, according to a Deloitte study, women's earning power is growing faster than men's in developing countries. Their earned incomes have increased by 8.1 percent, compared with 5.8 percent for men.[16]

IN BUSINESS OWNERSHIP

More and more women are shunning the corporate world in favor of entrepreneurship, thereby circumventing the impact of the glass ceiling altogether. The "State of Women-Owned Businesses Report" for 2013 (commissioned by American Express OPEN) reveals:

- Between 1997 and 2013, the number of women-owned firms has grown at one and a half times the national average;
- The number of women-owned and equally owned firms is nearly 13.6 million and they:
    - generate more than $2.7 trillion in revenues;
    - employ nearly 15.9 million people;
    - represent 46 percent of U.S. firms and contribute 13 percent of total employment and 8 percent of firm revenues.

IN POLITICS

More women are entering politics than ever before. The following statistics, however, show there is still a far way to go to reach parity with male political leaders.

Globally:[17]

- There are thirty-two female leaders in countries or self-ruling territories.

In the United States, women hold:

- 20 percent of seats in the U.S. Senate;
- 17.9 percent of seats in the U.S. House of Representatives;
- 23.4 percent of state-level elective offices.

As women realize their economic power and start leveraging it, these statistics will continue to improve. In addressing this global shift at the World Economic Forum, the International Monetary Fund's managing director, Christine Lagarde, talked about the power of what she termed "inclusive growth." She stated, "The evidence is clear, as is the message: when women do better, economies do better."

While I look at these statistics and applaud the progress women have made, and are making, I realize that there are many other women who still react to them with anger. Is there still progress to be made? Of course there is! Certainly, the fact that the glass ceiling is still holding down the number of women in the top executive positions and corporate boardrooms, as well as the fact that there is still a formidable pay gap between men and women, both continue to challenge women striving to excel in the corporate world.

But instead of focusing on the negatives, let's acknowledge the positive accomplishments of women leaders in business, both as corporate leaders and entrepreneurs, in politics and education today, and let's celebrate these women. Celebrate them for their courage, their success, and their leadership. Then let's come together as women to provide mentoring to younger women and tell them that they can be anyone, or do anything they want, as long as they work hard and focus on their goals. Women must help other women to succeed.

Facebook chief operating officer Sheryl Sandberg triggered a media blitz when she called for women to "lean in" and pursue their careers aggressively. In her book, *Lean In: Women, Work, and the Will to Lead*, released in 2013, she encouraged women to adopt traditionally "male" characteristics like working long hours, taking credit for performance, and being outspoken.

Many of her critics pushed back, saying she was an elitist and out of touch with middle-class working women who cannot afford expensive nannies, while others criticized her for focusing on internal issues that women face, rather than the external issues of equal pay and opportunity and condemning current male-dominated corporate executive suites and boardrooms for not inviting more women to join their ranks.

Both positions have valid issues; instead of criticizing each other, it is time to join forces for the betterment of all women.

Some of Sheryl's comments about the women, their struggles, and how to overcome them rang very true for me and I would like to share them:

> Throughout my life, I was told over and over about inequalities in the workplace and how hard it would be to have a career and a family. I rarely heard anything about the ways I might hold myself back.

> Don't put on the brakes. Accelerate. Keep your foot on the gas pedal. When more people [women] get in the race, more records will be broken. More female leadership will lead to fairer treatment for *all* women.

As I read her book, I saw Sheryl sharing her own successful career path as a woman, and the decisions that she made along the way, in the hope that it would provide inspiration to other women. One of her strongest messages is that women are taught that they need to limit their drive for power, which in turn limits their own ambitions and as a result often sabotages their careers.

I believe many, if not most, women do face self-confidence issues. While one woman may not be able to change the law regarding equal pay and opportunity, every woman can change her own internal dialogue about her ability to be successful. *Think and Grow Rich for Women* focuses on how women today can shed the chains of old thinking and old paradigms, and confidently create a life of success and significance.

I would highlight the fact that what helped successful women succeed in the past may not be the right advice for women seeking success in the future. While I agree that women need to face their own internal struggles, often about work/life balance, I believe that rather than telling women to be more like men, we should highlight the benefits found in female leadership that may be better suited for today's business environment.

As women have increased their numbers and influence in the workforce over the last decade, the business world as a whole has also been changing. We have moved from the Industrial Age into the Information Age, and there has been a spiritual change in the way business is done. The Industrial Age was one where competition was king. The competitive environment created a win-lose or dog-eat-dog philosophy in business dealings.

Today I see a very different business environment: one built on collaboration, strategic partnerships and alliances, and joint ventures; one that nurtures a win-win philosophy; and one where the parties will seek and find ways to leverage each other's strengths for the benefit of the ultimate consumer. This collaborative, cooperative environment is one where women do and will thrive.

Given the change in women's global influence and the change in the way business is done, I believe we are at a true *tipping point* for women. For years, women have told me they want a guide that is relevant to them, written by women who have created success in their own lives. I have studied successful women of the past, interviewed successful women of today, and analyzed *Think and Grow Rich* and its thirteen steps to success for women through the eyes and experience of these successful women. I have to admit I resisted writing a book for women for many years. But now is definitely the right time for *Think and Grow Rich for Women.*

The book addresses the issues women face today with real-life advice on how to overcome obstacles and seize opportunities—from family issues, to job advancement, to business ownership. For years, women have been taught that they should be able to have it all. They should be able to choose to work full-time or part-time, or work from home while still getting married, having children, and managing a household. But there were no rules or guidebooks on how to have it all—and keep your sanity in the process.

Think and Grow Rich for Women debunks the work/life balance guilt trip that women struggle with. I personally believe the word "balance" was created by a group of old male psychologists who saw the rise of women in the workplace and wanted to make sure they had a steady stream of female patients—women tormented with guilt and frustration with their inability to achieve the psychologists' definition of "balance."

In fact, I can't remember a time when a man has complained to me about work/life balance. Can you?

By the end of the book, my hope is that you will find your voice and that you will realize you have tremendous power and tremendous opportunity to create the life you choose. The most powerful word is "choice." You can replace the guilt from feeling out of balance with the power to make different choices. You can replace the goal of seeking work/life balance with the goal to seek one big life filled with love, family, satisfaction, success, and significance.

All that said, this is not a male-bashing book by any means. Although Napoleon Hill is the *only* man quoted in the body of the book, he is not the only man who has influenced my life for the better. Nevertheless, I wanted to focus exclusively on women as the sources for the book, and found it to be an unexpectedly huge task to find quotes by women for the subjects covered in each chapter—proof positive that we need this information and that we need to support one another as women of success and significance.

In the afterword, however, I invited some of the men I consider to be champions for women to share their thoughts on the importance of the messages found in *Think and Grow Rich for Women*.

Hill's original work, *Think and Grow Rich,* was written based on his interviews with more than five hundred of the most successful men of his time, as well as thousands of people who considered themselves failures. For *Think and Grow Rich for Women*, I invited many women to share their expertise with my own, in the desire to create a similar compilation of success for women. So, just as *Think and Grow Rich* was a compilation of success wisdom derived from many successful men, *Think and Grow Rich for Women* provides a compilation of wisdom derived from many successful women.

The book follows the same chapter outline as that of the original *Think and Grow Rich*. Each chapter begins with a contemporary review of the teachings of Napoleon Hill. The chapter review is followed by the personal stories of women thought leaders who have employed the lessons of that chapter to achieve success in their lives. Then I share how I have employed Napoleon Hill's lessons in my own life and the wonderful discoveries I have made along the way.

I include in each chapter a Sisterhood Mastermind. Napoleon Hill introduced the power of the Mastermind as an integral and necessary step to achieving success. So the Sisterhood Mastermind for each chapter shares a group of quotes from incredible women who further highlight the importance of the messages and lessons of that chapter. Think of every woman in the book as available for your personal Mastermind.

To wrap up each chapter I have added an Ask Yourself section. In order for us to achieve success, we must take action. This section takes the messages and lessons of the chapter and asks you to apply them to your own life. Use a personal journal to help you record your thoughts as you read how each of Hill's original steps to success is presented through the eyes of successful women. *Think and Grow Rich for Women* was truly written for you. You can find downloadable PDFs to assist you in the Ask Yourself section and additional resources at www.sharonlechter.com/women. This section will help you more quickly identify areas where you can ignite and accelerate your own path to creating the life *you* wish to achieve.

May you be blessed with success!

Sharon Lechter

Burning Desire

It's the Starting Point of All Achievement.
You Must Have Burning Desire.

■

I was a woman with a mission and
single-minded in the pursuit of my dream.
—ESTÉE LAUDER

DO YOU KNOW YOUR BURNING DESIRE?

You may be asking yourself, "Do I have a burning desire?" Different than a simple want for something, a burning desire may feel like a need to do something or accomplish something. It starts out as an idea or realization and grows to become a driving force behind your everyday actions. It is guided by your personal values and infiltrates your decision-making processes. In your dreams, expectation of yourself and your life, as well as your passions, you will most likely find your BURNING DESIRE!

You may instantly be reminded of a goal you have had for a while. It could be a personal, business, financial, physical, or spiritual goal. If you have yet to achieve the goal, ask yourself why. Is it possible that this goal has NOT been backed with the burning desire you needed to reach it successfully?

Now, turn the tables. Think of a time when someone has described you with one of the following terms: Passionate. Driven. Purposeful. Focused. Committed. Determined. Motivated. Single-minded. Compelled. Doggedly in pursuit. Devoted. Consumed with obsession. Pledged. Steadfast. Unswerving. Staunch. Dedicated. Headstrong.

More than likely, you were in pursuit of something for which you had a true burning desire.

When you combine a definite goal with a burning desire to achieve that goal, it will provide you with the necessary fuel (motivation, drive, stamina) to create and execute a plan that will allow you to realize that goal successfully.

In *Think and Grow Rich*, Napoleon Hill focused on burning desire as it related to financial wealth when he wrote:

> Every human being who reaches the age of understanding of the purpose of money, wishes for it. *Wishing* will not bring riches. But *desiring* riches with a state of mind that becomes an obsession, then planning definite ways and means to acquire riches, and backing those plans with persistence which *does not recognize failure*, will bring riches.

He provided six steps to take that are both definite and practical to turn your DESIRE for wealth into financial reality, summarized for you as follows:

First. Be definite about the *exact* amount of money you want (DESIRE).

Second. Commit to what you are willing to do in exchange for the money you desire. (There is no such reality as "something for nothing.")

Third. What is the exact (definite) date you intend to *possess* the money you desire?

Fourth. Create a definite plan of action, and begin it *at once.* A goal without a plan is simply a wish without burning desire. Do not procrastinate.

Fifth. Write a personal mission statement, a mantra, a clear, concise statement of the amount of money you want to acquire, the time limit you are giving yourself to acquire it, what you intend to give in exchange for the money, and describe clearly the plan, or action steps you will take to accumulate it.

Sixth. Read your mantra twice daily, once just before bedtime and once every morning.

AS YOU READ IT, SEE AND FEEL AND BELIEVE YOUR-SELF ALREADY IN POSSESSION OF THE MONEY.

Here is where a BURNING DESIRE will come to your aid. If you truly DESIRE money so keenly that your desire is an obsession, you will have no difficulty in convincing yourself that you will acquire it. The object is to want money, and to become so determined to have it that you CONVINCE yourself you will have it.

Only those who become money conscious ever accumulate great riches. "Money consciousness" means that the mind has become so thoroughly saturated with the DESIRE for money that one can see one's self already in possession of it.

This particular section of Hill's comments focused specifically on accumulating financial riches. In fact, his statement "'Money consciousness' means that the mind has become so thoroughly saturated with the DESIRE for money, that one can see one's self already in possession of it" has raised questions for some readers.

In fact, it gives me pause every time I read the book.

Many may react to this one line because of its apparent conflict with the biblical admonition "The love of money is the root of all evil."

Certainly there have been many examples throughout the history of money where excess wealth has brought out the worst in people, revealing who they really are inside their soul. If you are unkind, getting more money will just make you even more unkind. The inverse is true as well, however. If you are naturally generous, receiving more money will probably make you much more generous.

Since Hill was interviewing the richest people in the world, most of whom were also very philanthropic, I have chosen to reread this section as "money consciousness means that the mind has become so thoroughly saturated with the DESIRE for money, *so one can do more good works*, that one can see one's self already in possession of it." I believe he confirms this version of the statement when he continues the discussion referring to "great leaders":

> One must realize that all who have accumulated great fortunes, first did a certain amount of dreaming, hoping, wishing, DESIRING, and PLANNING before they acquired money.
>
> You may as well know, also that every great leader, from the dawn of civilization down to the present, was a dreamer.
>
> A BURNING DESIRE TO BE, AND TO DO is the starting point from which the dreamer must take off. Dreams are not born of indifference, laziness, or lack of ambition.

The resistance I felt about Hill's reference to desire for money is probably also partly due to the fact that I am a woman. A 2013 *Forbes Woman* article by Peggy Drexler, Ph.D., assistant professor of psychology in psychiatry at Weill Cornell Medical College, addresses how men and women define success in different ways.

> What does success really mean? The reason more women ask is because the answer is likely more complex for them than it is for men. Gender intelligence expert Barbara Annis believes

the definition of success for men is simple. It's winning. Success might come in the form of more money or a better job or a better parking space or a hotter wife. But success is about besting the competition, in any number of contests, period. Women, of course, want to win, too. But Annis argues they also want to be valued. She relates that in her experience as a consultant to a range of Fortune 500 companies, the number one reason women leave their jobs is that they feel their work is undervalued and their strengths are overlooked.[18]

"We've all bought into this male definition of success, money, and power, and it's not working," Arianna Huffington, cofounder and editor in chief of the *Huffington Post*, said on the *Today* show in June 2013. "It's not working for men, and it's not working for women. It's not working for anyone."

Huffington Post asked its Facebook and Twitter communities what success meant to *them*. I don't know if their efforts qualify statistically as a scientific survey, but I think the results speak volumes about how women are defining what it means to be powerful and what it means to be successful. In an article written by Emma Gray in July 2013, she shared Valerie Jarrett's statement from the *Huffington Post*'s Third Metric Conference: "You can have it all, but you can't have it all at the same time." She then shares the nineteen things that mean success from their survey.

HERE ARE NINETEEN THINGS THAT MEAN SUCCESS, ACCORDING TO *HUFFINGTON POST* READERS:
1. Doing something impactful and loving every minute of it.
2. Finding the good in life's imperfections.
3. Realizing that your contribution to the world is valued, if not by others, by you.
4. Making a difference by teaching *others* to achieve success.
5. Living and loving fully, without shame and without apology.

6. Promoting a just cause, such as the fight against ethnic profiling.
7. Going to the beach every day!
8. Making your family happy.
9. Playing an active role in achieving gender equality.
10. Having the ability to control your own schedule.
11. Being healthy—and having a job that helps other women do the same.
12. Having the strength to try, try again—even when you fall flat on your face.
13. Being proud of yourself.
14. Doing your best and being grateful for everything good in your life.
15. Finding a healthy balance between a loving home and a career you enjoy.
16. Having people in your life who can always make you smile.
17. Loving what you get to do for a living.
18. Knowing that your daughter will be able to stand up for what's right and is not afraid to be herself around others.
19. Learning to be in the moment instead of constantly going, going, going.[19]

While this survey may not have been performed scientifically, its answers are certainly consistent with my personal definition of success. When I have been asked to define success, my answer is: success is how you feel about yourself when you look in the mirror at night—and it has nothing to do with your reflection!

Does this mean women don't want to become wealthy? Absolutely not! But I do believe that women look at wealth much more holistically. They desire money for what they can do with it, not just for the money itself. Hill's advice related to acquiring financial success is equally applicable in the areas of personal, physical, spiritual, or business success. So let's review how Hill's six steps would read from that more holistic viewpoint:

Follow these same six steps, but focus them on the object of your BURNING DESIRE.

First. Be definite about the *exact* amount of impact you want to have, or change you want to see (DESIRE).

Second. Commit to what you are willing to do in exchange for achieving that impact. (There is no such reality as "something for nothing.")

Third. What is the exact (definite) date when you want to complete it?

Fourth. Create a definite plan of action, and begin it *at once.* A goal without a plan is simply a wish without burning desire. Do not procrastinate.

Fifth. Write a personal mission statement, a mantra, a clear, concise statement of what impact you want to have, the time limit you are giving yourself to complete it, what you intend to give in exchange for achieving it, and describe clearly the plan, or action steps you will take to accomplish it.

Sixth. Read your mantra twice daily, once just before bedtime, and once every morning.

Then, most important, SEE, FEEL, and BELIEVE that you are already successful in achieving your goal.

When you find yourself wanting to do something, or achieve something, to change something, or to become something so badly that you can think of little else, you are in a state of BURNING DESIRE.

You will find you become even more focused on your goal, and, more important, you will find peace of mind.

One of the greatest examples of someone who demonstrated a BURNING DESIRE that was certainly not financial in nature was Mother Teresa of Calcutta, who dedicated her life to helping the poor, the sick, and the dying around the world, particularly those in India. She felt a calling and burning desire to go out and help the poor while living among them and she inspired millions with her absolute devotion. She dedicated her life to instilling hope and creating joy where none existed.

Mother Teresa's own words describe her commitment and burning desire to promote unconditional love around the globe: "Let us not be satisfied with just giving money. Money is not enough, money can be got, but they need your hearts to love them. So, spread your love everywhere you go."

Blessed Mother Teresa was proof positive that one woman can change the world!

But she was not alone. While not as well known as Mother Teresa, Wangari Maathai was another great woman of history who was a great example of BURNING DESIRE set into action. Educated in the United States in biology, she became the first woman in east and central Africa to receive a doctoral degree and she was the first African woman to receive the Nobel Peace Prize.

She founded the Green Belt Movement in 1977, when she recognized that hundreds of thousands of women in Kenya were forced to walk miles for firewood and water. The country had been deforested and was plagued with drought and poverty. Her answer was simple: plant trees. So she began paying African women small amounts to plant the trees.

The trees helped prevent further erosion and eventually created firewood for fuel. The results from this one woman's tireless efforts can be seen and measured in the 51 million trees that women all over Africa have planted since 1977. She credited her success to education, service, a clear vision, personal responsibility, and self-determination, and she achieved clear results by taking action, with justice and integrity, not just advocating or complaining.

In her own words, "When we plant trees, we plant the seeds of peace and hope."

As to the source of her burning desire, she said, "I don't really know why I care so much. I just have something inside me that tells me that there is a problem, and I have got to do something about it. I think that is what I would call the God in me."[20]

But the very essence of a woman's journey for success and significance was best described by Oprah Winfrey, one of the most successful and wealthiest self-made women in the world, during her commencement speech to the graduates of Harvard on May 31, 2013. She shared that, while she is considered by most to be at the pinnacle of her success, she had to employ these same six steps when she found herself faced with "the worst period" in her professional life.

Even though it is hard to imagine someone like Oprah feeling stressed and like she had stopped succeeding, you will feel the power of her emotion as she describes how she found the BURNING DESIRE to succeed, gave herself a time limit, and created the plan that would turn her business around. The *Oprah Winfrey Show* had been number one for more than twenty years when Oprah ended the show and launched OWN, the Oprah Winfrey Network. After all those years of being the epitome of success, she had decided "that it was time to recalculate, find new territory, break new ground." She was used to success, had become "pretty comfortable" with the level of success that she had achieved with the *Oprah Winfrey Show.* She expected a similar triumph with OWN ("The initials just worked out for me"). OWN, however, did not initially live up to expectations. In Winfrey's words:

> . . . nearly every media outlet had proclaimed that my new venture was a flop. Not just a flop, but a big bold flop they call it. I can still remember the day I opened up *USA Today* and read the headline "Oprah, not quite standing on her OWN." I mean really, *USA Today*? Now that's the nice newspaper! It really was this time last year the worst period in my professional life. I was stressed and I was frustrated and quite frankly I was actually embarrassed.[21]

It was right around that time that Oprah received the invitation to address the Harvard graduates. Her confidence shaken from the panning of OWN, she had doubts: "What could I possibly say to Harvard graduates, some of the most successful graduates in the world, in the very moment when I had stopped succeeding?"[22]

As she described it, inspiration came to her in the shower (chosen in lieu of a bag of Oreos). She remembered the words of an old hymn: "By and by, when the morning comes. Trouble don't last always, this too shall pass." At that moment she committed to turn her network around, so she could share it with the Harvard graduates.

After thanking the graduates for providing her the motivation to drive the network to new heights of success, she went on to tell them that they should build résumés to tell their own stories, résumés that tell what they want to accomplish in life and why, not just with dates and lists of their accomplishments in life. She advised that it is their personal stories and their personal whys that will get them through those difficult times in life when they stumble and fall. Then she asked them each to think about their true calling, their true purpose.

Then Oprah shared her personal story of discovering her true purpose. Her inspiration came from a nine-year-old girl who had started collecting pocket change to help people in need. All by herself, the little girl had raised one thousand dollars. Oprah wondered what she could accomplish if she followed this little girl's example.

So Oprah then asked her viewers to start their own change collections. And in one month, Oprah's viewers sent in more than $3 million. She was able to send a student from every state in the United States to college. This began her Angel Network.

Oprah's Angel Network expanded dramatically; through the continued support and generosity of her faithful viewers it has been able to build fifty-five schools in twelve different countries and restored almost three hundred homes that were destroyed by hurricanes Rita and Katrina. Even though she had been on television for a long time, the success of the Angel Network helped Oprah redefine her purpose and redirect her influence on television. The goals of her shows, interviews, business endeavors, and philanthropy became focused on issues that unite rather than issues that divide.

I recommend you read her address to the Harvard graduates in its entirety. Oprah mesmerized the graduates, but her message was truly universal and applies to each of us. She pointed out that everyone falls down at some point in their life, but "[f]ailure is just life trying to move us in another direction." The key, she said, is to:

> . . . learn from every mistake because every experience, encounter, and particularly your mistakes are there to teach you and force you into being more who you are. And then figure out what is the next right move. And the key to life is to develop an internal moral, emotional G.P.S. that can tell you which way to go.[23]

She opened her heart to them in her closing statement, speaking with passion, sincerity, and great hope for their future:

> From time to time you may stumble, fall, you will for sure, count on this, no doubt, you will have questions and you will have doubts about your path. But I know this, if you're willing to listen to, be guided by, that still small voice that is the G.P.S. within yourself, to find out what makes you come alive, you will be more than okay. You will be happy, you will be successful, and you will make a difference in the world.[24]

It has been said that Oprah Winfrey is a great fan of *Think and Grow Rich* and Napoleon Hill. Certainly her belief that everyone should be responsible for their own lives is consistent with Hill's philosophy.

Most of us have grown up influenced by the major impact Oprah Winfrey has had in both media and philanthropy. But there is also a great movement among many younger women who are taking the reins of entrepreneurship and not only creating great financial success stories, but also coupling their financial success with philanthropic significance as well. Two of those women are Sara Blakely and Tory Burch.

Sara Blakely had a BURNING DESIRE to reform the women's undergarment industry, which has kept women in painful and ill-fitting undergarments for well over fifty years. From being a greeter on one of the rides at Disney World and a stand-up comedian to becoming the world's youngest female self-made billionaire, she is a fabulous example of how to turn your BURNING DESIRE into a fabulous success—and significance.

At the age of twenty-nine, Sara was frustrated when she couldn't find footless body-shaping undergarments to wear with her cream slacks and toeless shoes. She invested her life savings of five thousand dollars and SPANX was born. From having her new line of shaping underwear named one of Oprah's Favorite Things to creating an exclusive line called ASSETS for Target, Blakely has driven SPANX from a one-product company to an organization with more than a hundred styles and several hundred million dollars in annual revenue. She has retained 100 percent ownership in the private company and has never advertised.

Her advice: "Believe in your idea, trust your instincts, and don't be afraid to fail. It took me two years from the time I had the idea for SPANX until the time I had a product in hand ready to sell into stores. I must have heard the word 'no' a thousand times. If you believe in your idea 100 percent, don't let anyone stop you! Not being afraid to fail is a key part of the success of SPANX."

In 2006, she used her success to focus on helping others. She formed the Sara Blakely Foundation, which is dedicated to helping women globally through education and entrepreneurship. In 2013, at the young age of forty-two, she became the first female billionaire to sign the Gates-Buffett Giving Pledge.

Not only did Sara's fierce passion and commitment create incredible financial success for her and provide significance through financial support for so many young women around the globe through her foundation, but almost every one of us can say that we have benefited in our personal appearance by discovering the product of her BURNING DESIRE—SPANX! Thank you, Sara Blakely.

Sara is joined by yet another self-made female billionaire in her forties, Tory Burch. Tory created her success by seeing a void in the fashion market and stepping in to fill it. Tory launched her affordable, sophisticated, and ready-to-wear women's clothing line affectionately referred to as preppy-bohemian, from her kitchen table in 2004 with a clear vision and plenty of passion but only a basic knowledge of business.

In 2006, she launched her best-known product, a $195 pair of leather ballet flats, naming them Reva after her mother. Then, in 2010, Oprah included Tory's Reva flats in her final Favorite Things episode. According to *Forbes*, her company brought in close to $800 million in revenues in 2012, and in 2013 *Forbes* added her to its renowned billionaires list.

Inspired by her own experience as a successful businesswoman and a working mother, she launched the Tory Burch Foundation in 2009. Rather than simply start a charity to hand out money, she wanted to create opportunities for women to build their own businesses so they could find financial independence for themselves and their families. Through her foundation she provides loans ranging from five hundred dollars to fifty thousand dollars to women entrepreneurs in the United States through small business loans, mentoring programs, and entrepreneurial education. Its entrepreneurial education program is in partnership with Goldman Sachs 10,000 Small Businesses Program, LaGuardia Community College, and Babson College.

In an article for the *Huffington Post*, Tory also addressed the global initiative by Goldman Sachs when she wrote: "Over the last five years, Goldman Sachs 10,000 Women has proven that investing in women around the world is one of the most effective ways to reduce inequality and facilitate economic growth. When women are empowered it leads to healthier, better-educated families, and ultimately more prosperous communities."[25]

I find it quite interesting that both Tory Burch and Sara Blakely shared a spot on Oprah's Favorite Things lists. Oprah has catapulted so many businesses to new heights through her powerful recommendations and media exposure. In fact, I also experienced and was thrilled by Oprah's passion for financial education and for individuals taking responsibility for their own financial lives when, in 2000, she featured one of my books on her show. Oprah shared that she learned as a young girl, "if you want to move forward in life, you have to make it happen for yourself." She has certainly made it happen for herself— and helped millions of others along the way.

While Oprah, Sara, and Tory became self-made billionaires because they built their businesses from the ground up, many other women find success and financial independence from joining existing businesses. There are franchises as well as network marketing organizations that provide education, mentoring, and lower-risk opportunities for women wanting to build a business. Franchises usually cost a bit more than joining network marketing companies, but both offer proven models of success.

Donna Johnson shares her journey of a struggle of survival, and then great success and significance when she joined a network marketing organization and, to use her words, "Went all in!"

I grew up in Wisconsin in a middle-class family. We quickly moved to lower class when my father left our family (me and four brothers) with no child support and a mother determined to see us through. I soon learned to be grateful to have hand-me-down clothes from my cousin. My dad went to California to strike it rich in the printing business. Even when he was a success, he never sent money to help us, and told my brothers that "he expected the government to take care of us." He died young, leaving the majority of his wealth to employees.

I vowed never to be him and never to be helpless like my mom. This happened during my early teens, so I dove right into swimming, eventually competing at a national level.

I went ALL IN, which, I discovered later, was a pattern for me. Oftentimes, people will see their obstacles as a barrier for success, but I didn't know any better. I saw my obstacles as something simply to overcome. I kept my head down and focused, just like I did in the swimming lane I was competing in.

Since I didn't have the finances for college, I married young, started a family, and coached swimming. This of course is not a profitable endeavor. I coached for the sport and love of the children, but it certainly didn't put food on the table. When I found myself facing divorce with three small children, and an ex who didn't provide enough finances to support us, I realized I needed a plan. Not a job, a man, or a family to bail me out.

The first book I read on personal development and success was Napoleon Hill's *Think and Grow Rich*. I was completely blown away by the timeless concepts he taught, and was encouraged that someone like me, a poor kid from the poor side of town, could actually achieve success. I saw a glimpse of success with swimming, since those I competed against didn't have a sign on the starting blocks, saying they were more privileged or smarter than me.

I used my circumstances to dive ALL IN. I started my network marketing business with a goal to achieve five thousand dollars per month. That was twenty-six years ago, and I reached that goal in five months.

A few years later, I achieved six figures per month, and I've never looked back. I realized the only way I can make sure those I am helping earn what I'm earning is to keep going and do more. I also understood that if I wanted to make a difference, and help people, I could give more if I earned more.

I have supported a youth ministry, even when I was broke in the early days, and we support many orphanages around the world through my Spirit Wings Kids Charity.

I always teach my team, the book *Think and Grow Rich* is not "Grow Rich and Think." Don't put the cart before the horse. Be the person you see yourself in the future. You may not be able to give and serve at the scale you will when you reach your goals, but just start now and let it grow organically. Life is a journey, not a destination, and BE NOW, the person you always wanted to BE!

Have you noticed a common thread that runs through all of these women's stories? They each believe in the importance of giving back to, and serving, their communities and people in need. In fact, they are passionate about it. Napoleon Hill said, "You give before you get." It is a simple statement, but so very true. Let's review some of the supporting statistics released by the 2012 Bank of America Study of High Net Worth Philanthropy conducted by the Center on Philanthropy at Indiana University.

- 95 percent of high net worth households give to charity.
- 62 percent of high net worth donors cite "giving back to the community" as a chief motivation for giving.

In addition, the National Philanthropic Trust reports that:

- 64.3 million adults volunteered 15.2 billion hours of service, worth an estimated $296.2 billion.

A Harvard Business School study titled "Feeling Good about Giving: The Benefits (and Costs) of Self-Interested Charitable Behavior" reported that its findings supported the following theory:

> Happier people give more and giving makes people happier, such that happiness and giving may operate in a positive feedback loop (with happier people giving more, getting happier, and giving even more).

But the study also drew a distinction between giving for the sake of giving (without an attached self-interest) and giving in anticipation of a personal benefit, indicating further study is needed in the latter.

But there are other benefits to giving, either financially or of your personal time. There is the obvious, and well-publicized, advantage of the ability to deduct your financial contributions and certain aspects of volunteering for tax purposes.

More important are the personal benefits that come from giving back. The positive feedback loop, highlighted by the study from Harvard, itself has even greater rewards. The act of giving not only creates happiness, but will almost certainly improve your own sense of well-being and self-worth. You may discover your sense of purpose and inner satisfaction. In working closely with a charity you will become more educated about its specific purpose, whether it be social injustice or health related. Just by learning more about the charity you will be able to share it with your network of influence and "spread the word (and work)" of that particular cause.

Often people report that their spiritual lives were strengthened through their charitable work. Most certainly, you expand the opportunity to build your social networks and contacts while you are receiving the mental and spiritual benefits of your willingness to give back.

Debra Mesch, Ph.D., the director of Women's Philanthropy Institute (IUPUI), released a report called Women Give 2012, which revealed that boomer and older women are more likely to give to charity and give more than their male counterparts when other factors affecting giving are taken into consideration. They tend to make their donations for more personal reasons and tend to make more donations in smaller amounts than men do.

So Napoleon Hill's words "You give before you get" are validated not only by the women's stories shared in this chapter but also by the scientific studies and research.

CHAPTER IN PRACTICE—IN MY LIFE

My *burning desire* was lit when I was very young. As a little girl my father would ask me each night, "Sharon, have you made a difference in someone's life today?" Even though I lost my father years ago, I still ask myself that question each night.

From volunteering at school and church, to becoming a Girl Scout when I was young, to serving on several community and national nonprofits today, giving back and serving others has always been an important part of my life.

In business I have been fortunate to combine my passion as an entrepreneur, a woman, and a mother with my business endeavors. After starting a women's magazine and building the industry for talking books—children's books that make sounds when touched—my *burning desire* has become more focused in the last twenty years on financial education for young people and women, as well as business-building tools for entrepreneurs.

I don't call what I do work because it gives me back much more than I invest.

And as a result of the success I have been blessed with, I have been able to maintain my passion and combine my philanthropic endeavors with my business ventures. I support a financial initiative each year for high school students, work with many women's groups in providing financial seminars and coaching, as well as work with business owners helping them get to the next level. While these are my businesses, I reinvest a portion of the money I earn into providing those same services to people through my nonprofit initiatives. I receive the greatest joy when I see "the lights turn on" when a young woman trying to rebuild her life comes up with an idea as well as the courage to pursue it. This constant fuel keeps my *burning desire* burning strong!

THE SISTERHOOD MASTERMIND

Wisdom from women of success and significance on BURNING DESIRE:

MARY KAY ASH (1918–2001)
AMERICAN BUSINESSWOMAN AND FOUNDER
OF MARY KAY COSMETICS

"We must figure out how to remain good wives and good mothers while triumphing in the workplace. This is no easy task for the woman who works full-time . . . with your priorities in order, press on and never look back. May all of your dreams come true. You can, indeed, have it all. I want you to become the highest-paid women in America."

MAYA ANGELOU
BORN MARGUERITE ANN JOHNSON,
AMERICAN AUTHOR AND POET

"Ask for what you want and be prepared to get it!"

"You can only become truly accomplished at something you love. Don't make money your goal. Instead, pursue the things you love doing and then do them so well that people can't take their eyes off of you."

"Success is liking yourself, liking what you do, and liking how you do it."

MURIEL SIEBERT (1928–2013)
FIRST WOMAN TO OWN A SEAT ON THE
NEW YORK STOCK EXCHANGE

"If you are going to sit there and wait for other people to do things for you, you will soon be eighty years old and look back and say, 'Hey, what did I do?' My mother had a God-given voice, and she was offered a place on the stage, but nice Jewish girls didn't go on the stage in those days. So, I grew up with a woman who was frustrated her entire life. I certainly wasn't going to continue that role. I vowed I would do whatever I wanted to do."

INDIRA GANDHI (1917–1984)
INDIA'S THIRD PRIME MINISTER

"Have a bias toward action—let's see something happen now. You can break that big plan into small steps and take the first step right away."

MARGARET THATCHER (1925–2013)
PRIME MINISTER OF THE UNITED KINGDOM (1979–1990),
THE LONGEST-SERVING PRIME MINISTER OF THE TWENTIETH
CENTURY AND THE ONLY WOMAN TO HAVE HELD THE OFFICE

"What is success? I think it is a mixture of having a flair for the thing that you are doing; knowing that it is not enough, that you have got to have hard work and a certain sense of purpose."

"There can be no liberty unless there is economic liberty."

"You may have to fight a battle more than once, to win it."

TORY BURCH
AMERICAN FASHION DESIGNER AND BUSINESSWOMAN

"I think you can have it all. You just have to know it's going to work."

J. K. ROWLING, BORN JOANNE "JO" ROWLING
BRITISH NOVELIST BEST KNOWN AS THE AUTHOR OF THE HARRY
POTTER FANTASY SERIES

"Achievable goals are the first step to self-improvement."

YVONNE CHUA
PRESIDENT (2013–2014), LICENSING EXECUTIVES SOCIETY
INTERNATIONAL; PARTNER WITH WILKINSON & GRIST, SOLICITORS
& NOTARIES, HONG KONG

"Love what you do, and do what you love, with a vision of your own and respect for the support around you. Let the cream rise to the top."

I share these quotes from women whose words have inspired me in my life's journey in hopes that you will find something that ignites your BURNING DESIRE and drives you to incredible success and significance.

In the original *Think and Grow Rich*, Napoleon Hill warned: "There is a difference between WISHING for a thing and being READY to receive it. No one is ready for a thing, until he *believes* he can acquire it. The state of mind must be BELIEF, not mere hope or wish. Open-mindedness is essential for belief. Closed minds do not inspire faith, courage, and belief."

How do we transform our dreams, hopes, wishes, and BURNING DESIRES into total BELIEF in ourselves? The next chapter will guide you through successfully visualizing and believing in the attainment of your burning desire with the second step toward riches, FAITH.

ASK YOURSELF

Use your journal as you go through this section to identify your action steps, trigger your "aha" moments, and create your plan for achieving success!

Have you identified your BURNING DESIRE?

Take a moment to record it in your journal.

If you are having difficulty defining your BURNING DESIRE, close your eyes and try to remember a time when someone has described you as one of the following:

Passionate. Driven. Purposeful. Focused. Committed. Determined. Motivated. Single-minded. Compelled. Doggedly in pursuit. Devoted. Consumed with obsession. Pledged. Steadfast. Unswerving. Staunch. Dedicated. Headstrong.

Record the activity, project, or goal to which they were referring. You may have several different answers. Review them and measure your emotional reaction to each. It may help you identify, or refine, your BURNING DESIRE.

Now create goals and record them by identifying them by the following categories:

Personal
Business
Financial
Physical
Spiritual

For each goal, ask yourself the following questions and record your answers:

Is it really YOUR goal?
Is it ethical, moral, and attainable?

Are you willing to commit yourself to the goal, emotionally
and physically?
Is there a deadline to attain it? (If not, create one!)

Write the specifics of your plan on how you intend to
achieve the goal by the deadline given.
Can you visualize yourself reaching this goal?
Create a mantra, a personal mission statement for achieving the goal most closely aligned to your BURNING DESIRE.
Write it out on a sticky note and paste it on your bathroom
mirror.
When you look in the mirror tonight, say to yourself, "I am
fabulous. I can do this!" Then read your personal mission
statement.
Repeat morning and night until you realize your goal!

Giving Back

Record in your journal the ways you have given back to your
community, either financially or through volunteering your time
and talent.
How did it make you feel?
Are there other charities that you would like to support?
Can you commit to increasing your volunteer efforts each
month for the next six months?
Record what you are willing to do or give.

Congratulations on identifying your burning desire and committing to become more charitable. Your positive feedback
loop is engaged!
You are fabulous!

Faith

Visualization of, and Belief in, Attainment of Desire

■

Faith is the strength by which a shattered
world shall emerge into the light.
—HELEN KELLER

WHAT IS THE FIRST THOUGHT THE WORD "FAITH" TRIGGERS IN your mind?

Napoleon Hill challenged the notion that faith is only about religious belief. FAITH, or lack thereof, truly defines your destiny. It creates the road map that your subconscious follows. Negativity and lack of faith beget more negativity. On the other hand, optimism, positivity, and faith create the foundation from which success can be built.

The feeling and knowledge of faith carry tremendous power, wherever applied. Faith is fuel that drives us when our muscles are weak and our minds are tired, but our spirits are still on fire! Faith is the nourishment that will sustain us when the world seems to bear no fruit. Faith can be inspired but ultimately is found within each individual and therefore cannot be taken away. Faith is ours to discover, to lift us up, and to share with others so that they too may find faith in themselves.

What does faith look like? This will be different for each individual. You may demonstrate faith through encouragement of others. Perhaps you persist at the one task that is key to your definite purpose but that you have not yet mastered. It could be the impassioned debates you have with others who doubt your purpose. Faith inspires action!

When addressing the importance of faith, acknowledgment needs to be given to the forces that work against it—worry, anxiety, and self-doubt being among the main culprits. Although these tendencies may be part of the human condition, it is up to each of us to determine how big a role they play in our lives.

Hill stated that "FAITH is a state of mind which may be induced, or created, by affirmation or repeated instructions to the subconscious mind, through the principle of autosuggestion."

He also explained that when your FAITH combines with the vibration of your thoughts, it triggers your subconscious mind, which, in turn, communicates to Infinite Intelligence. He uses prayer as the example.

So ask yourself what you have really been praying for lately. What are you affirming in your mind and into your subconscious? Is it faith, or are you allowing faith's countermeasures to maintain power over you? Does your self-talk result in positive autosuggestion?

Worry and anxiety are both effective countermeasures to faith and ones to which women are particularly susceptible. It is so important for women to understand the role they play in their lives. They impact self-confidence, their FAITH in themselves, and their feelings of worthiness—all of which are major factors in achieving success—or not! You cannot have strong FAITH in yourself and be self-confident if you are suffering from anxiety and depression. So how is this any different for women than it is for men?

A January 2013 article written by the staff of the Mayo Clinic titled "Depression in Women: Understanding the Gender Gap" reports that approximately twice as many women as men experience depression—

and about one out of every five women develops depression at some point in her life. While there is much controversy as to the specific causes, hormonal changes (puberty, premenstrual problems, pregnancy, postpartum depression, perimenopause, or menopause), inherited traits, and life experiences all are known to contribute to depressive tendencies.

The article goes on to describe certain life situations, including cultural issues that are also stressors for women more than for men. The first is unequal power and status from the fact that women are more likely to live in poverty than men and don't feel in control of their lives. Certainly the well-known existence of the glass ceiling and the inequality of pay that still exists for men and women doing the same job both contribute greatly to women feeling unequal in power and status. The cultural realities that still exist in parts of the world where women are simply not valued enough for their contributions to family, community, and economy are certainly contributors as well.

The second life situation they refer to is work overload, where women who work outside the home still shoulder the domestic responsibilities for child rearing, household maintenance, and even caring for the older generation.

It is a natural result of these feelings of inequality, lack of status, and work overload that women would feel more insecure than confident, and more worrisome than faithful. It is almost impossible to be depressed and self-confident at the same time. Depression is destructive, while self-confidence and faith are constructive.

Regardless of the controversy over the exact causes of stress in women, what is important is that we focus on how to build, how to construct our self-confidence. In doing so, we are focusing positive thoughts and energy to create success in our life.

Let's review Hill's reminder definition of FAITH and the role it plays in creating success in your life:

Have Faith in yourself: Faith in the Infinite.

FAITH is the "external elixir" which gives life, power, and action to the impulse of thought!

FAITH is the starting point of all accumulation of riches!

FAITH is the basis of all "miracles" and all mysteries which cannot be analyzed by the rules of science!

FAITH is the only known antidote for FAILURE!

FAITH is the element, the "chemical" which, when mixed with prayer, gives one direct communication with Infinite Intelligence.

FAITH is the element which transforms the ordinary vibration of thought, created by the finite mind of man, into the spiritual equivalent.

FAITH is the only agency through which the cosmic force of Infinite Intelligence can by harnessed and used by man.

Sara O'Meara and Yvonne Fedderson are a testimony to Hill's definition of FAITH. They have lived their lives by FAITH, love, and definiteness of purpose. Together they founded Childhelp, America's largest nonprofit, meeting the physical, emotional, educational, and spiritual needs of abused children, and they are Nobel Prize nominees for their tireless work.

They share the story of the Faith Tree, how you can start with a seed of hope and faith, sustain that faith through difficult times while nourishing it and making it strong, and ultimately how to reap the benefits of the strength created and share its wealth with others, the greatest reward of all. They also share their Pocket Prayers, which can help you in your journey as well.

The Faith Tree: Growing, Surviving, and Thriving

GROWING

Money doesn't grow on trees, but faith does. Worry is interest paid on trouble before it is due, but Faith is like money in the bank. Napoleon Hill wrote: "Faith is the starting point of all accumulation of riches." We often find we are where we choose to be. Faith gives us the courage to make necessary changes in our lives and allows us to grow in a clear and positive manner. Every dream shaped into a goal begins with the faith that if we plant a seed of hope, tend our garden with care, and survive the storms that are sure to come our way, a thriving success will bloom.

When we began building our nonprofit, Childhelp, faith was the foundation; it became the soil in which we planted each advocacy center, residential treatment facility, hotline, adoption agency, foster care, and group home. Soon we saw the fruits of our labor branching into national legislation and flowering into prevention education. We knew that advocating for abused children was part of God's plan and we would be guided through each season. We worked hard in the field every day but never doubted that a Higher Power was enriching our soil, nourishing our vision, and ensuring the sun shone on our children.

But what if you have no faith? What if difficult times and disappointment leave you lacking the belief that you can be successful? The good news is that you can grow and know that you are growing. You can become stronger in faith, more knowledgeable in spirit and see it in yourself. A popular biblical parable posits that the smallest grain of faith, as minuscule as a mustard seed, can uproot trees and move mountains. Before you plant your tree, define successful growth and determine what will make your soil "rich."

When you choose to live your life in faith, desires and hopes will magnetize to you and you will begin to rise above the clouds. You will see beyond all seeming limitations and value yourself and others more. So ask yourself if you are solely seeking monetary wealth or the richness of spirit that comes from being in the service of others

SURVIVING

After the devastating attacks on America on September 11, 2001, a scorched tree with broken branches was discovered in the rubble at Ground Zero. It was a small Callery pear tree that had managed to sprout a few leaves beneath the destruction. Its discovery rejuvenated the spirits of weary rescue workers and became a symbol of recovery. They were determined to keep the tree alive and worked with local parks and recreation professionals to plant it at the site where so much had been lost. Even when a terrible storm uprooted it, the tree was replanted and once again flowered with white blossoms of hope. It was named the Survivor Tree.

Children who have been abused and neglected come to us with their spirits scorched and their lives uprooted. At each Childhelp Residential Treatment Village, there is a garden where the little boys and girls in our care nurture fruits and vegetables from seed to plate, learning the cycle of growth but embodying the importance of survival. We teach that there is no challenge of the past that can stop the fulfillment of a fruitful future. Like the Survivor Tree, they learn that a small seed can create something great that may be uprooted time and time again but always has the chance to branch out and become whole.

What if your past is blocking your progress or you keep experiencing setbacks? There is no need to look back except to acknowledge the lessons you have learned, taking only the positive from these experiences to draw upon in your future. Sorrow looks back, worry looks around, and faith looks up. Napoleon Hill asserts, "Faith is the only known antidote to failure" and 2 Corinthians 4:13–18 promises, "Though outwardly we are wasting away, yet inwardly we are being renewed day by day. For our light and momentary troubles are achieving for us eternal glory that far outweighs them all. So we fix our eyes not on what is seen, but what is unseen. For what is seen is temporary, but what is unseen is eternal." When you release your struggle to a Higher Power, you not only survive, you plant roots that will keep you strong forever.

THRIVING

Once you have grown in trust and survived the tests of your faith, you will enter a period of great power and responsibility. You will be victorious over your environment, weaknesses, and all obstacles in your life when you follow God's path. This is your time to thrive! You have become confident in overcoming struggles and watched your dreams manifest. Suddenly, you can see the way in which a bright idea becomes a concrete reality. This is the final plateau of faith that Napoleon Hill so deftly defines, "Faith is the 'eternal elixir' which gives life, power, and action to the impulse of thought."

It is important to live and do your work in such a way that when others see you, their evaluation is the evidence of Faith. When that happens, you reap the rewards you rightfully deserve. One of the most important lessons we have learned is that success is not an end point and our thoughts shape each and every day. From the children of Childhelp to our staff to our volunteers to our friends and families, we maintain this truth: our thoughts are our actions so positive thinking begets positive results. What's another word for positive thinking? Faith.

Matthew 12:33–37 speaks about using success responsibly: "The good person out of his good treasure brings forth good, and the evil person out of his evil treasure brings forth evil." The verse sums up perfectly: "Either make the tree good and its fruit good, or make the tree bad and its fruit bad, for the tree is known by its fruit." Thriving, then, is not just about how high you grow, it is ensuring that your branches never sprout poison bitter blossoms but rather that your fruit is always healthy and sweet.

Sara and Yvonne's Faith Tree certainly shows the depth of their giving natures, as well as their FAITH in each and every one of us. Let's review just a couple of their thoughts:

- We often find we are where we choose to be.
- Faith gives us the courage to make necessary changes in our lives and allows us to grow in a clear and positive manner.
- When you release your struggle to a Higher Power, you not only survive, you plant roots that will keep you strong forever.
- Thriving, then, is not just about how high you grow, it is ensuring that your branches never sprout poison bitter blossoms but rather that your fruit is always healthy and sweet.

Ask yourself the role that FAITH has played in your life and in your success. Try to remember a time when you "powered through" a difficult period in your life. What role did FAITH play?

In *Three Feet from Gold*, we introduced the Personal Success Equation, which demonstrates the absolute importance of faith in achieving success. It is as follows:

$$[(P + T) \times A \times A] + F = \text{Personal Success}$$

Just as Hill discovered the principles of success by research and study of the most successful people of his time, the personal success equation was derived by analysis of what was key to the success of modern industry leaders and their ability to overcome obstacles. When you combine your Passion and your Talent with the right Associations and then take the right Actions you are well on your way to success. But to ensure you truly succeed and overcome any obstacles that may stand in your way, you need Faith. Faith in yourself, your mission, and your ability to succeed will help you persevere when times are difficult and propel you to even greater heights of success.

The stories that follow are from women who credit faith as an integral part of their own success stories. You may recognize your own story of faith within one of theirs.

Liora Mendeloff, founder and president of Women Speakers Association, shares the moment she invested in her own FAITH:

> I realized that there is a sort of sweet surrender and this fine line to knowing one's purpose and not necessarily knowing how it's all going to look, how it has to look but moving forward anyway. So my life's journey has been learning who I am. It's not an external conversation. It's an internal conversation, and I've been sort of pushing myself out of the nest and learning to fly on the way down. Allowing myself to be carried and always landing on my two feet somehow. I don't know why, but by the grace of God, that's been the case.

Tess Cacciatore is the cofounder and chief operating officer of the Global Women's Empowerment Network (GWEN), a nonprofit organization dedicated to empowering women and helping them transform their lives beyond abuse. Tess is an award-winning producer, videographer, journalist, and social entrepreneur who has dedicated her life to advocating for peace, justice, and equality around the globe. In one of her endeavors, she worked to raise funds to feed 1.3 million children through social networking and to build thirty-eight homes in Sri Lanka after the 2004 tsunami.

When asked about the role FAITH played in her life, she responded:

I've been following Napoleon Hill's concepts for many years and four of the principles stand out to me as the cornerstone of how I operate my business. We have applied faith; we go the extra mile, we have a positive mental attitude, and we believe in teamwork. With those four principles I have been able to reach women and children around the world. Out of the four, applied faith would be the most important because through all the trials and tribulations that we're all going through in the planet today, I believe that my faith is the one that drives me the furthest, and gives me this positive attitude. It gives me the awareness and openness to create a team of people which I'm very proud to have witnessed and it gives me the lessons that I have experienced every day.

And then there is Rita Davenport, an incredible woman who has inspired, motivated, and entertained everyone who has had the pleasure of being around her. Not only did she have her own television show, she led a network marketing company as its president to nearly $1 billion in annual revenues and inspired all of its representatives to reach for their greatest potential. In her latest book, *Funny Side Up*, she shares the following fabulous advice:

You are worthy of success and will enjoy success to the extent—and only to the extent—that you believe in yourself. If you don't, everyone can spot it. Contrary to popular belief, people are not fools. If you don't believe in yourself it shows on your face and everyone else can see it. And if you don't believe in you, why should they? They're having enough trouble as it is maintaining their own belief in themselves!

Commit to seeing yourself in your highest possibilities, and act as if!

As evidenced by Liora, Tess, and Rita, FAITH not only creates positive attitude and self-confidence, it is an essential ingredient. Hill provides the following step-by-step formula for creating and building self-confidence. It begins with your Definite Purpose as analyzed in Chapter 1, and shows you how to apply and build your FAITH in achieving it.

SELF-CONFIDENCE FORMULA

Resolve to throw off the influences of any unfortunate environment, and to build your own life to ORDER. Taking inventory of mental assets and liabilities, you will discover that your greatest weakness may be lack of self-confidence. This handicap can be surmounted, and timidity translated into courage, through the aid of autosuggestion. The application of this principle may be made through a simple arrangement of positive thought impulses stated in writing, memorized, and repeated, until they become a part of the working equipment of the subconscious faculty of your mind.

First. I know that I have the ability to achieve the object of my Definite Purpose in life; therefore, I DEMAND of myself persistent, continuous action toward its attainment, and I here and now promise to render such action.

Second. I realize the dominating thoughts of my mind will eventually reproduce themselves in outward, physical action, and gradually transform themselves into physical reality; therefore, I will concentrate my thoughts, for thirty minutes daily, upon the task of thinking of the person I intend to become, thereby creating in my mind a clear mental picture.

Third. I know through the principle of AUTOSUGGESTION, any desire that I persistently hold in my mind will eventually seek expression through some practical means of attaining the object; therefore, I will devote ten minutes daily to demanding of myself the development of SELF-CONFIDENCE.

Fourth. I have written down a clear description of my DEFINITE CHIEF AIM in life, and I will never stop trying until I shall have developed sufficient self-confidence for its attainment.

Fifth. I fully realize that no wealth or position can long endure, unless built on truth and justice; therefore, I will engage in no transaction which does not benefit all whom it affects. I will succeed by attracting to myself the forces I wish to use, and the cooperation of other people. I will induce others to serve me, because of my willingness to serve others. I will eliminate hatred, envy, jealousy, selfishness, and cynicism, by developing love for all humanity, because I know that a negative attitude toward others can never bring me success. I will cause others to believe in me, because I will believe in them, and in myself.

I will sign my name to this formula, commit it to memory, and repeat it aloud once a day, with full FAITH that it will gradually influence my THOUGHTS and ACTIONS so that I will become a self-reliant and successful person.

CHAPTER IN PRACTICE—IN MY LIFE

I was nineteen when I first read *Think and Grow Rich*, and at that time the word FAITH meant going to church and saying my prayers each night. Life has taught me over and over, however, that FAITH is so much more than its religious connotation. Like most people, I have had many occasions that required me to evaluate my life, the decisions and actions I was taking, and how to move forward. Faith is what allowed me to take those steps, knowing and believing they were the best decisions.

I have had reminders of the important role FAITH plays along my journey. When preparing for a course I was teaching a couple of years ago, I came across a definition that changed my life. It was the definition of the word "worry." It read, "To worry is to pray for what you do NOT want!"

Mea culpa! I have been a worrier all my life. This simple definition has helped me learn to stop myself in the middle of my worry storms and allows me to refocus my thoughts and prayers from what I don't want to what I *do* want. It has a profound impact on my thoughts, my attitude, and my life.

Each time I read Hill's definition of FAITH, I catch myself being in awe of the power it holds. As I think about my personal journey in building and strengthening my FAITH, I realize I have received the greatest gifts from my spiritual teachers along the path. They have been my Angels on Earth, picked me up when I have fallen, lifted me up in prayer at my deepest moments, while gently reminding me of all for which I should be grateful. They walk the talk by living and demonstrating the greatest FAITH in their own lives, each and every day.

Sara O'Meara and Yvonne Fedderson have been two of the most impactful spiritual teachers in my life. I asked them to share their thoughts on FAITH so that you may share and benefit from their gift of FAITH and wisdom to me. I was very touched by how they expressed their vision and experience with FAITH.

As I review these four concise statements from their story again, I can see how each has played an important role in every turning point in my life.

- We often find we are where we choose to be.
- Faith gives us the courage to make necessary changes in our lives and allows us to grow in a clear and positive manner.

- When you release your struggle to a Higher Power, you not only survive, you plant roots that will keep you strong forever.
- Thriving, then, is not just about how high you grow, it is ensuring that your branches never sprout poison bitter blossoms but rather that your fruit is always healthy and sweet.

The words "choice," "courage," and "release" each have significance in my life. When I found the courage to make a different choice of direction in my life, I was most successful when I released the outcome to the guidance of a Higher Power. For instance, at twenty-six I left a successful career in public accounting to start building companies. Even though the decision turned out to be one of the worst business decisions of my life, my FAITH in making the move was rewarded because I met the love of my life, my husband and best friend for more than thirty-four years, Michael—definitely a win for me! I am only the woman I am today because I found the courage to make the choice to change careers and the FAITH to trust in God, the Higher Power in my life, when I did.

More recently I made the choice and found the courage to leave a highly successful company when I realized its mission was no longer in alignment with my Definite Purpose in life. They say "take a leap of faith," but I think it should be "take a leap WITH faith"! I had no idea what the future held for me, but released the worry about the future to God, and had faith that He had a plan for me. Within a short few months I received a call from Don Green, the CEO of the Napoleon Hill Foundation, asking me to work on the book *Three Feet from Gold*. Then Don asked and gave me the opportunity to bring to the world Hill's manuscript *Outwitting the Devil*, which had been hidden for more than seventy-four years. Now I have the opportunity to write this book, *Think and Grow Rich for Women*, an incredible honor.

These are just two examples from my life where I took a leap *with* FAITH.

THE SISTERHOOD MASTERMIND

Wisdom from women of success and significance on FAITH:

GAIL DEVERS
THREE-TIME OLYMPIC CHAMPION

"Keep your dreams alive. Understand to achieve anything requires faith and belief in yourself, vision, hard work, determination, and dedication. Remember, all things are possible for those who believe."

ELLEN G. WHITE (1827–1915)
AUTHOR, COFOUNDER OF THE SEVENTH-DAY ADVENTIST CHURCH

"Talk unbelief, and you will have unbelief; but talk faith, and you will have faith. According to the seed sown will be the harvest."

MARTINA MCBRIDE (MARTINA MARIEA SCHIFF)
KNOWN AS MARTINA MCBRIDE PROFESSIONALLY, AMERICAN
COUNTRY MUSIC SINGER AND SONGWRITER

"Faith that it's not always in your hands or things don't always go the way you planned, but you have to have faith that there is a plan for you, and you must follow your heart and believe in yourself no matter what."

HELEN KELLER (1880–1968)
AMERICAN AUTHOR

"Optimism is the faith that leads to achievement. Nothing can be done without hope and confidence."

EMILY DICKINSON (1830–1886)
AMERICAN POET

"Hope is the thing with feathers that perches in the soul and sings the tune without the words and never stops . . . at all."

Faith

KAY WARREN

STARTED SADDLEBACK CHURCH WITH HER HUSBAND IN ORANGE
COUNTY, CALIFORNIA, IN 1980

"Joy begins with our convictions about spiritual truths we're willing to bet our lives on, and truths that are lodged so deeply within us that they produce a settled assurance about God."

In the original *Think and Grow Rich*, Napoleon Hill closed the chapter on FAITH with these words:

> RICHES begin in the form of THOUGHT!
>
> The amount is limited only by the person in whose mind the THOUGHT is put into motion. FAITH removes limitations! Remember this when you are ready to bargain with Life for whatever it is that you ask as your price for having passed this way.

How do we strengthen our faith? I am constantly assessing my faith and looking for ways to strengthen it and have found the following poem brings me great clarity, especially during times of stress and worry.

FAITH by Family Friend Poems

To have faith is to defy logic.
It takes faith to think positively.
It takes faith to believe that there is a loving God who cares deeply
about our pain.
To believe in life, the universe, or yourself after numerous failures is
to have courage.
Faith is an act of courage.
It is choosing to get up in the morning and face our fears and believe
that God will help us.
Faith is choosing to believe that even though we may have failed one

hundred times before that we can succeed the next time.
www. familyfriendpoems.com-poems-life-faith

In fact, I have this poem posted in my bathroom as a constant reminder that "Faith is an act of courage." It forms a daily reminder and employs a strategy found in the next chapter. It will guide you on how to influence your subconscious mind, which is the third step toward riches, AUTOSUGGESTION.

ASK YOURSELF

Use your journal as you go through this section to identify your action steps, trigger your "aha" moments, and create your plan for achieving success!

How strong is your FAITH in yourself?

Do you recognize your natural talents?
Do you believe yourself to be capable?
When faced with uncertainty or obstacles, do you face them head-on or avoid them?
Is your self-talk positive?

Take a moment to record it in your journal.

Now think about your FAITH as it relates to the individual areas for which you created goals in the first chapter and record (honestly) the thoughts that first come to mind for each area:

Personal
Business
Financial
Physical
Spiritual

You may find that it was really easy to address your FAITH in some of these areas, but much more difficult for others. For instance, you may be very comfortable speaking about your FAITH related to your Spiritual life or Personal life but find it much more difficult to talk about FAITH in your Financial or Business life.

In which area, or areas, did you find it most difficult to address FAITH?

Take a moment to think about the thoughts that came to mind and record in your journal whether they were positive or negative. For instance, you may have had thoughts like, "FAITH in my financial life? Ha! I will never get ahead financially. I just can't catch a break!" That thought would be NEGATIVE!

Take the time to rewrite your NEGATIVE thoughts into POSITIVE thoughts. For instance, you might rewrite the previous example to read, "I have FAITH in my financial life. I have learned from my past mistakes and am prepared, determined, and optimistic about my Financial Future."

Hill stated, "Repetition of affirmation of order to your subconscious mind is the only known method of voluntary development of the emotion of faith."

In order to affirm your capability and renew your faith, practice the following application of Hill's self-confidence formula each day:

First. I will accept from myself no less than what I am capable of, which is the achievement of my Definite Purpose. I will require of myself specific action every day in order to reach this achievement.

Second. I realize that what I believe to be will be, and I create my own reality. I will become the person I desire to be by concentrating for thirty minutes each day on the characteristics and actions of the person I intend to be.

Third. I understand the importance of positive self-talk and of confidence in creating success. I will dedicate ten minutes each day to steps that develop self-confidence.

Fourth. I have clearly identified in writing my life purpose and will continuously work to develop the self-confidence needed to achieve this aim.

Fifth. I will build my success by being of service to others, living every day with integrity and being considerate of all who are impacted by my actions. I will engage the support of those who demonstrate the values with which I live my life, and through my faith in others, I will create faith in myself.

Repeat each step of this formula every day in writing or out loud in order to sustain the mind-set needed to live in faith and create success.

As you start training your thoughts from negative to positive, read the Pocketbook Prayers on pp. 44–45 that Sara O'Meara and Yvonne Fedderson have kindly shared in the hope that these will assist you in your efforts. In addition, you can come back to the Personal Success Equation and remember the importance that faith plays in determining the outcome of the formula.

$$[\, (\, P + T \,) \times A \times A \,] + F = \text{Personal Success}$$
$$[(\text{Passion} + \text{Talent}) \times \text{Association} \times \text{Action}] + \text{FAITH} = \text{Personal Success}$$

Although the last variable in the equation, faith is the most important and will be the catalyst to your success!

POCKETBOOK PRAYERS

FROM SARA O'MEARA AND YVONNE FEDDERSON

We would like to offer little Pocketbook Prayers for you to copy and keep in your purse. Pull them out when needed, meditate on the ideas, and invite a Higher Power to fill your heart with faith.

Pocketbook Prayer for Growth

As I begin this journey, I know I will feel excitement and energy as well as fear and frustration. I trust that your divine love is encouraging and forgiving. I believe that true success starts with a richness of spirit. Please enter my heart and help my faith to grow stronger every day. When it is as small as a mustard seed, show me how this tiny treasure-can create a forest. When my faith is as huge as a mighty oak tree, help me have the humility to see every small, helpless creature in its shadow and offer nourishment, shelter, and shade. Growing successful is my earthly goal, but growing in faith will remain my spiritual mission.

Pocketbook Prayer for Survival

When my spirit is scorched, my willpower is charred, or I have burned a bridge, remind me of the Survivor Tree. When uncertainty uproots my dream, exhaustion impedes my growth, and my heart is broken, show me the fruits of success and flowers of faith waiting to spring forth with a new tomorrow. Let every rainy day become a lesson learned. I need the rain to flourish. Let every sunny day become a gift earned. I will reach unimagined heights in the glow of your brilliant light.

Pocketbook Prayer for Thriving

Now that I have faith, help me use it and exercise it. I am prepared to be the master of circumstances, not the victim of negativity. With great gifts comes great responsibility. My faith has given me roots in solid soil and helped me weather every storm. Now I see the flowers of faith on this perfect day and give you the glory for this moment. As my blooms burst forth in beautiful colors, I will not let ego or pride compromise my spirit. A single tree is a success of faith, but a forest of trees is a miracle of life. Once again, I will become the humble gardener but this time tending to those that need me. Just as you have helped my faith grow, I must now plant the seed of hope in another heart.

Autosuggestion

The Medium for Influencing the
Subconscious Mind

*And life is what we make it.
Always has been, always will be.*

—GRANDMA MOSES (ANNA MARY ROBERTSON MOSES)

HAVE YOU EVER REALIZED YOU MADE A MISTAKE, ROLLED YOUR
eyes at yourself, and engaged in a round of sarcastic self-talk, clearly
identifying why it was not smart and why it should not have happened? What about a secret celebration, applauding yourself for doing
a great job, or realizing a win and affirming your fabulousness? Perhaps you have been able to get yourself through a tough situation or
a feeling of being stuck or frustrated by giving yourself a pep talk
and reiterating your belief that you will overcome that particular
challenge.

Most of us have somehow engaged in the use of self-talk, not realizing the role it has in our mind-set as well as our subconscious. Just
as these moments of constructive (or, in some cases, destructive) self-
feedback can magnify feelings of accomplishment or inadequacy,
AUTOSUGGESTION can directly influence our level of success and,
more important, our belief in its possibility.

The term AUTOSUGGESTION often brings reactions from people that clearly demonstrate that it is a misunderstood term. Many people immediately think it is New Age or relates to hypnotists performing on stage. Others believe it is somehow anti-Christian or non-religious. Let's set the record straight.

According to the *Merriam-Webster Collegiate Dictionary*, AUTO-SUGGESTION is "an influencing of one's own attitudes, behavior, or physical condition by mental processes other than conscious thought." This type of self-hypnosis had its first known use in 1890, well before the New Age movement.

Hill stated that "AUTO-SUGGESTION is the agency of control through which an individual may voluntarily feed his subconscious mind on thoughts of a creative nature, or, by neglect, permit thoughts of a destructive nature to find their way into this rich garden of the mind."

We each have the ability to consciously change our circumstances by intentionally concentrating on positive actions and thoughts, which in turn influences our subconscious mind to follow suit. This happens by focusing on achieving positive outcomes in our life, both what we WANT to receive, as well as what we are willing to give in exchange for receiving it.

To illustrate this concept, Crystal Dwyer Hansen shared her knowledge on the use of AUTOSUGGESTION. Crystal is certified by the American Board of Hypnotherapy and works with people all over the world to help them experience profound and lasting transformations in their relationships, careers, and health.

AUTOSUGGESTION is a tool that is constantly available to us. The more we use it, the more powerful we can become in our lives. Experiences and events can easily control our human experience, and often not for the better. When we're exposed to events that are laced with fear and other negative emotions, those events get recorded and organized in our minds and become the filtering system for our whole life experience.

Without deliberated intervention into this automatic process of living, through autosuggestion or self-suggestion, we begin to feel that forces outside ourselves are controlling us, and they are.

Any thought or thought form that has any influence whatsoever in your life, for good or for bad, was allowed in at some level by you. Once you become aware of this reality, you can begin to use the principle of self-suggestion deliberately, rather than allowing your subconscious to randomly select the stimuli from outside that set you up for failure and disappointments.

Women can be especially susceptible to negative thinking because our emotional and intellectual selves are so interconnected. We can think about many things at one time and because of that, negative or self-defeating thoughts can easily creep into our conscious minds, becoming anchored and established in our subconscious minds. In my years of work with the people in the realm of autosuggestion, I've found that women feel even greater levels of liberation than men, from negative thoughts and feelings and greater levels of power and control over their lives from using these techniques.

Napoleon Hill wrote: "Your ability to use the principle of auto-suggestion will depend, very largely, upon your capacity to CONCENTRATE upon a given DESIRE until that desire becomes a BURNING OBSESSION."

This principle is so very important. What Hill is referring to is a word that if learned to practice brings unlimited rewards. FOCUS. The two components of focus are *intention* and *attention* as the key to manifesting your greatest desires. The more you simply practice attention and intention, the more you will begin to feel and know the experience you desire, before you experience it in its full physical manifestation.

As you carry out the first six steps described in the first chapter, you want to be very clear about your desires, focusing not only on exactly how much money you desire, or impact you want to have, but on the feelings that will be present inside of you when you have exactly that much money, or impact. If your goal is money, how much more freedom will you feel with that amount of money? What burdens now will be lifted? How will having this amount of money, or impact, affect your joy, and the joy and freedom of the people you love?

Women are *feeling* creatures. God made us to be that way for very important reasons. Our brains have an elaborate, connected neural network between the right and left hemispheres, allowing us to feel things intuitively and then process them intellectually. It is a God-bestowed gift unique to women. My psychologist friend once told me, "Women have a superhighway between the feeling and the thinking side of the brain. Men have a dirt path." All kidding aside, we need to ask ourselves why we were given this gift and how we can utilize it better to serve the people we love and humanity at large.

As Hill suggests, "Hand over the thought suggested . . . to your IMAGINATION, and see what your imagination can, or will do, to create practical plans for the accumulation of money through transmutation of your desire."

Now that you're in touch with the feelings, the joy, and the enrichment this money, or impact, will bring into your life, you can plug those feelings into your imaginative mind;

the part of the mind I call your personal artistic canvas. Women are feelers, but we're also doers. Would you like to have a perfect financial plan that allows your kids to go to college, money for special events like buying homes, vacation houses, and travel? What about retirement? No matter what age you are right now, you can most likely look back and say, "Wow, I don't know what happened to the past five years. They've flown by!" Everyone wants to experience a greater level of freedom and security at some point in their lives. Retirement is not so much about an age anymore as it is about an amount of money.

If you are striving for impact, imagine a world that is better off as a direct result of your successful efforts. Start to paint the picture on the canvas of your imagination that represents your practical plans for the most important stages of your life.

And take to heart Hill's advice to be "DEMANDING AND EXPECTING, meanwhile that your subconscious mind will hand over the plan, or plans that you need. Be on the alert for these plans, and when they appear put them into ACTION IMMEDIATELY. When the plans appear, they will probably 'flash' into your mind through the sixth sense, in the form of an 'inspiration.' This inspiration may be considered a direct telegram from Infinite Intelligence. Treat it with respect, and act upon it as soon as you receive it. Failure to do so will be FATAL to your success."

Most people don't get what they want because they haven't created any space inside of themselves for those things to occur in their lives. AUTOSUGGESTION techniques like the ones Hill taught clear out doubts and fears and make a wide-open space to be filled in from Infinite Intelligence. You can deliberately direct what fills in that space, as you learn to use autosuggestion in your life. According to the laws of the Universe, it can only deliver what you're truly asking. You are the magnet. If you're uncertain or weak in your intention, you will get uncertain results.

It is usually our own limited expectation that prevents us from reaching more glorious levels of success in every area of life. When Hill talks about demanding and expecting that your subconscious will hand over the plan or plans you need, he is emphasizing how decisive and committed you must be to use autosuggestion to its fullest capacity and reap amazing results from practicing it.

Your own absolute resolve and expectation to see things change for the better will attract the power of Infinite Intelligence to you in the most *powerful* way. Expect answers and expect plans and ideas to be delivered to you from Infinite Intelligence. When you begin to get bursts of intelligence, ideas, and plans, *do not dismiss them!*

I have found that God (Source) speaks to everyone, but only some people listen. They doubt they're worthy of such high-level communication. Let's dispel that myth right now. You are worthy. You are created in the image and likeness of the Creator, and the Creator seeks to be one with you all the time. The more you're aware of it, the more you allow the gifts to flow to you.

Hill's next step in the process is "When visualizing the money you intend to accumulate, (with closed eyes), *see yourself rendering the service, or delivering the merchandise you intend to give in return for this money. This is important!*"

The laws of giving and receiving are crucial to its flow of abundance and wealth. It can never be a one-way street or your desire for wealth and success will go nowhere. To do this you must get in touch with your own value and then enhance your value tenfold through your beliefs and works. Women are famous for minimizing their own value, which is one of the primary reasons we don't get what we deserve for our efforts.

Do you practice AUTOSUGGESTION? If so, think of how it has helped you along the way. If not, it very well may be the answer you have been seeking. Ask yourself why not.

I had the pleasure of recently meeting Dina Dwyer, executive chairwoman of the Dwyer Group, a dynamic businesswoman who has led her company to fabulous success and opened the door of opportunity to thousands looking to open their own businesses. We were discussing the impacts our fathers had on our lives, and I learned that she was raised on the principles of Napoleon Hill, and most specifically AUTOSUGGESTION. I had to laugh when she shared her story of the sticky note! Where would we be without sticky notes?

The Power of the Sticky Note by Dina Dwyer

You can never start too young. That's what my father believed when he surrounded his children with the tools to succeed. Little did I know it at the time, but that started my journey on an incredible path that continues today as a wife, a mother, and a CEO.

Sticky notes were Dad's specialty. They were posted low on the bathroom mirror. Child height, you might say. We couldn't help but read these motivational statements and goal-setting triggers as we brushed our teeth and started our day. Before I knew it, something on that sticky note stuck.

Fast-forward and you'll find those same types of sticky notes on my mirror at home. If I have to travel, so do my sticky notes. I change them out regularly, but they are a constant reminder of what I want to achieve in business and in life.

Right now, my notes reinforce a business target—the EBIDTA we are on our way to surpassing at the Dwyer Group. There is also my spiritual reminder for the day. There is my timeline target. Then there is the chosen affirmation that gives me that extra boost: Something wonderful is about to happen.

There is no better way to start and end each day at the mirror. This exercise reinforces a popular phrase my father always promoted:

> *"Whatever the mind can*
> *conceive and believe, it can achieve."*
> —NAPOLEON HILL

I learned the power of positive thinking from my father, and it has been alive and well in my rituals since childhood. It wasn't long before it became incredibly useful and powerful to me as an adult too.

It was the early 1980s when the Dwyer Group was small, with eighteen or twenty of us building a corporate culture at our home office. We were responsible for leading *Think and Grow Rich* lessons, and we would have study time to benefit the company. I was only eighteen when I started getting involved at this level. So many things that I learned early in life, but never knew how to apply, suddenly benefited me in ways beyond belief. Soon I was managing several properties for Dwyer Real Estate with the confidence to learn from and then lead people much older than myself. I was no longer afraid of what I did not know, but excited about what I could learn and do as I moved up. Those sticky notes were only the beginning.

As an adult, I've continued to build on that foundation in other routines throughout my day. My computer password is an affirmation message directed toward myself. My Twitter account shares daily aspirational quotes to all who follow. I wear a widow's mite bracelet that I got on a trip to the Holy Land, which reinforces the biblical story of the poor widow who gave two mites—not much money in the minds of the wealthy, but all that she had. The Lord's message was that she gave the greatest gift and made the greatest sacrifice by comparison. I look at this bracelet and I'm always reminded and inspired to GIVE EVERYTHING I'VE GOT.

The mere practice of autosuggestion is peppered throughout my day in ways that are both second nature and exponentially powerful. They take no demands of precious time but give a lifetime of rewards.

Our mission at the Dwyer Group says: Our mission is to teach our principles and systems of personal and business success so that all people we touch live happier and more successful lives.

So, too, are my autosuggestions to myself each day. The key is to find what works and, as in the case of my sticky notes, stick with it!

CHAPTER IN PRACTICE—IN MY LIFE

As I look back over my life, AUTOSUGGESTION has played a major role, even when I didn't realize it at the time and didn't do it purposefully. When I was a child, my father would ask me each night, "Sharon, have you added value to someone's life today?" This nightly ritual made a huge impact on me and I believe may be largely responsible for my dedication and desire to serve others.

While my father's question was a major influence on me as a child, there have been many examples of the impact of autosuggestion since. It is because I spent time working with Crystal Dwyer Hansen during a particularly stressful period in my life that I know her ap-

proach to AUTOSUGGESTION works. I have also seen AUTOSUG-
GESTION play into my life's work, which I describe below, and I know
firsthand it is a critical element to the success of anyone, especially
women.

I shared in the chapter on faith about the turning point in my life
at age twenty-six when I took a leap WITH faith and left public accounting to start building businesses. As I struggled to make the decision I used the ever-faithful yellow pad and wrote out the pros and
cons of taking the new position offered to me. The list was quite
lengthy for both, adding to my frustration. As I sat on my bed reviewing the list, it was as if a higher power took over my hand and wrote
the words "Why not?" across the top of the page. Then I asked myself:

Why not try something new?
Why not give it a try?
Why not see where this exciting opportunity takes you?

Those two words have become the guiding principle in my life,
and I use them often as an autosuggestion. It helps me take a step
back and look at the bigger picture. It forces me to step outside my
box, step outside of what is comfortable and known. It also forces me
to visualize what could be.

So often you read or hear about finding your "why." Sometimes
your why, or burning desire, is behind the door that you have been
afraid to open. So first ask yourself why not. It may give you the courage to take a leap WITH faith.

A word of caution here: If there is a convincing answer to the question "Why not"? then by all means heed your intuition. On another
note, if it is illegal, it is best to not proceed. (Hope you are smiling.)

Another AUTOSUGGESTION technique I have used, and continue to use, that has brought me great peace and joy during times of
stress and worry was shared with me by a friend during the other

turning point I shared in the faith chapter. When I decided to leave the company, it was a very stressful time. Even though I never regretted the decision, the process of leaving was very painful and drawn out over eighteen months. A friend sent me a book called *The Prayer of Jabez*. This prayer, found in the Bible at 1 Chronicles 4:10 (New International Version) was a lifeline for me, and I still say it daily, and much more frequently during times of stress. It reads:

> Oh, that you would bless me indeed
> And enlarge my territory!
> Let your hand be with me,
> And keep me from harm so that I will be free from pain.

Again, it reminds me to look outside of myself. It reminds me that I have a responsibility to serve others, with FAITH, so that I can answer my father's question, "Sharon, have you added value to someone's life today?" each night.

Napoleon Hill describes AUTOSUGGESTION related specifically to achieving a specific goal, and I also use the method he describes. One of my burning desires and definite purposes in life has been to make financial education a requirement for high school curriculums, globally. I have that goal ever-present in all that I do. Serving on the President's Advisory Council and the AICPA Financial Literacy Commission allowed me to have a voice at the national level. To realize my goal, I focused my efforts locally first and have written the following goal, which I read every day.

> Before 2015, I will see financial education as a vital part of high school curriculums. I will begin in my home state, Arizona, bringing together nonprofits, community leaders, and government leaders in a collaborative effort to pass revenue-neutral legislation that will bring financial education to all Arizona students.

On June 20, 2013, Arizona governor Jan Brewer signed the bill into law, the first step in ensuring high school students have a proficiency in personal finance before they enter the real world.

I am now able to focus my efforts in seeing the curriculum implemented in Arizona as well as engaging other states to follow Arizona's lead, and then globally. In addition, I still travel the world advocating the need for financial education and enlisting others to take up the charge in their communities.

THE SISTERHOOD MASTERMIND

Wisdom from women of success and significance on AUTOSUGGESTION:

ALICE MEYNALL (1847–1922)
ENGLISH POET

"Happiness is not a matter of events, it depends upon the tides of the mind."

KATHERINE MANSFIELD (1888–1923)
NEW ZEALAND'S MOST FAMOUS WRITER

"Could we change our attitude, we should not only see life differently, but life itself would come to be different. Life would undergo a change of appearance because we ourselves had undergone a change in attitude."

AYN RAND (1905–1982)
AUTHOR AND PHILOSOPHER

"Every man is free to rise as far as he's able or willing, but the degree to which he thinks determines the degree to which he'll rise."

PEACE PILGRIM (1908–1981)
AMERICAN PEACE ACTIVIST

"Constantly through thought you are creating your inner conditions and helping to create the conditions around you. So keep your thoughts on the positive side, think about the best that could happen, think about the good things you want to happen."

BARBARA DE ANGELIS
AUTHOR AND RELATIONSHIP CONSULTANT

"No one is in control of your happiness but you; therefore, you have the power to change anything about yourself or your life that you want to change."

Do you recognize a familiar message? You can change your life, by identifying your Burning Desire, having Faith in yourself, and practicing AUTOSUGGESTION. But the fourth step toward riches is SPECIALIZED KNOWLEDGE. We introduced FOCUS in this chapter, and the next chapter will address the importance of acquiring Specialized Knowledge.

ASK YOURSELF

Use your journal as you go through this section to identify your action steps, trigger your "aha" moments, and create your plan for achieving success!

How do you see yourself? Take a moment and, with a pen and paper, write down your answers to the following question: Who am I?

You most likely came up with several answers. You may have written down wife, mother, sister, daughter, entrepreneur, businesswoman, or a variety of other responses.

Did you write down your own name?

The truth is, many women define themselves by how others see them or what role they play in the lives of others. However, unless we are clear on who we are and who we want to be, we cannot be the best in each of these other roles.

You are you, and with AUTOSUGGESTION you can realize the best you that you are capable of!

How do you talk to yourself?

Is your inner voice generally positive or negative?

The next time you are giving yourself feedback, take note of the tone and, if necessary, reframe it to be constructive. For example, if you've made a mistake, rather than focusing on what went wrong, identify what you learned and how you can use the experience to grow. If you are celebrating a win, frame it as the realization of your personal expectation. Remember, we become what we expect of ourselves.

READ THE ENTIRE CHAPTER ALOUD ONCE EVERY
NIGHT, UNTIL YOU BECOME THOROUGHLY
CONVINCED THAT THE PRINCIPLE OF
AUTOSUGGESTION IS SOUND, AND THAT IT WILL

ACCOMPLISH FOR YOU ALL THAT HAS BEEN CLAIMED FOR IT. AS YOU READ, UNDERSCORE WITH A PENCIL EVERY SENTENCE THAT IMPRESSES YOU FAVORABLY.

As you have followed the six steps described in the first chapter, and written your personal mission statement, it is now time to employ AUTOSUGGESTION to speed your path to realizing your goals. Write your personal mission statement and post it at home and at your office, so that you will have a visual reminder several times a day. Each time you see and read it, you are employing AUTOSUGGESTION.

Crystal shares three simple suggestions to help you along the way:

Step 1: Find a quiet spot where you can concentrate, undisturbed. Out loud, say the written statement of that which you desire, the date by which you wish to accomplish it, and what feeling you will experience for having realized your desire. When doing this, frame your statements in the affirmative, as if you have already achieved your goal. An example of this has been provided below.

It is January 1, 20___. I am so happy that I have received $100,000 in sales commissions for insurance sales. It feels so good to have received this money for the exchange of energy, time, and care I've put into helping people do the best possible plan for their future. I am enjoying making an important difference, helping people plan for the future, and my focus will always be on serving their highest need. I have delivered enormous value for this money and everyone is happy to have participated in this exchange. I was given a plan by Infinite Intelligence and clearly followed the plan I received. I am always aware and alert to the steps I need to take to continue to bring this glorious abundance of success and money into my life.

Step 2: Repeat this program every night and morning until you can literally see the money and the experience that comes from it, in your imagination. As you do this daily, make sure to suspend all disbelief and have the faith of a small child.

Step 3: Place your statement somewhere that you will see it each day and can review it right when you awaken and just before going to bed.

Specialized Knowledge

Personal Experiences or Observation: You Must Focus in One Area and Concentrate There

·

When you know better you do better.
—MAYA ANGELOU

HOW MUCH POWER DO YOU BELIEVE KNOWLEDGE HOLDS?

Napoleon Hill stated that "KNOWLEDGE has no value except that which can be gained from its application toward some worthy end." Have you ever learned something that you felt was important but you just weren't sure what to do with the information? Or perhaps you personally have sought out new information, in hopes it would add value to your skill set or to your business success.

The current economic turmoil, much like the Great Depression that was raging when Napoleon Hill originally published *Think and Grow Rich*, has forced thousands if not millions of people to find additional or new sources of income. Many have sought new education that would qualify them for a new position or new business venture.

Hill further discusses KNOWLEDGE by saying, "There are two types of KNOWLEDGE. One is general, the other is specialized. General KNOWLEDGE, no matter how great in quantity or variety it may be, is of but little use in the accumulation of money."

"KNOWLEDGE will not attract money, unless it is organized,

and intelligently directed, through practical PLANS OF ACTION, to the DEFINITE END of accumulation of money. Lack of understanding of this fact has been the source of confusion to millions of people who falsely believe that 'KNOWLEDGE is power.' It is nothing of the sort! KNOWLEDGE is only potential power. It becomes power only when, and if, it is organized into definite plans of action, and directed to a definite end."

We continue to hear today the phrase "KNOWLEDGE is power." Each time you hear it, rephrase it to Hill's accurate version, "KNOWLEDGE is potential power."

People must learn, in Hill's words, "HOW TO ORGANIZE AND USE KNOWLEDGE AFTER THEY ACQUIRE IT." This is the critical step, which is the ability not only to acquire the KNOWLEDGE but to also learn the critical thinking skills needed to apply that KNOWLEDGE.

The most successful businesses generally do one of two things:

1. Solve a problem;
2. Serve a need.

You can probably think of someone you know who is highly successful. More than likely she sought out and learned SPECIALIZED KNOWLEDGE in the area of her success, but more important, she then applied it to solve a problem or provide a service for which she was richly rewarded.

In today's environment, it has never been easier to acquire SPECIALIZED KNOWLEDGE. Just about anything you want to learn can be found on the Internet, and access to formal education through online platforms and flexible scheduling has made working toward advanced degrees extremely manageable as well. After validating the source of the information, the question is whether you will dedicate yourself to apply that KNOWLEDGE by taking action to solve a problem or serve a need.

Suzi Dafnis, the community director and CEO at Australian Businesswomen's Network, has built her business around providing specialized KNOWLEDGE and resources to businesswomen. Suzi built her own personal success through organizing live educational events both in Australia and the United States. Understanding the shifting dynamics of the industry and the need to shift to an online delivery, she formed the Australian Businesswomen's Network, an online-membership hub for female entrepreneurs. It provides online training, mentoring, resources, and support through the use of collaborative new media. She shares her experience from working closely with women entrepreneurs for more than twenty years.

At a time when more and more women are starting their own business, the area of SPECIALIZED KNOWLEDGE is an important contributor to business success. As the Internet and technology have opened up markets, so too have they opened up competition, making SPECIALIZED KNOWLEDGE a differentiator that no business owner can risk ignoring.

I have observed a number of traits among the most accomplished.

- All were lifelong students and continued to access new information and education to build on their skill set.
- They embraced changes in technology and leveraged these changes.
- They were thought leaders, exemplary in an area of KNOWLEDGE.
- They sought mentors and role models who had the KNOWLEDGE they sought.
- They surrounded themselves with networks of collaborators and supporters.

Let's explore these areas more closely.

EDUCATION IS A LIFELONG
CONTRIBUTOR TO SUCCESS

Technology, and life in general, is moving and changing quickly. In order to keep abreast of and ahead of trends, a commitment to ongoing up-skilling is essential. Not only are the fundamentals of business KNOWLEDGE (business planning, sound financial skills, marketing and operations) essential, but so too is the ongoing adoption of new technology.

TECHNOLOGY AND LEARNING

Over the last five to ten years, how we learn has changed. Today, the busy business owner rarely has time to attend industry conferences and after-work networking sessions in person. Online learning, available both on-demand and in real time (and across a multitude of media) is a powerful way to up-skill and learn from local and international experts without leaving your desk. Podcasts (audio programs available via iTunes), videos (widely available on how to do practically anything), webinars (Web-based seminars) and blogs, online newsletters, and social networks offer access to thought leaders in every area.

MENTORS AND ROLE MODELS

The opportunity to learn from experts anywhere in the world, at the time and on the device of your choice—think smartphone, tablet—means that our options for the acquisition of specialized KNOWLEDGE from role models and mentors are mobile and amplified. Role models can sow the seeds of KNOWLEDGE and mentors (carefully selected for their experience and KNOWLEDGE in areas in which you wish to grow) are a secret weapon worth seeking out.

THOUGHT LEADERSHIP, MICRO BRANDING, AND THE BUSINESSWOMAN

No matter how large or small your business, your brand is what will differentiate you as a KNOWLEDGE expert. Often branding is thought of as a big-business requirement. That couldn't be further from today's truth—that in order to survive, and to differentiate your business from your competition, your brand must speak clearly about who you are and what you stand for. Your brand, and congruence with it, allows you to demonstrate your own thought leadership. And the use of new media and social tools allows you to leverage your KNOWLEDGE and to position yourself as an expert that others can rely on and trust.

BUSINESS NETWORKS AND YOUR BUSINESS SUCCESS

Let's look at the act of networking and your network separately. A powerful network of peers and collaborators is an important part of business and can move you in the direction you wish to go, and provide ideas, feedback, and support. Nurturing the contacts you already have, authentically supporting those who support you, and actively seeking to help others and share KNOWLEDGE is a more effective way of networking than attending a networking event looking to sell your wares. You can extend your network using social networking tools, attending conferences, and getting face-to-face with potential clients. Successful networkers are NOT those that push their wares on the unsuspecting, though; it's those successful networkers who genuinely offer value to those they meet without expectation or self-interest.

Suzi confirms in the last part of her essay that being of service (providing valuable and desired solutions to the needs of others) is a critical element of expanding your network. It can also make the difference when seeking out mentors and working to engage partners who can provide the specialized KNOWLEDGE that you wish to gain.

Mentoring is an effective method for gaining specialized KNOWLEDGE as well as demonstrating proficiency and finding ways to apply the KNOWLEDGE. Once you have acquired the KNOWLEDGE, employ it by mentoring others. This serves a dual purpose as it allows you to give back and at the same time demonstrate the ability to put that KNOWLEDGE to work by considering its use in a variety of situations, utilizing a variety of plans for the intention of wealth generation.

Renee James was named president of Intel in 2013. In an interview about being the first woman chosen in her field, she shared that early in her career she was uncomfortable speaking at women's events because she wanted to be thought of as capable for her position, not because of her gender. Then she went on to say, "Now, I realize that I am a role model. I feel more of a responsibility to give back to other women." Thank you, Renee, for being an incredible role model.

Women mentoring one another are critically important to our success. Let's give the good old boy network a run for its money with the great, *but never old*, women's network!

These networks and mentoring opportunities are beginning to form in high school and college as women come together to support each other. As shared in the introduction, 140 women graduate with a college degree at some level for every hundred men. This means more women will excel in areas of Specialized Knowledge as they achieve these advanced degrees.

The Pew Charitable Trust released a report titled "How Much Protection Does a College Degree Afford?" that explored the differences between college graduates and less-educated groups and how each was impacted by the recent economic recession. It revealed that a four-year college degree helped shield people from unemployment, low-skill jobs, and lesser wages. Even though all twenty-one- to twenty-four-year-olds suffered declines in employment and wages during this time, it was much more severe for those with only a high school or associate degree.

In fact, the following chart issued by the Bureau of Labor Statistics graphically shows the relative unemployment rates and median weekly earnings in 2012 based on the level of education achieved:

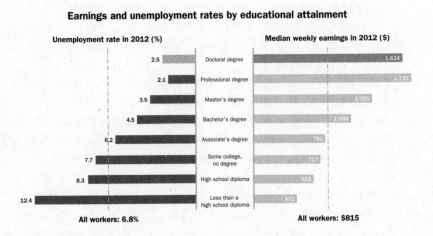

Earnings and unemployment rates by educational attainment

Unemployment rate in 2012 (%)		Median weekly earnings in 2012 ($)
2.5	Doctoral degree	1,624
2.1	Professional degree	1,735
3.5	Master's degree	1,300
4.5	Bachelor's degree	1,066
6.2	Associate's degree	785
7.7	Some college, no degree	727
8.3	High school diploma	652
12.4	Less than a high school diploma	471

All workers: 6.8%   All workers: $815

So as more and more women earn these higher degrees, they will have greater opportunities for higher earnings and financial success.

Teresa Sullivan, the first female president of the University of Virginia, founded by Thomas Jefferson, shared her passion for providing the finest education possible in her speech titled "A Founder's Perspective: Today's University of Virginia (U.Va.) through Jefferson's Eyes." She stated: "Jefferson's aspirations for this University's students are summed up neatly in a letter he wrote in 1821. In personal terms, he described, . . . 'the sweet consolation of seeing our sons rising under a luminous tuition to destinies of high promise.' Today, of course, we have both sons and daughters pursuing their destinies of high promise at U.Va.—in fact, more daughters than sons now enroll each fall."

In addition to the obvious advantage of a college education, President Sullivan also highlights the importance of specialized knowledge in the quest for success. She shares:

> Specialized knowledge refers to detailed information concerning a specialty, which is a limited area of human inquiry. As the volume of human knowledge has grown exponentially, no single individual is able to acquire all the information needed to sustain a complex economy and society. Specialists are people who have acquired detailed, in-depth information about a specific area of information; in many cases, the specialist has also acquired research techniques, or the means to continue discovering new information in the specialty. In the field of medicine, for example, all medical doctors acquire basic information about many areas of human health and the diagnosis, progress, and treatments for specific diseases. A doctor may then become a specialist in a particular area of medicine—say, neurosurgery—by undergoing additional years of learning and training. While all doctors have some knowledge about the human brain and spine, the neurosurgeon has specialized knowledge about the structure and function of the brain down to the cellular level, as well as much more information about diseases and treatments for various brain malformations, diseases, or degeneration. Some specialized knowledge is associated with every profession and occupation.

President Sullivan's comment, "As the volume of human knowledge has grown exponentially, no single individual is able to acquire all the information needed to sustain a complex economy and society," is extremely important and highlights the importance of collaboration. Having and leveraging specialized KNOWLEDGE does not mean that you have to personally have the KNOWLEDGE. When the needed KNOWLEDGE is accessible and you know how to find it, this is just as impactful as if you have the KNOWLEDGE yourself.

Katharine Graham led the *Washington Post* to greatness when she assumed the reins of the company and of the *Post* after Philip Graham's suicide. As the only woman in such an executive position with a publishing company, she realized she had no female role models. She felt many of her male colleagues and employees did not take her seriously. In her memoir she shared her lack of confidence and distrust in her own KNOWLEDGE. But she succeeded by finding the talent she needed to be successful—Benjamin Bradlee as editor and Warren Buffett for his financial advice. She led the paper for more than two decades.

When you combine the fact that more women are graduating from college than ever before, thereby acquiring SPECIALIZED KNOWLEDGE, with our natural talent for collaboration, the opportunity for women achieving great success is very bright!

CHAPTER IN PRACTICE—IN MY LIFE

The term SPECIALIZED KNOWLEDGE seems pretty self-explanatory. If you need brain surgery, you want the best-trained brain surgeon around. If you want to learn how to paint using oils, you want training specializing in oil painting, not watercolors.

At an early age, I learned from my dad SPECIALIZED KNOWLEDGE on how to, and how not to, pick oranges. I also had to learn how to change the oil and tires on my first car before I could drive away in it. At the time, of course, I certainly didn't see this type of "KNOWLEDGE" as anything very useful to me.

I like to contrast my school smarts from my street smarts. I did very well in school, but the most "real" life lessons I learned from the "street" with my dad. He challenged me constantly to think about what I was learning in school and how it would benefit me in real life.

He would then add his street-smart lessons and ask me about current issues in the news and how I would address them. My ability to think critically, problem solve, and practically apply what I learned came from those street lessons.

He often told me that I had two choices when faced with a question I didn't know how to answer. Find the answer on my own, or know who to call for it. He demonstrated this throughout his life. My father only had a third-grade formal education, but ended up practically running the engineering school at the Great Lakes Naval Station before he retired from the Navy. He was totally self-taught. My love of learning came from my father, not my years of schooling. He taught my sister and me how to think, how to problem solve, and how to dedicate ourselves to do whatever it took to complete a task, and complete it well.

Even though I achieved great success in traditional schooling and earned my credentials as a certified public accountant (CPA), when I started in the publishing industry, I was like a fish out of water. After learning a few street lessons, I focused on learning everything I could, from paper stock to various types of printing to distribution methods. I trained myself by researching (at that time in the library because there was no Internet), by visiting printing companies, and getting competitive quotes. I was a sponge, soaking up as much KNOWLEDGE as I could so I would be able to make the best decisions possible.

As the world of publishing continues to change dramatically, I make every effort to keep abreast of the latest trends. But I also seek advice from those on the front lines who see the bigger picture and may know of a resource that could benefit me. I continue to follow my father's two-step rule—either educate myself, or know who to ask.

When I began investing in real estate, I recognized that I needed more specialized KNOWLEDGE. I sought out successful real estate investors and asked them to mentor me. I went to real estate seminars and did my research on market trends. First I concentrated on investing in apartment complexes, and then moved to single-family homes when the market dictated. While both are considered real estate investing, each requires different KNOWLEDGE and investing strategies.

In Pay Your Family First, I recognize the ever-changing nature of online curriculum and community building as well as Internet marketing. I also know that I will never be able to educate myself on what is new, what works, and more important, what is a waste of money. So I find the best people who possess the specialized KNOWLEDGE I need and enlist their help. Then I put them on speed dial.

Each new initiative I engage in requires specialized KNOWLEDGE of some kind. From publishing to real estate and now to ranching, I have embraced each with a passion for learning while keeping a keen eye for opportunities to solve a problem or serve a need.

In Hill's words, "The accumulation of great fortunes calls for POWER, and power is acquired through highly organized and intelligently directed specialized KNOWLEDGE, but that KNOWLEDGE does not, necessarily, have to be in the possession of the man [woman] who accumulates the fortune."

The women I include in this Sisterhood Mastermind have all gained tremendous Specialized KNOWLEDGE, and great POWER along with that KNOWLEDGE. They have shaped the future for us.

THE SISTERHOOD MASTERMIND

Wisdom from women of success and significance on SPECIALIZED KNOWLEDGE:

SANDRA DAY O'CONNOR
FIRST WOMAN TO SERVE ON THE U.S. SUPREME COURT

"Do the best you can in every task, no matter how unimportant it may seem at the time. No one learns more about a problem than the person at the bottom."

"We don't accomplish anything in this world alone . . . and whatever happens is the result of the whole tapestry of one's life and all the weavings of individual threads from one to another that creates something."

"Young women today often have very little appreciation for the real battles that took place to get women where they are today in this country. I don't know how much history young women today know about those battles."

"I think the important thing about my appointment is not that I will decide cases as a woman, but that I am a woman who will get to decide cases."

DR. SALLY RIDE (1951–2012)
FIRST AMERICAN WOMAN IN SPACE

"We have come a long way."

"There are lots of opportunities out there for women to work in these fields. . . . Girls just need support, encouragement, and mentoring to follow through with the sciences."

"My parents didn't have a scientific bone in their body, and their daughter was pursuing a career in astrophysics. They didn't even know what astrophysics meant, but they supported me."

BARBARA BARRETT
TRAINED ASTRONAUT, FORMER U.S. AMBASSADOR TO FINLAND, AND FORMER INTERIM PRESIDENT OF THUNDERBIRD SCHOOL OF GLOBAL MANAGEMENT

"Knowledge is the gateway to the future. Like most gateways, knowledge is rarely the end in itself; knowledge represents the threshold beyond which opportunity and rewards await."

QUEEN RANIA

QUEEN OF JORDAN AND THE WIFE OF KING ABDULLAH II

"Social media are a catalyst for the advancement of everyone's rights. It's where we're reminded that we're all human and all equal. It's where people can find and fight for a cause, global or local, popular or specialized, even when there are hundreds of miles between them."

CONDOLEEZZA RICE

FIRST FEMALE AFRICAN-AMERICAN SECRETARY OF STATE

"Education is transformational. It changes lives. That is why people work so hard to become educated and why education has always been the key to the American Dream, the force that erases arbitrary divisions of race and class and culture and unlocks every person's God-given potential."

GIA HELLER

CEO, THE NATIONAL BUSINESS EXPERTS

"It's difficult to be 'expert' at anything if you do 'everything.'"

Hill emphasizes, "If you have IMAGINATION this chapter may present you with an idea sufficient to serve as the beginning of the riches you desire. Remember the IDEA is the main thing. Specialized KNOWLEDGE may be found just around the corner—any corner!"

The importance of his statement is found in realizing that once you have your Definite Purpose and Burning Desire, and the idea on how to accomplish comes to you, do not be afraid if you lack the immediate KNOWLEDGE you need to realize it. You can find the specialized KNOWLEDGE, maybe even at the comfort of your own home computer. The next chapter will delve into IMAGINATION, the Workshop of the Mind.

ASK YOURSELF

Use your journal as you go through this section to identify your action steps, trigger your "aha" moments, and create your plan for achieving success!

What is my specialized KNOWLEDGE?

This may be a difficult question because women often do not give themselves the credit they deserve or do not feel comfortable doing what may feel like bragging. Once you have identified what kind of specialized KNOWLEDGE you can employ, however, you are better empowered to add value to the lives of others while creating the life you desire.

On a piece of paper, answer the following questions:

1. What natural talents do I have?
2. What topics do people most often ask me questions about?
3. What areas of expertise do I have access to through my contacts?

Who is on your team? Are you able on a regular basis to reach out and find answers to the questions you do not have the KNOWLEDGE to address? Or do you frequently find yourself "stuck" or unsure of what to do? If it is the latter, it is time to find ways to expand your network or work toward gaining additional specialized KNOWLEDGE yourself.

What certifications do I have and to what associations do I belong?

What service or need does my burning desire or life purpose address? What kind of specialized KNOWLEDGE is required to do this? If I do not already have this KNOWLEDGE, how can I go about getting it?

Certification?

Mentorship?

Degree?

What method of acquiring this KNOWLEDGE will provide the
best leverage to build wealth or achieve my purpose?

If I do not wish to acquire this specialized KNOWLEDGE,
who can I engage as part of my team to provide it?

Service professionals?

Members of associations?

Business executives?

Educators?

In order to successfully engage these people, first identify
where you might find them and what value you are willing to
offer in exchange for their specialized KNOWLEDGE. If you are
seeking them for purposes of a business deal, are you offering monetary compensation or equity? Perhaps there is a
trade for services that will benefit both parties. If enrolling
specialists for the purpose of a nonprofit or community project, are you offering public acknowledgment, potential for
great networking, or will the nature of the project and the mag-
nitude of its impact be enticements all on their own?

Once you have identified your KNOWLEDGE or the KNOWL-
EDGE from someone else that you intend to leverage, have a
clear plan for how you intend to use it and what specific outcomes will result that put you closer to achieving your burning
desire.

Imagination

The Workshop of the Mind

·

*Imagination is not only the uniquely human capacity
to envision that which is not, and therefore the fount
of all invention and innovation. In its arguably most
transformative and revelatory capacity, it is the
power that enables us to empathize with humans
whose experiences we have never shared.*

—J. K. ROWLING

HAVE YOU EVER HAD A GOOD IDEA? OF COURSE YOU HAVE. HAVE
you ever made money from one of your good ideas? If your answer is
yes, congratulations! If not, this chapter may help you identify ways
that your next great idea can become your next successful business. In
addition, you will discover why imagination will have a huge role in
solving so many needs that currently exist around the globe.

As so well expressed by J. K. Rowling, creator and author of the
Harry Potter fantasy series, "Imagination is the fount of all invention
and innovation." Certainly she is an incredible and obvious example
of imagination at its best through her work, but she very importantly
highlights that imagination is necessary in all invention and innovation. Imagination is at the core of every successful business as well. As
shared in the last chapter, the most successful businesses do one of
two things:

- Solve a problem;
- Serve a need.

Your imagination will help you identify the problem and/or need and will lead you to the solution as well!

Hill described it so well: "The IMAGINATION is literally the workshop wherein are fashioned all plans created by man [woman]. The impulse, the DESIRE, is given shape, form, and ACTION through the aid of the imagination faculty of the mind. It has been said that man [woman] can create anything which he [she] can imagine."

You can find IMAGINATION in its purest form by remembering yourself as a child or by watching young children at play. Watching them with their imaginary friends, with the forts they build and defend, and the castles they create from plastic building blocks, you see them reveal their fertile and unencumbered imaginations.

What happens to that zestful IMAGINATION? These very same children start formal education and training and learn that they must conform their behavior to acceptable standards. Well-intended teachers and caregivers feel unbridled imagination may lead to unruliness, so it is often put in a box and allowed to peek out only during structured playtimes.

As adults, we use terms like "multitasking," "focused," "driven," or "overwhelmed" to explain away or make excuses for our lack of free, creative time. It is during this free time when our imaginations could soar, and possibly identify and create the next business opportunity. For a few moments, close your eyes and imagine yourself as the Entrepreneur of the Year being recognized for creating the latest and greatest new invention that _____! (Did you fill in the blank?)

In a deeper analysis of imagination, Hill identifies the following two forms of imagination:

SYNTHETIC IMAGINATION: Through this faculty, one may arrange old concepts, ideas, or plans into new combinations. It works with the material of experience, education, and observation with which it is fed. It is the faculty used most by the inventor, with the exception of the "genius" who draws upon the creative imagination, when he cannot solve his problem through synthetic imagination.

CREATIVE IMAGINATION: Through the faculty of creative imagination, the finite mind of man has direct communication with Infinite Intelligence. It is the faculty through which "hunches" and "inspirations" are received. It is by this faculty that all basic, or new, ideas are handed over to man. It is through this faculty that thought vibrations from the minds of others are received. It is through this faculty that one individual may "tune in," or communicate with the subconscious minds of other men.

One of the greatest examples of Synthetic Imagination I have seen was demonstrated by Leila Janah, founder and CEO of Samasource. She took an existing business model and imagined how it could be flipped upside down to positively impact the masses. In discussing the origination of her business idea, she said:

I had an "aha" moment: why not use this model of outsourcing to address poverty, rather than send the work to big, for-profit companies like my client? I thought, outsourcing has made billionaires out of a few businessmen. Why not use the same model to provide a few dollars to the billions of people at the bottom of the pyramid?

That idea grew into Samasource, which I formed in September 2008. The core concept was to apply the ideas of fair trade to the outsourcing industry, and redirect a small part of the $200 billion-plus spent on outsourcing to poor women and youth in developing countries. I thought if we could move even one percent of this large amount of wealth to poor and marginalized people through a smart model that integrated with the global economy, we'd make a tremendous difference in the health, education, and well-being of people who are so often left out. And we'd do it by using money that would normally flow between large corporations, and by helping companies meet their existing needs for data services. I thought of this model as a win-win for people, for businesses, and for governments, who could either spend less on foreign aid, or direct the aid to more useful programs.

Since then, with the help of a tremendous team and hundreds of clients, donors, and advisors who believed in the impossible, what started as a pipe dream has morphed into reality. Samasource has generated over $5 million in contracts from leading companies and institutions, including Google, eBay, Microsoft, LinkedIn, Eventbrite, and Stanford University, directly employing 3,500 and benefiting over 10,000 marginalized people in sub-Saharan Africa, South Asia, and the Caribbean, including refugees, youth, and women from conservative communities.[26]

By looking at an existing business model from a different point of view, Leila Janah was able to build a successful business that is helping thousands of people around the world. She started from humble beginnings but imagined what could be and then coupled it with her burning desire.

When I think of people with creative imagination, I think of writers like J. K. Rowling selling more than 400 million copies of Harry Potter worldwide. Rowling has shared that she was on a train when she began to imagine the first book of the series, saying, "Harry just strolled into my head fully formed." Even though she was unemployed, receiving government assistance, and living below the poverty line with a small child in a small flat in Edinburgh at the time, she never stopped writing.

The first book became an overnight success and the Harry Potter phenomenon was launched. Today J. K. Rowling is a billionaire, but she has not forgotten her humble beginnings. She's now pushing the British government to increase its support for single parents and Britain's poor.

In addition to authors who tap into their creative imaginations, inventors and problem solvers also use their creative and sometimes synthetic imaginations to create innovative solutions to challenges or needs in our society. I did a little research to find women inventors and was surprised by what I found.

In the early years of the United States, a woman could not get a patent in her own name. Patents were considered property, and until the late 1800s laws forbade women in most states to own property or enter into legal agreements in their own names, so women could not own patents. Instead, a woman would have to secure a patent in the name of her father or husband.

As an example, Sybilla Masters is believed to be the first American woman inventor. In 1712 she developed a new corn mill, but couldn't get a patent because she was a woman. In 1715 her husband filed the patent in his name but referenced her within the patent itself.

Some of the female inventors who made historic impacts on all our lives are highlighted below. You may recognize a couple of them from their well-known names and may be surprised by the significance of their inventions. Most of the others you may not recognize by name, but you will most certainly be aware of their inventions and the incredible impact they have had on the world. The vast majority of these women started from humble beginnings and used their synthetic and/or creative imaginations to solve a problem or serve a need they identified. Most likely you will think that of course this would have been invented by a woman!

1897—Anna Connelly invented the first outdoor fire escape. Such fire escapes have been credited with saving hundreds of thousands of lives over time.

1898—Marie Curie is best known as the discoverer of the radioactive elements polonium and radium and as the first person to win two Nobel Prizes. She went on to discover X-ray technology in 1901.

1903—Mary Anderson invented the windshield wiper. She noticed that streetcar drivers had to open the windows of their cars in order to see, so as a solution she invented a swinging arm device with a rubber blade that the driver could operate from within the vehicle using a lever. Windshield wipers became standard for all American cars by 1916.

1904—Elizabeth Magie invented the board game concept that became Monopoly. It was originally called the Landlord's Game, to highlight the evils of land ownership and monopolies and intended as an educational tool. Her game was later apparently "pirated" by Charles Darrow, who patented the game as Monopoly in 1933 and later sold his patent to Parker Brothers with a royalty due to him on future sales of the board game, making him a millionaire. In a clear effort to protect their rights to Monopoly, Parker Brothers purchased Elizabeth Magie's game and patents for only five hundred dollars and future manufacturing rights.

1930—Ruth Wakefield invented chocolate chip cookies when she was making cookies for guests at her Toll House Inn and ran out of baker's chocolate. In an effort to improvise, she broke up pieces of a Nestlé semisweet chocolate bar assuming they would melt during baking, but they didn't. The Toll House chocolate chip cookie was born.

1940—Dr. Maria Telkes invented the first home solar-heating system. Interested in solar power from when she was in high school, she devoted her career to it, inventing in the process one of the first successful solar ovens, solar heating systems, and a solar water distilling system for making seawater potable. She became known as the Sun Queen.

1941—Hedy Lamarr, a famous film actress and world-renowned beauty, coinvented wireless communication and spread spectrum technology, the first wireless communications used to combat the Nazis in World War II, which led to today's Wi-Fi and GPS.

1950—Marion Donovan invented disposable diapers but was told by manufacturers that they were impractical. Ten years later, Pampers were created by Victor Mills utilizing similar ideas.

1958—Bette Nesmith Graham invented Liquid Paper. She saw painters decorating windows for the holidays. When they made mistakes, rather than remove their mistakes entirely, the painters simply covered them up with an additional layer of paint. The quick-thinking Graham mimicked their technique by using a white, water-based tempera paint to cover her typing errors.

1966—Stephanie Kwolek invented Kevlar. While looking for a light-weight solution for making tires, she developed a material that was considered a failure for tire use. Fortunately, she recognized that it was innovative and could be used elsewhere. Not only was it stronger than nylon, but it was also five times stronger than steel. The new field of polymer chemistry quickly began and by 1971, modern Kevlar was introduced. Thousands of lives have been saved by Kevlar bulletproof vests and other products.

1999—Randi Altschul invented the disposable cell phone. She is a perfect example of when the lack of expertise in a certain field need not restrict you from becoming an inventor and creating an exciting new product in that area. As a successful New Jersey toy inventor, she became frustrated while driving down the highway when her cell phone connection became weak and she has been quoted as wanting to throw her cell phone out the window. She has referred to this as a "eureka!" moment. Why not create a disposable cell phone? It was her first endeavor into electronics, but she was utilizing her experience in the toy field, where toys have limited life expectancy, and applied it to mobile phones. She worked with an engineer to develop the super-thin circuitry that would go inside the phones. She was issued a series of patents for the wireless, prepaid cell phone as well as the circuitry, in November 1999. While she never commercialized her version, many other manufacturers utilize her technology in the production of disposable cell phones today.

Imagination and creativity are often thought of in the context of the unpractical and unreal. Even with imaginary play as children, however, we are finding solutions to problems. When a child needs a fort to stake out in case of "enemy attack," does she wait for one to appear, or go to task draping blankets over chairs and boxes, securing her walls with pillows—as did the women listed above? When the rules of a traditional game get boring, do children give up and go sit down? No! They make up their own rules, creating interest and entertainment for themselves and their friends.

Each of the women listed above used creativity to identify a solution to a problem. Some solutions were for problems that the world had not acknowledged yet, and these imaginative thinkers were criticized or ridiculed for their ideas. However, once the world saw value in what they had to offer, each woman was recognized and rewarded for her contribution.

Masterminding, which will be covered more thoroughly in a later chapter, is a fabulous exercise in creativity and imagination. The ability to brainstorm with others helps ignite the combined creativity of the group. This is when you truly see the power of the question. When you ask a question, it ignites creativity. Instead of saying, "I can't," say, "How can I?" "I can't" is a statement that closes the mind, but "How can I?" opens the mind and triggers creativity.

Try it out the next time you are with friends, business associates, or children. It is amazing. You will quickly see why they say the person asking the questions is in control of the situation, and is typically the leader.

It is through this brainstorming that you can transform an idea created from IMAGINATION into an organized plan. As Hill reminds us, "Transformation of the intangible impulse, of DESIRE, into the tangible reality, of MONEY, calls for the use of a plan, or plans. These plans must be formed with the aid of the IMAGINATION."

CHAPTER IN PRACTICE—IN MY LIFE

When I thought about the role IMAGINATION has played in my life, it was illuminating, to say the least.

I grew up in a pretty serious, middle-class, hardworking home. My dad was career Navy and discipline was pretty strict in our household. I was an excellent student in school, got good grades, and following the rules (for the most part). But as I now look back, I believe that my creativity was stifled in that school environment. After I graduated and became successful in public accounting, I found myself once again in a structured and defined corporate environment, where many people thrive, but I did not.

Once I left the corporate world and became an entrepreneur, I realized that I had found a sense of freedom that allowed my creativity to be unleashed and expressed.

Today, I am most energized when I am problem solving or discovering new ways to do something. I start with the problem and a white board and brainstorm the possibilities for solutions. It is exhilarating. It is an extension of my "Why not?" philosophy. By asking myself that question, I allow myself to take the path less traveled and experience new things.

At times when I feel stuck, I force myself to do something new. I often will go to the ocean. The water lapping on the shore, the sunsets, and ocean sounds are food for my soul and reignite my creativity. In fact, I have visited the ocean at least once for every book I have written.

When Don Green, CEO of the Napoleon Hill Foundation, asked me to review an original manuscript of Hill's that had been undiscovered for more than seventy-three years, I went to the ocean in San Diego. I had to be in the right environment to read it when I learned that I was to be only the fourth or fifth person ever to read the manuscript, which Hill had titled *Outwitting the Devil*. What an incredible honor—and responsibility. I read it within just a few hours, and it changed my life forever.

Outwitting the Devil reveals how self-limiting beliefs hold us back from achieving the success we deserve and how negativity can paralyze us in our pursuit of success. It provides a seven-step plan to conquer that negativity and free you from those self-limiting beliefs.

Hill's wife had been concerned by the title and forbade it from being published during her lifetime. I believe, however, there was also a greater power at work and that the book was truly meant to be published for our current times. So many people today are paralyzed by fear, unable to break through their own self-limiting beliefs.

When Don Green asked me to edit the manuscript and annotate it for the modern reader, I was thrilled—and overwhelmed by the awesome responsibility. As I sat overlooking the ocean, I prayed for guidance in honoring Hill's work while highlighting its relevance to our world today. What transpired during my writing I can only describe as what Hill describes in his definition of "creative imagination . . . the finite mind of man has direct communication with Infinite Intelligence. It is the faculty through which 'hunches' and 'inspirations' are received. It is by this faculty that all basic, or new ideas are handed over to man."

There were times during my writing when I just stared at the ocean, opening my mind and asking for inspiration. Then I would start writing furiously, and find myself surprised by what I had written. Of all the books I have had the honor to write, I can honestly say that *Outwitting the Devil* has had the greatest impact on my life. We constantly hear from people who have felt similar impact from reading it.

Recently I was again at the ocean in Los Angeles contemplating this book and the power and importance of imagination in our quest to succeed. The following inspiration came to mind:

"As kids we use imagination to play and create, as adults it seems we most often use imagination to escape."

I see many of my friends "escaping" into books or movies in an effort to avoid dealing with issues in their lives. If only they could unleash their imaginations in a creative way, they could find ways to conquer their problems and create new avenues of success in their lives.

During a particularly stressful time in my life, I found myself at our ranch in the middle of the Tonto National Forest in Arizona. The incredible beauty was overwhelming and it helped me put my own issues and/or troubles into perspective. To see God's vast abundance and beauty helps you realize how any current issue you are dealing with is just a blip in his overall plan for your life.

Just creating a change of scenery will often trigger new thoughts and creativity.

THE SISTERHOOD MASTERMIND

Wisdom from women of success and significance on IMAGINATION:

RITA DOVE
AMERICAN POET AND AUTHOR, FIRST AFRICAN-AMERICAN TO SERVE AS POET LAUREATE, CONSULTANT IN POETRY TO THE LIBRARY OF CONGRESS (1993–1995)

"You have to imagine it possible before you can see something. You can have the evidence right in front of you, but if you can't imagine something that has never existed before, it's impossible."

ANNE SULLIVAN MACY (1866–1936)
IRISH-AMERICAN TEACHER, BEST KNOWN AS INSTRUCTOR AND
COMPANION TO HELEN KELLER

"We imagine that we want to escape our selfish and commonplace existence, but we cling desperately to our chains."

SYLVIA PLATH (1932–1963)
AMERICAN POET AND AUTHOR

"And by the way, everything in life is writable about if you have the outgoing guts to do it, and the imagination to improvise. The worst enemy to creativity is self-doubt."

EMILY DICKINSON (1830–1886)
ONE OF AMERICA'S GREATEST POETS, AND WELL KNOWN FOR
LIVING A LIFE OF SELF-IMPOSED SOCIAL SECLUSION

"The Possible's slow fuse is lit by the Imagination."

L. E. LANDON (1802–1838)
ENGLISH POET AND NOVELIST, BETTER KNOWN BY HER
INITIALS, L.E.L.

"Imagination is to love what gas is to a balloon—that which raises it from earth."

LAUREN BACALL
AMERICAN ACTRESS AND MODEL

"Imagination is the highest kite that can fly."

MARIE VON EBNER-ESCHENBACH (1830–1916)
AUSTRIAN WRITER NOTED FOR EXCELLENT PSYCHOLOGICAL
NOVELS

"Without imagination, there is no goodness, no wisdom."

NANCY HALE (1908–1988)
FIRST WOMAN REPORTER FOR THE *NEW YORK TIMES*,
AND NOVELIST

"Imagination is new reality in the process of being created. It represents the part of the existing order that can still grow."

MARIAN ANDERSON (1897–1993)
DEEMED ONE OF THE FINEST CONTRALTOS OF HER TIME AND THE
FIRST AFRICAN-AMERICAN TO PERFORM WITH THE NEW YORK
METROPOLITAN OPERA, IN 1955

"When you stop having dreams and ideals—well, you might as well stop altogether."

DR. JOEL MARTIN
FOUNDER, TRIAD WEST INC.

"You've probably heard the expression, 'Get out of the box.' Well, transformation is inventing your box and making it large enough to handle and generate more of what you want personally, professionally and in your relationships."

In summarizing the chapter on Imagination, Hill emphasizes, "The story of practically every great fortune starts with the day when a creator of ideas and a seller of ideas get together and worked in harmony." In the next chapter he reveals that even with the greatest imagination, you need to be skilled in ORGANIZED PLANNING.

ASK YOURSELF

Use your journal as you go through this section to identify your action steps, trigger your "aha" moments, and create your plan for achieving success!

How would you assess your IMAGINATION?

From time to time each of us will need to recharge our creative juices so that our imaginations can soar.

The following list includes various ways to recharge your IMAGINATION. Go through each item and ask yourself the last time you experienced each one.

Physically

1. Get enough sleep.
2. Get sufficient exercise.
3. Take a walk outdoors, sit and enjoy nature.
4. Become comfortable with silence.
5. Read a book.
6. Listen to music.

Mentally

7. Daydream.
8. Rid yourself of self-limiting beliefs, and do not compare yourself to others.
9. Suspend disbelief.
10. Believe anything is possible.

Actions

11. Keep a notebook and pen with you to take notes.
12. Go away to an unfamiliar territory.
13. Become more spontaneous, try new things.
14. Ask yourself more questions, like "Why not?"

15. Take creative breaks.
16. Brainstorm with your family and friends.
17. Play.
18. Create.

Challenge yourself to schedule "imagination" time during the next few days and learn to make it part of your everyday schedule.

What will you plan to do to energize your IMAGINATION?

Get paper and pencil (colored ones are best) and start mindlessly doodling. Give yourself at least thirty minutes of drawing time. What thoughts came to mind as you were drawing? Were they creative, or judgmental?

In your journal begin to write anything that comes to mind. Write for at least thirty minutes, and repeat daily for at least a week. At the end of the week, ask yourself what new ideas came to mind. Did you experience emotion as you wrote?

Practice using the power of the question to trigger your IMAGINATION. When in a group, ask a general question and witness how it ignites the conversation within the group. You will see the energy of the group increase as a result of the discussion.

Ask yourself what environment is most conducive for your creativity and IMAGINATION. Go there and allow your creativity and IMAGINATION to soar. What inspiration did you receive?

If you are a parent, plan something with your children that will create imagination time for them as well. Talk about it with them—you will be amazed by their creativity.

Organized Planning

The Crystallization of Desire into Action

·

In the end it is the quality and character, a leader's
understanding of how to be, not how to do, that
determines the performance, the results.
—FRANCES HESSELBEIN

SO YOU HAVE THAT BURNING DESIRE TO ACCOMPLISH A DEFI-
NITE PURPOSE, and FAITH in yourself and your ability to accom-
plish it, you have the SPECIALIZED KNOWLEDGE needed and your
IMAGINATION is in high gear. You create your PERSONAL MIS-
SION STATEMENT and follow the six steps outlined in the first
chapter to employ AUTOSUGGESTION.

The LAW of ATTRACTION says, "Think good thoughts and
good things will happen for you," or "You can attract into your life
whatever you think about." Napoleon Hill said, "What your mind can
conceive and believe, your mind can achieve."

So your SUCCESS should be assured, right?

In the chapter on FAITH, I shared the Personal Success Equation
from the book *Think and Grow Rich: Three Feet from Gold* and how
important having FAITH is in your success. Another essential com-

ponent of that formula is taking ACTION. In order to assure attraction of that which you want or need, you must also take action!

Actually, Hill also said you need to "go the extra mile," and need to have DEFINITE PLANS. So where do these plans come from?

As you task your imagination with your BURNING DESIRE it will generate both the strategy and the DEFINITE, practical PLANS that will make your success a reality.

Most success and leadership pundits lay out the process for Success in some form of the following four-step process.

1. VISION—**What** goal are you striving to accomplish?
2. STRATEGY—**How** are you going to accomplish it?
3. PEOPLE—**Who** is going to do it? Get the right people in the right positions.
4. LEADERSHIP—**You** lead your handpicked team to SUCCESS.

This is where Hill's philosophy stands apart from traditional thought and may reveal a very important distinction for anyone truly wanting to achieve success. He emphasizes that you must keep in mind these two important facts:

First. You are engaged in an undertaking of major importance to you. To be sure of success you must have *plans* that are faultless.

Second. You must have the advantage of the experience, education, native ability, and imagination of other minds in *creation of the plans.*

So under Hill's philosophy, you must have the "who" in place before you create your strategy and plans, so that you will derive benefit from the Mastermind's experience, education, native ability, and imagination. You employ the team to help you create the most effective strategy and definitive plans. You bring them in *before* you create the STRATEGY and get the benefit of their IMAGINATION in the process. In doing this, you develop a plan that is not only well organized, but can be executed with efficiency and success.

1. VISION—**What** goal are you striving to accomplish?
2. DEVELOPMENT TEAM—**Who** is on your Mastermind team to help you strategize and create the specific plan to do it?
3. STRATEGY—**How** are you and your team going to accomplish it?
4. DEFINITE PLANS—Created with, and approved by, the members of your MASTERMIND alliance.
5. PEOPLE—**Who** is going to do it? Put the right people in the right positions.
6. LEADERSHIP of the TEAM.

There is another distinction. Not only does Hill's leader involve and employ the power of the MASTERMIND, he distinguishes a different type of leadership, leadership by consent of and with the sympathy of the followers. This is in contrast to the other style of leadership, which is leadership by force, without the consent and sympathy of the followers.

Another way to contrast the two types of leadership would be to call the first Leadership by Collaboration and the second Dictatorial Leadership. By way of emphasizing his point, Hill points out, "History is filled with evidences that Leadership by Force cannot endure. The downfall and disappearance of dictators and kings is significant. It means that people will not follow forced leadership indefinitely."

The importance of leadership in organized planning cannot be overemphasized. Leaders "steer the boat" according to the plan and know how to leverage the best qualities of individuals in order to execute the well-thought-out plan of which all parties take ownership.

We celebrate LEADERSHIP BY CONSENT or COLLABORA-TIVE LEADERSHIP and agree that it is the best formula for SUC-

CESS. Since women excel at this type of leadership, they will continue to fill more and more leadership roles, and succeed.

A wonderful example of a woman leader with these skills is Frances Hesselbein, the president and CEO of Leader to Leader Institute. Prior to this role, she served as the CEO for the Girl Scouts of the USA for fourteen years (1976–1990). She is credited with reigniting the Girl Scouts through her organizational skills and leadership, as well as by increasing its diversity and establishing the Daisy Scouts program for younger girls. Under her leadership, the Girl Scouts grew to a membership of 2.25 million girls with a primarily "volunteer" workforce of 780,000. She was awarded the Presidential Medal of Freedom for her work.

When asked about leadership, her simple but powerful response is, "Leadership is a matter of how to be, not how to do it." In an article written by Joanne Fritz, who had been part of the Girls Scout organization under Hesselbein's leadership, she shared: "I have worked in business, education, and nonprofits during my career, and none measured up to the sheer organizational beauty of the Girl Scouts." Hesselbein's leadership philosophy includes the following recommendations:

1. Find mentors who are the best minds in the field.
2. Make your organization a learning organization. In her words: "The first item in your budget should be learning, education, and the development of your people."
3. Let go of any hierarchy. She placed the leader in the middle of the organizational chart instead of at the top, calling it "circular management." In her words: "We developed leaders at *every* level, and we discovered that circular management liberates the energy of our people, liberated the human spirit."
4. Respect the feelings of your dissidents. By doing so, you can turn antagonism into cooperation.

5. Do your research. Listen to the customer, and focus on needs, not your own assumptions. After research, run pilots to test ideas and/or programs.

Women approach leadership differently than men. The company McKinsey studied more than a thousand managers from a wide range of companies, and found that differences exist between the leadership styles of men and women. The following table shows what strategies each is more likely to employ in leadership positions.[27]

FREQUENCY OF USE OF MAJOR LEADERSHIP BEHAVIORS

Women Use More	Men Use More	Both Genders Use Equally Often
People development	Individualistic decision making	Intellectual stimulation
Expectations and rewards	Control and corrective action	Efficient communication
Role model		
Inspiration		
Participative decision making		

Today, the executive leadership of the Girl Scouts continues to innovate and focus on building leaders for tomorrow. Anna Maria Chavez, CEO of the organization, says, "Research shows that girls look at leadership differently than boys." The Girl Scout mission statement reads: "Girl Scouting builds girls of courage, confidence, and character, who make the world a better place." Its Three Keys to Leadership are:

Discover: Girls understand themselves and their values and use their KNOWLEDGE and skills to explore the world.

Connect: Girls care about, inspire, and team with others locally and globally.

Take Action: Girls act to make the world a better place.

With this type of training, we will continue to see great women leaders develop from the Girl Scouts.

When looking at women business leaders today, many people point to the fact that women currently hold only twenty-three Fortune 500 CEO positions (as of January 2014). This percentage has been consistently increasing year to year, however, and in 2012 women held 51.5 percent of U.S. management, professional, and related positions, which demonstrates growth in the number of women leaders.

FORTUNE 500 WOMEN CEOs (PERCENT)

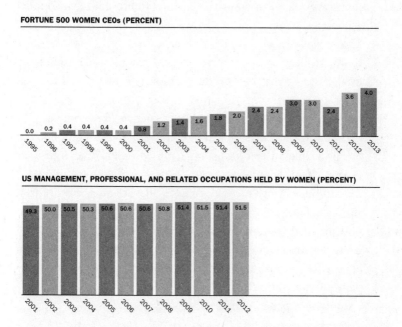

US MANAGEMENT, PROFESSIONAL, AND RELATED OCCUPATIONS HELD BY WOMEN (PERCENT)

Let's focus on the progress women are making and cheer them on as their influence grows in the workplace, boardroom, and CEO suites. Let's replace the negative talk about the lack of women CEOs with the positive talk about the advances that have been made, and are continuing to be made, by women in all levels of management.

Recognized as one of the women Fortune 500 CEOs as well as one of the Most Powerful Business Women in the World, Indra Nooyi, CEO of PepsiCo, calls her leadership style "performance with purpose" and has shared five leadership lessons that are important for global leaders in the twenty-first century.

1. Balancing the short term with the long term. Effective leaders need to find a balance, producing earning results in the short term but with vision for the long-term view of the business.
2. Develop public/private partnerships. These types of collaborations can create win-win strategies and improve local and global economies.
3. Think globally, act locally. She advocates breaking corporate silos, creating cross-corporate collaboration, while embracing local customs that can produce innovative and out-of-the-box ideas.
4. Keep an open mind, and be ready to change. She promotes asking probing questions to facilitate dialogue and exploration, and being flexible, instead of having a closed mind. Lead with your head and your heart.
5. Leaders must bring "their whole selves to work every day." In fact, she wrote letters to the parents of her executive team, telling them how proud they should be of their children. Apparently it paid great corporate culture dividends. Her executive team's passion and sense of purpose were energized in executing the company mission. [http://snyderleadership.com/2013/05/07leadership-lessons-from-pepsico-ceo-indra-nooyi/]

Indra Nooyi also has a meaningful message for women: "We women must listen to our inner voice. It is easier for women to do this as they are not afraid to say what they feel. We must keep both our femininity and our strength. As a leader, I am tough on myself and I raise the standard for everybody; however, I am very caring because I want people to excel at what they are doing so that they can aspire to be me in the future."

She recommends always having a positive attitude and intent. She warns that when you have a negative attitude, you deal from anger. If you face a negative situation with negativity, you have two negatives fighting each other. If you instead take away that anger, and react to a negative situation with positive intent, you will be amazed. You will diffuse the situation and your emotional maturity increases because you are not random in your response.

Napoleon Hill realized the ability of women to lead. His foundation presented its Gold Medal Award to Mary Kay Ash, founder of Mary Kay Cosmetics, in 1983. In presenting the award to her, trustee Jim Oleson of the foundation board echoed Hill's belief when he said, "It's the first, it's an historical event and in this day and age where woman are proving that they can get out and do the job that a man can do . . . if not better."

In her acceptance speech, Mary Kay shared: "I read [*Think and Grow Rich*] first through like a novel, and then I read it through one chapter every single day. I read that chapter every day for a week until I began to practice what it had said in those words. And at the end of that book and the end of those weeks . . . my life had turned around . . . I've come to feel that women can do anything in this world they want to do . . . if they want to do it bad enough. And it's that message that I try to instill in all our people across this nation and the other countries, 'You can do it, you can do anything . . .' So, yes, anything a man can do a woman can do better."

Mary Kay's pathway to success embodies the teachings of *Think and Grow Rich*. She had the BURNING DESIRE when she started her company with her life savings of five thousand dollars. Her goal was to provide women with an unlimited opportunity for personal or financial success. She had FAITH and IMAGINATION, and she had a good idea—allow women to advance by helping others to succeed. She demonstrated great PERSISTENCE, and she was a great leader.

As a leader she valued the individual worth of people and believed:

> Everybody wants to be somebody, to accomplish something, and have some worth;
>
> Nobody cares how much you know until they know how much you care;
>
> Everybody needs somebody;
>
> You can't achieve greatness by yourself.
>
> Anybody who helps somebody influences a lot of people. (Either directly or indirectly you are helping everyone within that person's circle of influence.)

When asked about her leadership style, she shared: "We treat our people like royalty. If you honor and serve the people who work for you, they will honor and serve you."

Each of these women I have mentioned are shining examples of true leaders and embody the following major attributes of leadership outlined by Hill in the original *Think and Grow Rich*:

THE ELEVEN MAJOR ATTRIBUTES OF LEADERSHIP

1. Unwavering courage
2. Self-control
3. A keen sense of justice
4. Definiteness of decisions
5. Definiteness of plans
6. The habit of doing more than paid for
7. A pleasing personality

8. Sympathy of understanding
9. Mastery of detail
10. Willingness to assume full responsibility
11. Cooperation. Leadership calls for *power*, and power calls for *co-operation.*

In addition to knowing the attributes of being a good leader, it is equally important to understand what may cause you to fail in your quest to become a good leader. Hill specifies ten major causes of failure in leadership because he felt it was just as important to know WHAT NOT TO DO as it is to know what to do:

THE TEN MAJOR CAUSES OF FAILURE IN LEADERSHIP

1. Inability to organize details
2. Unwillingness to render humble service
3. Expectation for pay for what they "know" instead of what they do with that which they know
4. Fear of competition from followers
5. Lack of imagination
6. Selfishness
7. Intemperance
8. Disloyalty
9. Emphasis on the "authority" of leadership
10. Emphasis on title

Let's focus on the "Definiteness of Plans" and "Mastery of Detail" as specific attributes needed by a great leader, as well as the "Inability to Organize Details" as a cause of failure in leadership. As Hill emphasized, "Your achievement can be no greater than your PLANS are sound."

Your plans need to be definite, they need to be both short term and long term, and they must be coupled with specific goals. If the first plan you make doesn't work, devise a new one, and if that new one fails to work, replace it with still another one, and so on until you find the plan that works. This comes from PERSISTENCE. Many of us meet with failure because we quit before we find the plan that works. Again, Hill reminds us that

A quitter never wins—and—a winner never quits.

Each of these women had great vision, courage, and tremendous persistence to achieve SUCCESS. But they also had specific DEFI-NITE PLANS and were organized in their strategies to employ those plans.

Ingrid Vanderveldt, the founder of Dell Innovator's Credit Fund and the Entrepreneur in Residence at Dell, highlights the importance of planning in one simple but powerful statement, "A desire without a roadmap is a dream that remains a wish. To 'Make the Impossible, Possible' or rather, to create and live the life you imagine—one that creates wealth for yourself and others—it's critical to develop a plan around your goal with measurable milestones that you hold yourself accountable to."

Think about your own life. Do you have definite plans? Did you enlist the power of a Mastermind in creating your plans? Are you organized, or could you be more organized? The topic of Organized Planning may not be the most exciting, but it is one of the most important in achieving success. Judith Williamson, director of Napoleon Hill World Learning Center, oversees the extensive library of Hill's work and shares her strategy for Organized Planning, providing practical advice we can all employ.

The Payoff in Organized Planning

Organized planning is essential to everyone's success. From writing a book, to constructing a dollhouse, to preparing a dinner, all demand advance planning and preparation. The same is true in building a successful career or business. An organized, and detailed, plan is critically important for charting your course to success.

Once my overall plan is set, I construct a daily to-do list of ten or more essential items I want to accomplish that day that will help me reach my long-term goals. The simple task of crossing it off the list makes me feel great, as I have accomplished something. I challenge myself to start with the least appetizing item on the list, as accomplishing it will jumpstart my day.

Since we all multitask, it is important to address issues related to our spiritual, physical, mental, social, emotional, and financial goals, so that we care for our whole being. If not, you could find yourself successful financially, but not healthy enough to enjoy it.

By beginning your itemized list with verbs such as 1) *wash* the car, 2) *clean* the bathroom, and 3) *write* the chapter, it will help you be motivated to take the action listed, and it will be easy to discern at the end of the day whether you accomplished your goal.

As you accomplish smaller objectives that contribute to larger goals, inch by inch, step by step, and yard by yard, the process begins to take on a life of its own.

As an example, when noticing things around the house, aren't you ever astonished as to how quickly things accumulate? Newspapers that arrive daily stack up to create a heavy load by the end of the week. Mail scattered on the dining room table soon covers the tabletop horizontally and begins to stack up vertically if left unsorted. Refrigerators filled with leftovers for "later" literally soon begin to take on a life of their own. These are just mundane examples of how the tendency is for things to accumulate. By creating a to-do list and focusing on your intention to declutter for a reasonable period each day, you will find that you have achieved a great deal by the end of the month. This cosmic pattern can be replicated for all our desirable goals and objectives once we understand how to put this natural law to our best use.

I perform best when I am organized. A former boss used to tell me that a folder for each project I was working on would be all the organization I needed to succeed. When I navigated from one project to the next, I would place whatever notes, receipts, memos, etc., I had accumulated into the folder. I also keep a printout of my calendar with related appointments and phone calls to help jog my memory later. The folder is always waiting for me the next time I need it. It's a simple system that works, if you use it.

Organized planning is crucial to anyone's success. But even the most organized individual needs to have a pleasing personality, creating friendly and authentic human relationships. With trust, sincerity, and genuine common interest in everyone's betterment and achievement and by intentionally following the golden rule of "do unto others as you would have others do unto you," we can begin the process of making the world better—starting with bettering ourselves.

The only person we can truly change lives inside of us. Fundamentally, the truth is that change begins with us, and when we change, everything around us changes also. By getting ourselves organized, we will be better able to lead others in accomplishing theirs.

Judy's advice emphasizes the importance of being organized, and suggests some simple systems we can use to become better organized on a daily basis. When you are not an organized leader, it is easy to become overwhelmed and lose focus. Getting organized may take a little time today but will provide long-term benefits, including:

1. Higher productivity—making a list allows you to prioritize, and you can then focus on each task as you address your to-do list;
2. Reduced stress—with organization, you gain confidence, and with confidence, stress is reduced;
3. Better working environment—by reducing clutter, you will have more space on your desk and be able to access important information more quickly.

But at the end of the day, the trick will be to stay organized! That requires establishing new habits that support your definiteness of purpose. Allyn Reid, a publisher and married to my *Three Feet from Gold* coauthor Greg Reid, shared her truth about habits, "The key thing about habits, they're difficult to form, they're difficult to keep up. If you have faith in yourself that the habits will work then allow yourself to have consistency. From there you'll find your life will move so much faster and more things will come to you. Just follow those two things, understanding your purpose and having amazing habits."

CHAPTER IN PRACTICE—IN MY LIFE

At the beginning of my career, I felt I needed to know everything, that asking questions would reveal my lack of KNOWLEDGE and make people think less of me. I believe this fear was the result of years of schooling where I was graded on my individual performance.

It didn't take long for me to realize how silly this was, but it did take a long time for me to break the habit of wanting to always have the right answer. I call myself a recovering straight-A student.

During this recovery process, I have discovered the tremendous energy and excitement that comes from the Mastermind process. The brainstorming process creates an environment of exponential ignition of imagination, as multiple minds feed each other. The process includes throwing out ideas, without judgment, followed by a lot of what-if questions and others that expand the group's thinking. The leader of the Mastermind needs to become more of a facilitator to make the process work. I was quite complimented at one such meeting when one of the members of the Mastermind told me, "I have never seen anyone able to 'lead' a roundtable with such grace and yet with such direction and focus."

It was during such a Mastermind that my husband, Michael, and I were searching for ways to share our newly acquired ranch, Cherry Creek Lodge in Young, Arizona. One of our friends "at the table" asked if we had been featured in *Arizona Highways,* and if we hadn't she would reach out to the publisher on our behalf. Eureka! Our ranch was featured on the cover of the January 2010 issue, and later that year the *Arizona Highways* television show filmed a special on the ranch, which continues to air from time to time.

While it may sound like a simple public relations opportunity, it was at that meeting that we created the various revenue engines that we would employ at the ranch, which included lodging (bed and breakfast), tours of historical sites where the Pleasant Valley War had been fought, horseback rides, all-terrain-vehicle rides, shooting courses, and special-event planning. Going into the meeting, we simply wanted to find ways to make the ranch generate a little revenue; coming out of the meeting we had collectively created a real business, with a real business model and a business plan, marketing strategies, promotional plans, and a vision for the future.

During a similar Mastermind meeting for my company, Pay Your Family First, we had shared with the team that we had been struggling getting our board game, ThriveTime for Teens, into the schools. We went into the meeting looking for help and strategies to get through to the administrators and principals in order to convince them of the importance of financial education, and the impact our game would have in preparing teens for the economic world they would face. Our strategy completely changed as a result of that meeting. We refocused our energies on offering the program to individual teachers at the high school, highlighting winners at each school, with a statewide tournament where the top winners would receive college scholarships.

The what-if questions were flying:

What if we pay the school a stipend for allowing us in?
What if we pay the top three winners at each school a small amount of prize money to encourage participation?
What if we invite the winners to a statewide tournament?
What if we have lots of prizes and a raffle at the state tournament?
What if we see if a major university will sponsor the state tournament?
What if we ask community leaders to help sponsor the initiative, showing collaboration?
What if we ask businesses to sponsor the event, further showing a public-private collaboration?
What if we perfect the model here in Arizona, so it can be duplicated in other states and other countries around the globe?

And the ThriveTime Challenge was born. Our added bonus has been that each year a major university has not only sponsored the state tournament, but they have also matched our scholarships for the winners. All from the power of a group of individuals with shared passion, a focused mission, and organized plans.

I must admit that my team may smirk at me being called an organized planner. While I call myself a multitasker, they affectionately refer to my shotgun focus. I call myself flexible, they call me entrepreneurial. In any event, I know my personal weakness is not the ability to create definite plans, but the inability to stick to them—which is why I make sure my team complements that weakness. The COO of Pay Your Family First, Angela Totman, has worked with me for more than twelve years. She is focused, organized, and she is a disciplinarian with a velvet hammer.

But more important, she has developed the leadership skills we have discussed in this chapter.

There are several habits I have adopted to assist myself in staying focused and organized with my plans. In addition to the to-do lists referred to by Judy Williamson, I make myself a stop-doing list. On it, I list the things that I do (that I use my time for) that could be done, usually more efficiently, by someone else. I find a way to stop doing it. In fact, I started having someone else clean my house and do my laundry twenty years ago so I would have more time to spend with my family and to get my writing done. Even though my husband still complains about how his socks are folded, it was the right decision for me. It reduced my stress at trying to do everything and I have absolutely no guilt about it!

I also created the "2-2-2 plan." It helped me establish a habit of focusing on the future of my business each and every day. Before I turned my computer off each evening, I would reach out to six people who could help open new opportunities for my business. Originally it stood for two phone calls, two handwritten letters, and two faxes (which tells you how long I have been in business). Today, it stands for two social media postings, two e-mails, and two handwritten notes, but the intent is the same—to always keep my focus on following the plans I have for growing my business. Creating the habit has helped me keep a measure of my efforts, and it allows me to show my gratitude to the people who have helped me grow.

We have all heard that gratitude is very important to living a happy life. But the importance of gratitude was brought home to me when I heard Brené Brown, Ph.D., L.M.S.W., a research professor at the University of Houston Graduate College of Social Work, address it in one of her TED talks. She shared: "[I] never talk about gratitude and joy separately, for this reason. In twelve years, I've never interviewed a single person who would describe their lives as joyful, who would describe themselves as joyous, who was not actively practicing gratitude."

So straight from the expert with proof, I now truly believe that:

Actively practicing gratitude brings you joyful results.

In addition to learning the power of gratitude along my journey to become a more effective leader, I also learned that I had to first lead myself to making better decisions. The next chapter focuses on making decisions that will not only make you a more effective leader, but will also speed your journey to success.

THE SISTERHOOD MASTERMIND

Wisdom from women of success and significance on ORGANIZED PLANNING:

ELEANOR ROOSEVELT (1884–1962)

LONGEST-SERVING FIRST LADY OF THE UNITED STATES, DURING HER HUSBAND PRESIDENT FRANKLIN D. ROOSEVELT'S FOUR TERMS IN OFFICE. PRESIDENT HARRY S. TRUMAN LATER CALLED HER THE "FIRST LADY OF THE WORLD" IN TRIBUTE TO HER HUMAN RIGHTS ACHIEVEMENTS

"It is not fair to ask of others what you are not willing to do yourself."

MEG WHITMAN

PRESIDENT AND CEO, HEWLETT-PACKARD

"A business leader has to keep their organization focused on the mission. That sounds easy, but it can be tremendously challenging in today's competitive and ever-changing business environment. A leader also has to motivate potential partners to join."

ELIZABETH DOLE
AMERICAN POLITICIAN AND
FORMER HEAD OF THE AMERICAN RED CROSS

"We aim to give a 'wake-up call' to businesses, to alert them to the fact that the next 'fair-haired boy' of their organization just might be a woman."

JOANNE HARRIS
BRITISH WRITER AND AUTHOR OF *RUNEMARKS*

"A man may plant a tree for a number of reasons. Perhaps he likes trees. Perhaps he wants shelter. Or perhaps he knows that someday he may need the firewood."

CONNIE LINDSEY
EXECUTIVE VICE PRESIDENT AND HEAD OF CORPORATE SOCIAL RESPONSIBILITY AT NORTHERN TRUST, AND NATIONAL BOARD PRESIDENT OF GIRL SCOUTS OF THE USA

"Great leaders are great servants."

HARRIET WOODS (1927–2007)
AMERICAN POLITICIAN AND U.S. SENATOR

"You can stand tall without standing on someone. You can be a victor without having victims."

MARGARET THATCHER (1925–2013)
PRIME MINISTER OF THE UNITED KINGDOM (1979–1990)

"Being powerful is like being a lady. If you have to tell people you are, you aren't!"

GOLDA MEIR (1898–1978)

FOURTH PRIME MINISTER OF ISRAEL

"It's no accident many accuse me of conducting public affairs with my heart instead of my head. Well, what if I do? Those who don't know how to weep with their whole heart don't know how to laugh either."

GLORIA STEINEM

AMERICAN FEMINIST LEADER AND JOURNALIST

"Planning ahead is a measure of class. The rich and even the middle class plan for future generations, but the poor can plan ahead only a few weeks or days."

ABIGAIL ADAMS (1744–1818)

WIFE OF JOHN ADAMS,
SECOND PRESIDENT OF THE UNITED STATES

"Great necessities call forth great leaders!"

JUDI SHEPPARD MISSETT

FOUNDER AND CEO OF JAZZERCISE, INC.

"Surround yourself with people who will lift you up, and then lead by letting other people become the emerging stars."

As Hill shared the importance of Organized Planning and Leadership as essential tools for success, he was preparing us for the next chapter. We are in control of our own destiny, and we must make the DECISION to want to succeed. It goes back to the Action element of the Personal Success Equation.

ASK YOURSELF

Use your journal as you go through this section to identify your action steps, trigger your "aha" moments, and create your plan for achieving success!

While this chapter is titled ORGANIZED PLANNING, it emphasized the importance of LEADERSHIP. In your journal record the following attributes of a good leader as identified by Hill and describe how you rate yourself for each attribute.

The Eleven Major Attributes of Leadership

1. UNWAVERING COURAGE
2. SELF-CONTROL
3. A KEEN SENSE OF JUSTICE
4. DEFINITENESS OF DECISION
5. DEFINITENESS OF PLANS
6. THE HABIT OF DOING MORE THAN PAID FOR
7. A PLEASING PERSONALITY
8. SYMPATHY AND UNDERSTANDING
9. MASTERY OF DETAIL
10. WILLINGNESS TO ASSUME FULL RESPONSIBILITY
11. COOPERATION

Leadership calls for POWER, and power calls for COOPERATION.

Now review your notes, and pick out two or three areas where you know you can make improvements in yourself. Record them, make an organized plan to work on them, and then commit to work on your plan in the next thirty days.

In addition to knowing the attributes of being a good leader, it is equally important to understand what may cause you to fail in your quest to become a good leader. Hill specifies the ten Major Causes of Failure in Leadership because he felt it was just as important to know WHAT NOT TO DO as it is to know what to do. In your journal record the following causes of failure in leadership that Hill has identified and how each may have hindered you at some time in your life.

The Ten Major Causes of Failure in Leadership
1. INABILITY TO ORGANIZE DETAILS
2. UNWILLINGNESS TO RENDER HUMBLE SERVICE
3. EXPECTATION FOR PAY FOR WHAT THEY "KNOW" INSTEAD OF WHAT THEY DO WITH THAT WHICH THEY KNOW
4. FEAR OF COMPETITION FROM FOLLOWERS
5. LACK OF IMAGINATION
6. SELFISHNESS
7. INTEMPERANCE
8. DISLOYALTY
9. EMPHASIS ON THE "AUTHORITY" OF LEADERSHIP
10. EMPHASIS ON TITLE

Now review your notes, and pick out two or three areas where you had a "tap on the shoulder" when you were reading them. How can you make improvements in yourself to get past them? Record them, make an organized plan to work on them, and then commit to work on your plan in the next thirty days.

Create your stop-doing list. Think of at least three things, no matter how small, that you can, and should, stop doing so that you will have more time to devote to your Definite Plan for Success. I will stop doing . . .

Create your own "2-2-2" plan for creating the habit of working on your plan for your future each and every day.

Engage with your Mastermind. Get a group of associates and/or friends together and discuss these attributes and

causes of failure. You will learn from them, and they may identify an area you need to work on that may be a surprise to
you. Or, you may also find that your associates and friends
have a higher opinion of your leadership skills than you do!
Enjoy!

Decision

The Mastery of Procrastination

*When you make the right decision, it doesn't
really matter what anyone else thinks.*
—CAROLINE KENNEDY

HAVE YOU EVER PROCRASTINATED? PUT SOMETHING OFF UNTIL
some point in the future? Waited until the last minute to do something, then squeezed it in just before the deadline?

Do you ever justify delaying a project, saying to yourself that you
work well under pressure, so it will all work out?

Hill defines PROCRASTINATION as the opposite of DECI-
SION and as the common enemy that we all must face in our quest
for success.

His study of successful people, who had accumulated fortunes,
showed that "*every one of them* had the habit of REACHING DECI-
SIONS PROMPTLY, and of changing these decisions SLOWLY if and
when they were changed." Conversely, "People who fail to accumulate
money, *without exception* have the habit of reaching decisions, IF AT
ALL, very *slowly*, and of *changing these decisions quickly and often.*"

When you combine your DEFINITE PURPOSE with your

BURNING DESIRE, you can more easily reach decisions promptly and are much less likely to procrastinate. If, however, you are easily influenced by the opinions of others, it will impact your ability to reach a decision. Think of a time when a family member or close friend, while not meaning to do so, put a damper on something you wanted to do simply by expressing concern or an opinion that made you rethink your intention. "You want to do *what*? Are you crazy?" Often they will use humor, but it comes across as ridicule.

As Hill shared: "Thousands of men and women carry inferiority complexes with them all through life, because some well-meaning, but ignorant person destroyed their confidence through 'opinions' or 'ridicule.'"

In *Outwitting the Devil*, Hill went even further when he introduced the concept of "drifting." A drifter is "someone who permits himself to be influenced and controlled by circumstances outside his own mind . . . one who accepts what life throws in his way without making a protest or putting up a fight." The devil shared that he wouldn't bother with people who were nondrifters because they had their definiteness of purpose and were driven to achieve it by their burning desire and could not be swayed from their goals. However, it is the drifters, who are easily swayed by the opinions of others, that the devil enjoys messing with the most by derailing them at every turn.

This habit of indecision typically begins during someone's youth and can only be counteracted when they find their definiteness of purpose and the desire to succeed.

Can you think of someone you know who you would consider a drifter? Do they have difficulty in making decisions? Do they go with the flow?

Now think of someone who is very successful. More than likely you would consider them a nondrifter. They use their own mind, and reach their own decisions.

Then there are those people who want to "look successful" and impress you with their knowledge. They generally do too much talking and not enough listening. As Hill warns, "Keep your eyes and ears wide OPEN—and your mouth CLOSED, if you wish to acquire the habit of prompt DECISION. Those who talk too much do little else. If you talk more than you listen, you not only deprive yourself of many opportunities to accumulate useful knowledge, but you also disclose your PLANS and PURPOSES to people who will take great delight in defeating you, because they envy you."

Hill then explains, "Genuine wisdom is usually conspicuous through modesty and silence." Today, we hear the phrase "actions speak louder than words."

Those people who can decide and take action quickly often become the leaders in their chosen field. This definiteness of decision requires courage. Courage is not the absence of fear, but acting in spite of the fear.

Hill gives this example: "The 56 men who signed the Declaration of Independence staked their lives on the DECISION to affix their signatures to that document. ECONOMIC FREEDOM, financial independence, riches, desirable business and professional positions are not within reach of the person who neglects or refuses to EXPECT, PLAN, and DEMAND these things. The person who desires riches in the same spirit that Samuel Adams desired freedom for the Colonies, is sure to accumulate wealth."

While the Declaration of Independence is an incredible example of courage that may seem unparalleled, it is not. There are people making decisions every day who demonstrate their courage to forge new paths toward achieving their goals.

There are many women who have shown great courage in opening opportunities for other women. One such woman was Amelia Earhart. As the first female pilot to fly solo across the Atlantic Ocean, she received the Distinguished Flying Cross for this record. She was also instrumental in the formation of the Ninety-Nines, an organization to support and encourage other female pilots. Her message to other women was profound in its simplicity:

The most difficult thing is the decision to act, the rest is merely tenacity. The fears are paper tigers. You can do anything you decide to do. You can act to change and control your life; and the procedure, the process is its own reward.

There are women facing difficult life situations every day. Many of them find the courage to make the decision to do whatever it takes to provide for themselves and their families. One such woman is Margie Aliprandi, who shares her story of how she made the decision to build a business to support her children, and in the process provided hope and opportunity to thousands of women around the world. This is her experience:

Twenty-six years ago I stood at the crossroads of my life, filled with doubt in the face of daunting circumstances. I was a single mom with three little kids. I had a big vision. I knew that my job as a junior high school music teacher would never support it. So when an opportunity to build my own network marketing business came along, I made the whatever-it-takes decision that unbeknownst to me would change our lives and the lives of hundreds of thousands around the world.

I had no business experience and no start-up capital. But I did have a definite major purpose. It was my children and my burning desire to give them a wonderful life. That definite major purpose kept me on track to make clear, nonnegotiable, committed decisions, easily and promptly. In the presence of clear, committed decisions, there can be no procrastination.

Procrastination is a symptom of many things, including the lack of a definite major purpose. But women are wired to desire meaning and purpose. We have an innate need to infuse our days and our actions with meaning. To do this we have two choices: either think differently about our daily routines so they feel purposeful and grand, or flat-out find things that have deep meaning and light us up. Your definite major purpose will provide that deep meaning. When your life purpose aligns with your business purpose, you are unstoppable. Then let the magic begin.

Our quest for meaning and purpose makes us great businesspeople. We're team players, collaborators, and good listeners. We're multitaskers, people-connectors, and nurturers. We're transparent, intuitive, and empathetic. We're always looking for the win-win, and we're happy to share the credit. Combine these natural traits with the mother instinct that drives us to stand so tenaciously when challenged and you have the firm decision maker.

One of the gifts of a clear, committed decision is that it makes life easier. You stay centered and strong when it seems that nothing is going right and the challenges are coming at you rapid-fire. You don't need to waste time and energy re-thinking things when obstacles get in your way. When you make a nonnegotiable decision, you burn bridges. You leave no chance for retreat, no back door, no escape hatch. You may fall down ninety-nine times but you'll get right back up again. You let nothing stop you from moving forward.

A whatever-it-takes decision means having courage, knowing yourself, trusting yourself, seeing a big vision, staying focused, and being persistent. Early on in my case, it also meant driving to distant states in my Subaru wagon because I couldn't afford airfare; sleeping in my Subaru wagon because I couldn't afford hotels; dressing in gas station restrooms and bouncing into meetings that sometimes consisted of a handful, or one, or even none of the expected audiences.

But in year one, my tenacity paid off and I made more money in a month than I would have made in a year of teaching. In year three, I made my first million dollars. Today I have a team of more than two hundred fifty thousand, which is one of the largest network marketing teams in the world. One night my unwavering whatever-it-takes policy meant making the wrenching decision of tearing myself away from a sobbing three-year-old boy pleading, "Mommy, don't go!" I was on my way to a meeting and he came running barefooted and pajama-clad into the street. I got out of the car, held little Todd in my arms, and wept with him. I promised that one day I'd take him and the other children everywhere. I knew this meant lots of sowing before I could reap; and I had no idea when the harvest would come.

I decided on short-term sacrifice for long-term gain.

If I had stayed home and just listened to the crying, I would never have built the business that enriched the lives of all four of my children, allowed us to travel the world, and helped me to lead them by example into a self-sufficient, caring and responsible adulthood. It turns out that I had not only planted seeds of financial abundance, but also seeds that in some small way contributed to who those kids are today. I modeled dedication, hard work, and keeping commitments. By steadfastly pursuing my dream, I showed them that their dreams matter too. Now, what my children mirror back every day is the most precious harvest of all.

And so, dig deep for your definite major purpose. Decide what you really want. Decide with clarity and commitment that you will get it. When your decisions are clear and committed, you will not abandon them. You will achieve mastery over procrastination, and you will be set free to succeed. As Napoleon Hill said, "Those who reach decisions promptly and definitely know what they want, and generally get it."

Margie's story is very inspirational and is echoed by many successful women who found their definiteness of purpose through their steadfast love for their family and burning desire to provide the best future possible for their family. In hearing about my work on *Think and Grow Rich for Women*, a young woman reached out to me with the earnest desire to share her story. I found it to be fascinating, both representative of issues many women are facing today, as well as inspirational in how Kimberly Schulte chose to make different decisions in her life.

Kimberly Schulte shares her story:

I sat at my kitchen table, feeling completely devastated and void of hope. Emotions of despair and anxiety consumed me, the fear so thick that it was suffocating my ability to even breathe. Unable to see a way through, I became a paralyzed prisoner to my depression. All I could think was, "When and what ball will drop next?" What used to be excitement and zest for life had turned to a feeling of dread. In denial of my own reality, all I could wonder was, "How did I become a single mother approaching forty, who went from a very comfortable, luxurious lifestyle to a failed marriage and being financially destroyed with tens of thousands of dollars of debt?"

Driven by my fears, I had become mastered by indecision. What I didn't realize at that time was that every decision I had *not* made led me here. It was not until later that I became wise with the knowledge that indecision IS a decision— it is simply deciding not to decide.

Indecision plants the seed of procrastination, which was my best friend. Avoidance of making decisions had become my immediate drug of choice to numb the pain of anxiety. But this quick fix payoff never lasted, and the long-term consequences always cost me greatly. I hated my habit of procrastination, yet I chose it over and over again.

As I started to slowly conquer my depression, I got the

help that I needed to make positive choices that resulted in forward movement. My progress seemed to exponentially multiply, however, after I decided one day to read *Think and Grow Rich* by Napoleon Hill. This book did not change my life but rather inspired me to become empowered to make decisions, take action, and change it myself!

I was getting clear and distinct messages from several people all within a short period of time that I need to read *Think and Grow Rich*. If I have learned one thing clearly in my experiences, when you get taps from God that you are being led to something, you heed the message and follow it! It was no accident that Mr. Hill's book came to me at the divine right time, when I was most ready to receive its profound message.

As the Buddhist proverb says, "When the student is ready, the teacher will appear."

I did not just read the book, I studied it. I took notes, meditated on it, and even bought the audio version. My car became a *Think and Grow Rich* classroom that fed my mind and soul during my long commute for work. Napoleon Hill's thirteen principles are brilliant. The one principle that hit me dead-on like an arrow to my heart, however, was Principle #7: DECISION.

Mr. Hill explained that people who had accumulated fortunes all had one major thing in common. They had a habit of reaching quick and definite decisions promptly, yet changing them slowly, if and when they were changed. No wonder I was stuck—I was living in reverse! Living in fear, I had formed a habit of indecision. Making decisions requires courage. What if I was wrong? What if it didn't work? What if I failed?

My habit needed to change, but where to start? I chose to *start at the start*. In other words, I began. I made that first decision, and then followed through by taking action on it. Then the next decision became easier, and I was building momentum.

I chose to reframe my old thinking patterns and deliberately think thoughts of only empowering outcomes. Deciding to move through my fears even though I was still afraid, my thoughts reframed to: What would my life be like if I stepped out in faith? What if I learned what didn't work so that I could do what did work? What if I succeeded? How would I feel on the other side when I had completed what I had been avoiding?

Inspired by my changed perspective, I began making one decision at a time and took action on purpose to follow through. My fears began to fade with each decision. More courage developed, more self-confidence grew, and it became easier and easier to make the next choice. I felt light, happy, and empowered. This was freedom!

As I sifted through what was left of my worldly possessions, I had a new epiphany. I was cash poor but "thing" rich with stuff I no longer needed or wanted. At the time, things that seemed so important to have, for myself, my home, my family, and for my kids, had now become heavy, burdensome, and useless to me. I was downsizing to a home less than half the size of the one I was forced out of. It was time to purge. I picked up each item, one by one, assessing, keep it, donate it, or pitch it.

Ironically, I recalled practically every dollar amount I had spent on each item. I thought, this item cost me fifty dollars, this one a hundred, this thousands . . . But now, with only memories of purchases without meaning, I was either giving items away or throwing them out. I couldn't afford a storage unit, so only what I really needed or loved would stay.

I no longer wanted to buy "things." I decided right then and there that I would pay my debt off and invest in myself. I would spend my money more deliberately, wisely, and purposefully. My decision was clear. I would spend money on educating myself in specific skills that would give me a lifetime of value instead of short-term pleasure. As I learned from *Think and Grow Rich*, I decided to take massive action, making decisions quickly and definitively. I invested in myself with education in my passions: coaching, yoga, and fitness.

Because of this, I am blessed to live a life of significance by making a difference in the lives of hundreds of people that I have coached and inspired!

I decided from this moment on, I would spend my money on learning new skills that I was passionate about, and teach my children to do the same in their lives. As a family, we would respect ourselves by making mindful choices with our money. Deciding to invest and spend our money wisely on experiences, travel, culture, nutrition, and of course still some luxury items! Reading and applying Napoleon Hill's seventh principle, DECISION, helped me shift from a life of consumption to a life of contribution. I now add value to the world every day in the work that I am doing. What a blessing this has paid forth in my life and in the lives of others!

Just five years ago, I was financially devastated, on the brink of declaring bankruptcy and utterly consumed in indecision and procrastination. Today, I am elated to share that I am nearly debt free! Better yet, I have acquired the mind-set that I can create whatever income I desire and the skills to make it a reality. I radically shifted my thinking so that I could truly Think and Grow Rich. It all started with the choice to move from indecision to being in decision. Teach-

ing and inspiring my children and others to do the same in
their own life is my passion.

Indecision is a decision!

Kimberly's message that indecision is a decision is incredibly
important. Her journey demonstrates the path we each can take to
change our lives for the better, to shift from lives of consumption to
lives of contribution. In doing so, we are able to not only create success
in our lives, but also lead lives of significance.

When you fully commit and invest yourself in deciding to create
the future you want, doors will fly open and you will be better able to
recognize new opportunities. Loral Langemeier is a perfect example
of someone who made the decision to change direction in her life,
from a successful corporate career to becoming an entrepreneur to
teach people how to create financial independence in their lives. Her
advice to other women is priceless:

> I'm here to tell you, you can have everything you've ever
> wanted in every area of your life—a fulfilling family life, a
> successful career, a hot body, a sizzling relationship—and it's
> easier to achieve than you might think.
>
> See, most women get it all wrong. They think that in
> order to HAVE it all, they must DO it all . . . that having a
> "balanced" life means handling everything in it. Well, that is
> neither correct nor sustainable. The real way to live a healthy
> and balanced life, and to truly have it all, is to start making
> very prompt and firm decisions about what you want and
> what you need to do to get there. The rest doesn't matter.
>
> This is exactly what I did to build a multimillion-dollar
> business and create the life of my dreams. The first thing I
> did was decide I was going to get what I wanted. It sounds
> simple, but it's probably the most important decision you can

make. Most women don't do this. They don't give themselves permission to go after what they truly want. This is the key.

Next, I asked myself, "How much is it going to cost me to have the life I want?" I challenge all of you reading this to start thinking about what that number is for you. And have the courage to play big, design big! Where do you want to live? What kind of vacations do you want to take? Who will you hire to make it happen?

Once I got that number, I simply demanded it of my business. I decided it would reach that level, no matter what. This gave me clarity and direction in my business and it fueled my desire to get there.

Now, of course, I didn't do it alone. I had the support and input of a lot of amazing folks. But keep in mind, input is different from opinions. We women are conditioned to seek opinions and the approval of others and this is holding us back. I don't want you to seek opinions, I want you to find input from strategic thinkers who have experience and evidence of results! You need to surround yourself with people who plan a bigger game in order to level up.

It all started for me when I met Sharon Lechter and she presented me with an entrepreneurial opportunity to sell and teach her company's financial education game. This decision illuminated my path to freedom and my way out of corporate America; 120 days later, I quit my job. If you're feeling stuck in a job, know that there is a way out. You have special gifts and talents that you can monetize. This is exactly what our work in *Think and Grow Rich for Women* is going to help you with. All you need to do is decide to finally live the life you want.

From there I created my own company, Live Out Loud, and created my own educational platform and programs. My first year in business, I earned hundreds of thousands of dollars. By year two, I was making millions and I haven't stopped. Live Out Loud is now a $24 million international company. Now, I'm not saying this to brag or sound arrogant. I just want you to see this is possible for you. If a farm girl from Nebraska can do it, so can you. You just need to DECIDE.

Following this advice got me to #1 on the *New York Times* bestseller list, landed me a gig as Dr. Phil's money expert, and had me featured on major national media outlets all over the world.

How do you get there? I'm challenging all you women out there to step up. You have a God-given talent and if you truly believe in the power of your product—both in how it can serve you and the world—then it's your birthright to play a bigger game. You really have only one choice to make and the economy depends on it.

Stop overthinking it and stop procrastinating. Procrastination breeds indecision and indecision breeds procrastination. Move forward promptly with discipline and consistency. It may seem like a struggle at first, but that's just because those muscles are weak and atrophied. The more decisions you make, the more momentum you'll gain, and the easier it will become. And remember, don't do it all! As women, we are grand collaborators. Find a role model, mentors, and team members to propel you forward. Start by deciding that you're worth it.

You can do this. Live by courage and faith. Say yes and figure out how. It's all waiting for you.

Loral's advice is right on the mark. Have you ever said to yourself, "Easy for her to say, I will look for, or become, a mentor when I am a little further along," or "When I make more money I can start giving to charity"? This is procrastination at its best. These are both examples of decisions of indecision. Make the decision that you are worthy, and that you can design your life of success and significance.

CHAPTER IN PRACTICE—IN MY LIFE

Most of my life, I have been quick to say things like "I work best under pressure" and "I do my best work when I am facing a deadline." Reading Hill's chapter on Decision in *Think and Grow Rich* caught me right between the eyes. It made me realize I had just been making excuses with those statements, when I really had become a champion procrastinator. Many of us tend to put off difficult decisions. While it is a form of procrastination, I think it is also because of the fear of the consequences or fear of change. Some may also call it fear of rocking the boat.

On a very personal note, one of the most difficult decisions of my life was choosing to leave the Rich Dad organization. I had given birth to it, and poured my soul into building it for more than ten years. Every book was like one of my children. For several years, however, I had felt a disconnect with my partners. We were no longer aligned in the mission of the company. They wanted to transform the company into a franchise model and sell franchises, and I wanted to continue creating affordable products for people wanting to take control of their financial lives. The environment in the office vacillated from celebratory one day to very difficult and negative the next. It was quite the roller coaster.

Weekly, I would ask myself, "Is staying good for Sharon?" Which I would quickly answer, "No!" Then I would ask myself, "Is staying good for the company, am I still making a positive impact?" Which would be answered, "Yes." So for several years, I had continued to make the decision to stay in an environment that was not healthy for me.

I procrastinated for two years before making the decision, which ultimately ended up improving my life. In fact, I realized that procrastination itself had become a habit. Every time you procrastinate, you are reinforcing the negative action. The longer you procrastinate, the more you program your subconscious mind to associate procrastination and laziness with the activity you are trying to avoid. It will become a damaging habit with negative consequences.

The day I made the decision to leave, I felt tremendous relief. I have never regretted it. When I finally did what was best for me, other doors of opportunity opened for me. I was asked by President George W. Bush to be on his Advisory Council on Financial Literacy, and I served both Presidents Bush and Obama in that capacity. It was a tremendous honor, one I would not have experienced had I stayed at Rich Dad.

Then I received the call from Don Green, asking me to work with him to reinvigorate the work of Napoleon Hill—first working with coauthor Greg Reid on *Three Feet from Gold*, and then annotating the hidden manuscript of Hill's provocatively titled *Outwitting the Devil*. What an incredible honor, to be able to step into the largest personal development brand in the world, after building the largest personal finance brand. I was truly blessed!

But the lesson was so important. I lived through several years of frustration that impacted my health in very negative ways. I gained weight and had to take blood pressure medication due to the constant stress I was under. Once I made the decision that was RIGHT FOR ME, my world turned around. I have lost weight; I no longer need blood pressure medication. I can focus on my business goals without the added stress of being in a difficult environment.

I have heard that it takes three weeks to establish a new habit (hopefully, a good one), but I think I tend to skew that average because it took me closer to two years to make a DECISION to form better habits.

My current goal is to commit even greater effort to improving my health, through exercise and better eating habits. I will shed my negative procrastinating habit of not exercising enough and replace it with daily positive action toward better health.

Many women are like me and tend to put themselves last, taking care of their families, jobs, businesses, and households first. One of my goals is to help women, including myself, learn to take better care of themselves. By doing so, we will be even better able to take care of our families, jobs, businesses, and households.

THE SISTERHOOD MASTERMIND

Wisdom from women of success and significance on DECISION and Mastering Procrastination:

VIRGINIA "GINNI" ROMETTY
CHAIRWOMAN AND CEO, IBM

"Actions speak louder than words is one thing I think I always took from my mom. And to this day, I think about that in everything I do. The second thing, you know, I think about that, she did some things that were unbelievable. So, nothing is insurmountable after that. You come to believe nothing is insurmountable. And I think the third thing she taught us was you define yourself. Don't let others define you. You define yourself."

KATHIE LEE GIFFORD
TELEVISION HOST, SINGER, AND SONGWRITER

"I wasn't ever interested in marrying someone else's career or bank account."

MURIEL SIEBERT (1932–2013)
THE FIRST WOMAN TO OWN A SEAT ON THE NEW YORK STOCK EXCHANGE AND THE FIRST WOMAN TO HEAD ONE OF THE NYSE'S MEMBER FIRMS

"There were no female role models, so I just blazed my own path."

"I fought like a son of a bitch to get ahead."

"I didn't create my business simply by pounding on the door and saying, 'I'm a woman, I'm entitled.' I made my success by slugging it out with the boys."

"Part of my career goal was 'Where can I go where there is no unequal pay situation?' That's why I decided to buy a seat on the stock exchange and work for myself."

MIA HAMM
RETIRED AMERICAN PROFESSIONAL SOCCER PLAYER,
MEMBER OF THE NATIONAL SOCCER HALL OF FAME

"Follow your heart, and make it your decision."

CLARE BOOTHE LUCE (1903–1987)
THE FIRST AMERICAN WOMAN APPOINTED TO A MAJOR
AMBASSADORIAL POST, SERVING AS AMBASSADOR TO ITALY
AND BRAZIL

"In the final analysis there is no other solution to man's progress but the day's honest work, the day's honest decision, the day's generous utterances, and the day's good deed."

SHERYL SANDBERG
CHIEF OPERATING OFFICER, FACEBOOK

"But women rarely make one decision to leave the workforce. They make lots of little decisions along the way."

"I do not have the answers on how to make the right choices for myself, much less for anyone else. I do know that I can too easily spend time focusing on what I am not doing. When I remember that no one can do it all and identify my real priorities at home and at work, I feel better— and I am more productive in the office and probably a better mother as well. Instead of perfect, we should aim for sustainable and fulfilling."

CARLY FIORINA
AMERICAN BUSINESS EXECUTIVE AND CEO,
HEWLETT-PACKARD (1999–2005)

"Quitting law school was the most difficult decision of my life. But I felt this great relief that this is my life and I can do what I want with it."

SOLANGE KNOWLES
AMERICAN SINGER-SONGWRITER (SISTER OF BEYONCÉ),
WHO AT TWENTY-SEVEN WAS STRUGGLING TO
FIND A WORK/LIFE BALANCE AND MADE
THE DIFFICULT DECISION TO CANCEL UPCOMING
PERFORMANCES IN ORDER TO FOCUS ON FAMILY

"Any decision I make is based on myself, and the only person I have to give an explanation to is God."

ANN MCNEILL
PROFESSIONAL DEVELOPMENT EXPERT

"Your destiny is not a matter of luck, it is the result of the choices you make on a daily basis. These choices will either elevate you or cause your dreams to sink. Decide today to be everything you have been created to be and everything you deserve. Your success is in your hands."

SHEIKHA LUBNA AL QASIM
UNITED ARAB EMIRATES' FIRST FEMALE MINISTER

"It is up to us as women to decide . . . what it is that we can do and not do."

MARIA SIMONE
TRANSFORMATIONAL BUSINESS AND
FUNDING STRATEGIST, SPEAKER, AND AUTHOR

"The more clear we become about what we want to accomplish, the peo-

ple we want to attract, and the life we want to live, the easier it can be-come. It's the lack of choosing—that living by default and dealing with whatever shows up—that creates chaos and disappointment. Allow your heart and soul to share truth and see what shows up. Commit to the al-lowing and stop denying yourself the very things you want simply because they don't seem logical or others are telling you there's no way. There's always a way."

SHANDA SUMPTER
FOUNDER AND QUEEN VISIONARY, HEARTCORE BUSINESS

"Wealth is created by how you make your decisions, not how many op-portunities you get. You can put yourself in the flow of opportunity."

CLARISSA BURT
FORMER INTERNATIONAL SUPERMODEL AND ACTRESS

"Maybe you are using a desire you can't fulfill to distract you from truly engaging the blessings you already have."

ASK YOURSELF

Use your journal as you go through this section to identify your action steps, trigger your "aha" moments, and create your plan for achieving success!

Can you think of a time when you were lost in indecision or procrastinated?

How did you deal with it?

Here are some steps that may help you conquer procrastination.

1. Set clear definitive goals. Make sure they are SMART goals:
   a. Specific
   b. Measurable
   c. Achievable
   d. Realistic
   e. Time-bound
2. Share your goals with your family and friends. It will make your goals more real.
3. Eliminate distractions that may keep you from focusing on your goals.
4. Recognize your bad habits—maybe you start thinking about answering e-mails, or wanting to get something to drink; these are signs you are starting to procrastinate. Recognize them and stop yourself.
5. Don't worry about perfection, just get started.
6. Break the task into smaller ones.
7. Create "little wins" along the way, and celebrate achieving each one.
8. Simply do it now!

Decide today to create your own blueprint. Visit sharonlechter.com/women for additional resources to assist you in creating the success you so richly deserve.

Persistence

The Sustained Effort
Necessary to Induce Faith

◾

*Never give up, for that is just the place and
time that the tide will turn.*

—HARRIET BEECHER STOWE

THERE YOU ARE, SO CLOSE TO YOUR GOAL OR FEELING THE FIRE
within to start something new—and a wall rises in front of you. How
will you scale and overcome the wall?

You get unexpected news. Life changes immediately and you cannot begin to imagine how it will turn out. How do you make it through
the uncertainty?

You have been working so long. You feed your passion with action
and have faith that your determination to continue will one day be
rewarded. How do you trek on down what seems like an endless road?

If you have ever found the light at the end of the tunnel, have ever
faced down fear and been the victor, or have ever answered doubt and
criticism with achievement, you already have the answer inside you.
PERSISTENCE is the key to successfully batting obstacles back that
life catapults in your way. This is the weapon that causes enemies such
as fear, doubt, and negativity to crumble.

Hill observed in his study and synthesis of the philosophy of achievement: "Will power and desire, when properly combined, make it an irresistible pair."

Young children provide a great demonstration of this. When we are young, we are inherently persistent. Have you ever seen a parent worn down by a child relentlessly insistent upon something? Whether for a new toy, a tasty dessert, or an opportunity to play with a friend, children often combine their desire with persistence to meet their desired end.

Over time, this persistence is diluted when children are taught that making mistakes and receiving criticism is always a bad thing and that drawing outside the lines is not acceptable in most environments.

According to Hill, persistence is a state of mind, meaning it can be cultivated by anyone. A person training herself to be persistent would require a foundation for this training that includes the following eight factors:

1. DEFINITENESS OF PURPOSE. Knowing what one wants is the first and perhaps the most important step toward the development of persistence. A strong motive forces one to surmount many difficulties.
2. DESIRE. It is comparatively easy to acquire and to maintain persistence in pursuing the object of intense desire.
3. SELF-RELIANCE. Belief in one's ability to carry out a plan encourages one to follow the plan through with persistence. (Self-reliance can be developed through the principle described in the chapter on AUTOSUGGESTION.)
4. DEFINITENESS OF PLANS. Organized plans, even though they may be weak and entirely impractical, encourage persistence.
5. ACCURATE KNOWLEDGE. Knowing that one's plans are sound, based upon experience or observation, encourages persistence; "guessing" instead of "knowing" destroys persistence.

6. COOPERATION. Sympathy, understanding, and harmonious cooperation with others tend to develop persistence.
7. WILLPOWER. The habit of concentrating one's thoughts upon the building of plans for the attainment of a definite purpose leads to persistence.
8. HABIT. Persistence is a direct result of habit. The mind absorbs and becomes a part of the daily experiences upon which it feeds. Fear, the worst of all enemies, can be effectively cured by forced repetition of acts of courage.

For women, implementation and application of some of these eight factors may come with great challenge, while others with surprising ease.

As caregivers, supporters, confidantes, and peacemakers, women often put themselves and their desires last. For some women, establishing a definiteness of purpose may feel selfish. It is important to realize that in contrast, having a definite purpose and working toward it will set a good example and that by creating positive impact we are improving all lives that we touch. This could be a close-knit group, such as immediate family, but is more likely to extend to friends and community members.

This same innate calling to be of service to those in need and willingness to sacrifice our own needs may put a woman's self-reliance at risk. Understand that providing yourself an opportunity to be the best individual woman and reaching maximum potential will better prepare you to then fulfill any natural desire to nurture, empower, or in turn help others reach their best potential. This first starts with the belief that you deserve it, are worthy, and that you are capable of self-reliance. If you have doubts related to any of these statements, allow yourself additional time to understand and employ AUTO-SUGGESTION.

Planning, accurate knowledge, and cooperation provide an opportunity for women to leverage characteristics that come naturally to most. Because women are less reluctant to ask for help, they are able to put together a sound plan with the support and utilizing the knowledge of others where needed. In addition, as natural collaborators, women are easily able to engage others. When we see others get excited about what we are doing, it helps us maintain energy, enthusiasm, and the tenacity needed to persist.

The tendency of women to be more emotionally driven than men can influence willpower and habit either positively or negatively. A woman who is able to direct her emotions and energy in order to concentrate on an end goal and the repetitive actions needed to achieve her desired purpose will be more likely to achieve success.

Michelle Patterson shares how her own PERSISTENCE gave her the willpower to keep going with the California Women's Conference when everyone around her was telling her she should cancel it. She had a dream and a vision and doggedly pursued it even in the face of major obstacles.

Persistence is one of the biggest keys to success. It means that you keep moving forward even when you feel like quitting. Many people give up on their dreams at the first sign of opposition or misfortune. Nothing in life worth achieving ever comes easily. Sometimes you need to fight for your dream. Sometimes you need to let your sheer will and persistence carry you through despite all the negativity and opposition you might face.

Since its founding three decades ago, the California Women's Conference has been bringing together women from all over the world to learn from each other and to grow. The purpose of the conference was to address the failure rate of women in business in California. For most of that time, the event was organized by the first lady of California, the governor's wife. But in 2012, Governor Jerry Brown's wife decided to discontinue the event. Mrs. Brown's decision really affected and inspired me. As an experienced producer of large-scale events, I decided to take over the conference, determined to keep it alive. I locked down a venue, built my team, developed a plan, and started to execute. I had a burning desire and a definite plan of action.

Over the next few months, I signed up thousands of attendees, brought in more than 250 exhibitors, and secured more than 150 speakers. Everything was off to a great start, but as the event grew closer, things were not going according to plan. I had two big setbacks that jeopardized my dream and the event. First, the team outsourced to handle sponsorships missed their projections; they were nowhere near what they should have been. Second, the funding that was expected to come for the business failed to materialize. When a payment came due for the production, I realized my business was $1.8 million in the hole. The event was in danger of being canceled, and we had just seventeen days to save it.

This was the moment when it felt like I just couldn't go on anymore. After months of hard work and putting everything I had into this event, people were telling me that I had to shut down the event! One of the most common reasons for failure in any endeavor is giving up too soon. Persistence allows you to keep taking action even when you don't feel motivated to do so, and therefore you keep accumulating results. You keep moving forward no matter what.

That's exactly what I did.

With a definite goal—to put on this event and to provide resources to thousands of women who needed it—against all odds, I kept at it. No matter how many people told me to shut down the event, I just kept the end result in mind and stuck to the plan. I pulled in all my resources together and stuck to the plan.

Together with my team of advisors, I went from being

shut down and considering bankruptcy to reducing what was owed from $1.8 million down to $150,000. By persisting and having a positive attitude I was able to make the 2012 California Women's Conference extremely successful.

In the following year after the conference so many great things started happening. The size and scope of women's initiatives the conference focused on has grown to nearly every issue that is important to women, not only in California but also across the country. Today, my objective for the conference along with our new organization, the Women Network Foundation, is to harness the passion and ambition the conference embodies and take it around the globe.

We are able to make a bigger impact on the world by forming partnerships with the United Nations and other major women's groups. By also creating a digital platform where women can come together to be a part of an online global community that provides resources and education, I was able to bring inspiration from the two-day California Women's Conference to be available 365 days of the year.

I often reflect on what would have happened had I given up out of fear and let my ego get the best of me, but by not accepting defeat, the loss was nothing more than a temporary roadblock. Had I given up when I was at my lowest, none of this would have been possible. By persisting and just taking one step at a time, I was able to create an organization that has an impact on thousands of women worldwide.

Michelle's story not only demonstrates persistence, but also how she continues to employ the eight factors Hill defined as key to developing it.

You may be thinking that you know your definite purpose, have clearly defined your desire, and envisioned your achievement and the plan that will get you there, only to have the rug pulled from under you, unsure of why things did not work out. What was the missing piece, disabling your persistence?

Hill identified the following Symptoms of Lack of Persistence, stating, "Here you will find the real enemies which stand between you and noteworthy achievement."

1. Failure to recognize and to clearly define exactly what one wants.
2. PROCRASTINATION, with or without cause. (Usually backed up with a formidable array of alibis and excuses.)
3. Lack of interest in acquiring SPECIALIZED KNOWLEDGE.
4. Indecision, the habit of "passing the buck" on all occasions, instead of facing issues squarely. (Also backed by alibis.)
5. The habit of relying upon alibis instead of creating definite plans for the solution of problems.
6. SELF-SATISFACTION. There is but little remedy for this affliction and no hope for those who suffer from it.
7. Indifference usually reflected in one's readiness to compromise on all occasions, rather than meet opposition and fight it.
8. The habit of blaming others for one's mistakes, and accepting unfavorable circumstances as being unavoidable.
9. WEAKNESS OF DESIRE, due to neglect in the choices of MOTIVES that impel action.
10. Willingness, even eagerness to quit at the first sign of defeat. (Based upon one or more of the six basic fears.)
11. Lack of ORGANIZED PLANS, placed in writing where they may be analyzed.
12. The habit of neglecting to move on ideas, or to grasp opportunity when it presents itself.
13. WISHING instead of WILLING.
14. The habit of compromising with POVERTY instead of aiming at riches. General absence of ambition to *be*, to *do*, and to *own*.

15. Searching for all the shortcuts to riches, trying to GET without GIVING a fair equivalent usually reflected in the habit of gambling, endeavoring to drive "sharp" bargains.

16. FEAR OF CRITICISM, failure to create plans and to put them into action, because of what other people will think, do, or say. This enemy belongs at the head of the list, because it generally exists in one's subconscious mind, where its presence is not recognized. (See the Six Basic Fears in a later chapter.)

As you review these adversaries to persistence, ask yourself if any have an influence on your life. Although it is difficult to hold a mirror to ourselves and take inventory of our actions and decisions, doing so empowers us to know what changes need to be made in order to be successful. A woman who can identify and be honest regarding any obstacle she has allowed to impact her is much more courageous than one who fears what she might discover or allows pride to stand in her way, thereby choosing to be stopped in her tracks by the obstacle.

"There may be no heroic connotation to the word 'persistence,' but the quality is to the character of man (woman) what carbon is to steel."

Hill offered the following advice for building momentum when developing PERSISTENCE: "You may find it necessary to snap out of your mental inertia . . . moving slowly at first, then increasing your speed, until you gain complete control over your will. Be PERSISTENT no matter how slowly you may, at first, have to move. WITH PERSISTENCE WILL COME SUCCESS."

Notice that Hill referred to starting slowly at first and then increasing speed. This means taking one step to get started, then another to progress and then another, not waiting for life to create the circumstances you need for success.

Many people believe that material success is the result of favorable "breaks." The only "break" anyone can afford to rely

upon is a self-made "break." These come through the application of PERSISTENCE. The starting point is DEFINITE-
NESS OF PURPOSE.

Tracy Trottenburg is the founder of Amazing Woman International and shared the importance that persistence and perseverance
played in her success: "I had a lot of highs and a lot of lows throughout
my career and in my business and to really dig deep and keep perse-
vering has been phenomenal and that book [*Think and Grow Rich*]
reminded me that it wasn't just about—going and going and keeping
going just for the sake of it, but actually what happens to that part of
you—that part of me that really came out when I just dug deeper and
I didn't stop; that's number one, and number two was really about that
faith.

As I really dug in and let that sink in and believe it while I was
reading the book and working the book, my business grew
exponentially, with ease and grace.

Paula Fellingham, founder of the Women's Information Network,
shares how persistence not only helped her build a global network of
women, but also how she sees women all around the world utilizing
persistence to build success for themselves and their families.

I believe this is the most magnificent time in history to be
a woman. Right now there is a rising and awakening of
the women of the world that is more far-reaching and fast-
moving than anything ever before experienced in history.

Yes, women around the globe are squaring their shoulders and lifting their heads as they understand, like never
before, that this is our time. Humanity is watching this global
phenomenon and some are concerned. Most are rejoicing.

I've observed that one of the powerful contributing components to the surge in women's progress is their persistence. Indeed, many women who are part of today's global feminine breakthroughs embody this value. They understand that persistence is a critical key to success in their personal lives and in their businesses.

As the founder of the Women's Information Network (WIN), I have witnessed profound persistence in action as I meet with women in many countries. One remarkable role model is Edel Quinn. She tirelessly works in the Kibera slums in Nairobi, Kenya, where nearly one million people live in one square mile. Edel teaches women how to start small businesses so they can eventually leave the slums and provide better lives for their children.

One rainy afternoon as I walked with Edel through the slums and talked with the women there, I was deeply impressed with their positive attitudes and emotional strength. Those I met were cheerful, hopeful, and tenaciously persistent in their efforts to release themselves and their families from their dire circumstances. Our sisters in Kibera truly embody the definition of persistence, which is "to continue steadily despite problems or obstacles."

Napoleon Hill remarked, "There is no substitute for persistence! It cannot be supplanted by any other quality!" Mr. Hill maintained that persistence is a state of mind, as well as a character trait. I wholeheartedly agree.

Women who persist are those who believe in their goals strongly enough to keep trying and working through the tough times. We women all know what tough times feel like because each of us has experienced a "refiner's fire" in our lives to some degree. When the "heat" increases, some women whine and blame and quit. Others shine and work and persist.

Women today recognize that we stand upon the shoulders of those heroic women throughout history who exemplified persistence. Amelia Earhart is one of my favorites. After numerous international successes as a pilot, in 1937 she died in her attempt to be the first woman to fly solo around the world. In her final letter, Amelia answered her concerned husband's question. He asked why she persistently tried to reach such lofty goals. Amelia wrote: "I want to do it because I want to do it. Women must try to do things as men have tried. If they fail, their failure must be but a challenge to others."

As women who are traveling through life together during the twenty-first century, let us joyously celebrate our progress and also eagerly serve our sisters in need. We should persist in doing good—every day—no matter what.

I leave you my love and my invitation to connect heart-to-heart with your sisters during this exciting global rising and awakening of the women of the world.

CHAPTER IN PRACTICE—IN MY LIFE

Have you ever been called stubborn, dogged, tenacious, or determined? All of these adjectives are synonymous with being persistent.

I have to admit that I have always been very persistent. As a child, I had to find the right, and complete, answer for every homework assignment I was given. In high school and college, I spent many all-nighters making sure term papers were as perfect as possible (thank goodness for Wite-Out!).

This has carried over into my business life, sometimes to the extreme. I have a hard time letting go of every book I write because every time I go over the manuscripts I think of more I want to add. I have learned to impose deadlines on myself in order to force completion for each book.

And once the book is complete, true persistence is needed to properly promote the book. Many authors have the "write it and it will sell" attitude and are sadly disappointed when their book sales don't explode. Successful authors know that they are their best marketing tool. You must doggedly promote, consistently reach out to media and scheduled events, capitalize on social media to spread the news, and commit to persistently promote your book for it to succeed.

You may know that *Rich Dad Poor Dad* was on the *New York Times* bestseller list for more than seven years. What you may not know is that it took three years for us to get it there. I was shipping books from my dining room table and going to the post office every day to fill orders. When the post office told me I couldn't bring such large quantities into that facility anymore, it jolted me into action and I found a fulfillment house to take over the shipping.

At the three-year mark, after constant, never-ending promotion and doing whatever it took to spread our message, we hit the lists. That was when the major publishing houses came after us. They hadn't been interested when we had originally offered the book to them, but once we showed our success, they were knocking on our door.

In concert with my publishing efforts over the last twenty years has been my passion to get financial education into school curriculums. It has been an uphill battle, filled with red tape, people who openly resist any change, as well as school administrators who are too overworked with their daily issues to even spare the time to listen to our initiative. In June, however, we achieved our first major win, when the governor of Arizona signed a bill into law that provides the first major step in ensuring Arizona high school students will have a proficiency in personal finance when they graduate.

I have just completed a college curriculum called "Your Financial Mastery, Financial Literacy for the Real World," which we will be marketing, with persistence, to colleges and universities that covers every aspect of personal finance. Our hope is that it will help college students stay out of monumental student debt, and better prepare them for the financial future they face. Our task will be convincing college administrations that such a course is so important and necessary that they will both adopt it and then encourage their students to take it. It will take great persistence.

Today, when someone calls me stubborn I simply smile and say, "Thank you, and yes I am!"

THE SISTERHOOD MASTERMIND

Wisdom from women of success and significance on PERSISTENCE:

ESTÉE LAUDER (1906–2004)
COFOUNDER, ESTÉE LAUDER COMPANIES

"When I thought I couldn't go on, I forced myself to keep going. My success is based on persistence, not luck."

ROSA PARKS (1913–2005)
AFRICAN-AMERICAN CIVIL RIGHTS ACTIVIST

"If I have to face something, I do so no matter what the consequences might be. I never had any desire to give up. I did not feel that giving up would be a way to become a free person."

DOLLY PARTON
AMERICAN COUNTRY MUSIC SINGER-SONGWRITER, ACTRESS, AUTHOR, AND LITERACY ACTIVIST

"The way I see it, if you want the rainbow, you gotta put up with the rain. We cannot direct the wind, but we can adjust the sails. Storms make trees take deeper roots."

HELEN KELLER (1880–1968)

AMERICAN AUTHOR AND POLITICAL ACTIVIST

"Character cannot be developed in ease and quiet. Only through experience of trial and suffering can the soul be strengthened, ambition inspired, and success achieved."

MARIAN WRIGHT EDELMAN

PRESIDENT AND FOUNDER, CHILDREN'S DEFENSE FUND

"You're not obligated to win. You're obligated to keep trying to do the best you can every day."

CHIN-NING CHU (1947–2009)

CHINESE-AMERICAN BUSINESS CONSULTANT AND BEST-SELLING
AUTHOR IN ASIA AND THE PACIFIC RIM

"Without the strength to endure the crisis, one will not see the opportunity within; it is within the process of endurance that opportunity reveals itself.

MARILYN MONROE (1926–1962)

AMERICAN ACTRESS, MODEL, AND SINGER

"Just because you fail once doesn't mean you're gonna fail at everything."

ELEANOR ROOSEVELT (1884–1962)

LONGEST-SERVING FIRST LADY OF THE UNITED STATES DURING
HER HUSBAND PRESIDENT FRANKLIN D. ROOSEVELT'S
FOUR TERMS IN OFFICE. PRESIDENT HARRY S. TRUMAN
LATER CALLED HER THE "FIRST LADY OF THE WORLD"
IN TRIBUTE TO HER HUMAN RIGHTS ACHIEVEMENTS

"We gain strength, and courage, and confidence by each experience in which we really stop to look fear in the face . . . we must do that which we think we cannot."

MARY PICKFORD (1892–1979)
SILENT FILM ACTRESS KNOWN AS "AMERICA'S SWEETHEART"
AND COFOUNDER OF UNITED ARTISTS

"You may have a fresh start any moment you choose, for this thing that we call 'failure' is not the falling down, but the staying down."

RICHELLE E. GOODRICH
AMERICAN CONTEMPORARY AUTHOR

"Is anything truly impossible? Or is it that the path to our goals appears too unclear to follow? It seems to me that if you seek hard enough, pray hard enough, you usually stumble across a scattering of bread crumbs that marks the trail leading to the goal you once considered beyond your reach."

GISELA RICHTER (1882–1972)
CLASSICAL ARCHAEOLOGIST AND ART HISTORIAN

"A series of failures may culminate in the best possible result."

ASK YOURSELF

Use your journal as you go through this section to identify your action steps, trigger your "aha" moments, and create your plan for achieving success!

Am I persistent?

If you are unsure of the response, review the eight factors essential for PERSISTENCE and Hill's Symptoms of Lack of Persistence and be truthful in taking inventory of those that apply to you.

To further help you determine your level of PERSISTENCE, ask the following:

1. Have people ever referred to you as having "fighter's will"?
2. Do you rise under pressure or tend to feel overwhelmed?
3. Do you have tools for overcoming emotions seeded in negativity?
4. Is your self-talk primarily empowering, ensuring yourself that you can succeed, or do you tend toward negative self-talk?
5. Do you wait for opportunity to come to you, or do you make your own breaks?

If you find that you aren't built for challenges or wish you had more emotional fortitude, rest assured that these are things that are fully under your control! You have the power to change.

Think back to a time when you were required to choose between two situations, neither of which was appealing. There you were, not sure of what to do and yet you had to make a choice. It does not matter whether you made the right choice. The fact of the matter is that you persisted in spite of adversity to get beyond that moment—and here you are today, better for it.

How did it feel to be on the winning side of adversity? Think back to the relief, the joy, or whatever positive emotion rewarded you. Let this be your kindling as you build your persistence fire!

Hill furthers our instruction on developing persistence with these four steps:

There Are Four Simple Steps That Lead to the Habit of PERSISTENCE. They Call for No Great Amount of Intelligence, No Particular Amount of Education, and but Little Time or Effort. The Necessary Steps Are:

1. A DEFINITE PURPOSE BACKED BY a BURNING DESIRE FOR ITS FULFILLMENT.
2. A DEFINITE PLAN, EXPRESSED IN CONTINUOUS ACTION.
3. A MIND CLOSED TIGHTLY AGAINST ALL NEGATIVE AND DISCOURAGING INFLUENCES, including negative suggestions of relatives, friends, and acquaintances.
4. A FRIENDLY ALLIANCE WITH ONE OR MORE PERSONS WHO WILL ENCOURAGE ONE TO FOLLOW THROUGH WITH BOTH PLAN AND PURPOSE.

Have you identified your definite purpose and burning desire? If you have, take a few minutes to review it now. If you have not by the time you finish this book, go back and revisit DEFINITE PURPOSE in order to explore your passions and ultimately determine your purpose.

Do you have a plan in place in order to fulfill your definite purpose? Now is the time to start or revisit your plan to be sure you have defined specific actions in order to keep moving forward.

Is negativity a pervasive nuisance in your life, or have you taken steps to guard your mind against it? Take control of your environment and what you allow to influence you in order to eliminate the effect negativity has on you.

Who in your life is most encouraging? Find ways to nourish persistence by surrounding yourself with people who will support you and help you follow through until you have achieved your purpose.

Power of the Mastermind

Surround Yourself with Mastermind.
It's Your Driving Force.

■

Alone we can do so little;
together we can do so much.
—HELEN KELLER

YOU HAVE HEARD THE SAYING "TWO HEADS ARE BETTER THAN one!" This has never been more true than today. The business world is shifting. Where for many years business was based on intense competition and created a win-lose environment, thankfully we are now seeing a transformation where collaboration and cooperation create a win-win platform for business.

Did you ever play team sports? Do you remember group projects that were tremendous fun when you were in school? Or maybe you remember other projects where you wanted to eject a team member or two. Do you belong to a membership organization that supports your learning or achievement of your personal and business goals? Think of how good you feel when you leave a meeting where you have had an "aha" moment.

Napoleon Hill first wrote about the POWER OF MASTERMIND

in the early 1900s. His description of the MASTERMIND starts by describing the power that is generated from the benefits of the collective thought from a group of individuals.

POWER IS REQUIRED FOR THE ACCUMULATION OF MONEY! POWER IS NECESSARY FOR THE RETENTION OF MONEY AFTER IT HAS BEEN ACCUMULATED!

The power he refers to is not dictatorial power, but rather the power that is gained from acquiring knowledge. He shares that there are three sources of organized knowledge:

1. Infinite Intelligence—which is drawn upon through Creative Imagination as described in the chapter on Imagination (see chapter 5).
2. Accumulated Experience—This is where Hill includes all formal education, as well as knowledge that is recorded and available in a public library. Today you would include information accessible through the Internet, with the warning that you need to validate the sources of the information.
3. Experiment and Research—While Hill referred to scientists who seek out new knowledge, through experiment and research, I believe this also refers to anyone seeking new territory—building new businesses, taking the less-traveled path, where again Creative Imagination comes into play.

If power is achieved through accumulating all three types of knowledge, Hill points out that it would be difficult for one person to accomplish this task alone. In order to be truly successful, you must find a team of people to work with you so that the knowledge can be attained more quickly to achieve your definite purpose.

This is the essence of the POWER of the MASTERMIND. Hill defines the MASTERMIND as follows:

The Mastermind is the coordination of knowledge and effort, in a spirit of harmony, between two or more people, for the attainment of a definite purpose.

He then describes that there are two distinct advantages of the MASTERMIND. First, the obvious economic advantages from the results gained through collective effort. You gain the advantage of the experience, education, native ability, and imagination of the other minds in your MASTERMIND. This type of cooperative alliance generates the foundation of almost every great fortune.

Second, he describes the spiritual benefit of the group effort: "No two minds ever come together without, thereby, creating a third, invisible, intangible force which may be likened to a third mind." This SPIRIT OF HARMONY creates increased energy that becomes available to each individual in the group. He describes this as the "psychic" phase of the MASTERMIND.

The saying "The whole is greater than the sum of its parts" refers to this spiritual element. Can you remember a time when you were involved in a team project, where the interaction provided this increased energy, usually adding an element of fun to the project itself?

Now the opposite is true as well. When you are involved with a group initiative where there is DISHARMONY, the increased negative energy may be expressed through conflict or increased frustration, and can make the attainment of the group's defined definite purpose that much more difficult to accomplish. This is particularly true when the "leader" takes a dictatorial role over the MASTERMIND, which dramatically impacts the collective brainstorming ability of the group.

It appears that women are more receptive to working in groups than men are. Katherine Crowley, a Harvard-trained psychotherapist, and Kathi Elster, a management consultant and executive coach, wrote the book *Mean Girls at Work: How to Stay Professional When Things Get Personal*, which focuses on female bullies in the workplace and how many women leaders still do not help other women succeed.

They also share their insights into differences between men and women within the work environment. One brief synopsis of their philosophy: "Men are from the combat zone, women are from the support circle." In an interview they shared:

> Most women join companies with the desire to be part of a team, to connect with the other players, and to deliver outstanding results. While men are friendly towards their colleagues, women often relate to coworkers, clients and vendors as friends. Men, on the other hand, seem to assume and accept that the workplace is a competitive environment.

This appears to be validated by the *Los Angeles Times*, which reported that a recent survey by Ernst & Young revealed that 90 percent of the businesswomen executives surveyed indicated that using teams was their number-one choice for handling business problems. In addition, 82 percent of the women surveyed indicated that an organization made up of smoothly functioning teams was a key to reaching their business goals.[28]

That survey, however, was administered to women executives in large corporations with more than $250 million in annual revenues. So how do women find team members or support groups when they are in smaller organizations, own their own businesses, or have an issue in their personal life? For personal issues, women tend to reach out to their circle of friends or find local support groups, both of which could be considered MASTERMIND groups. To answer the need for this type of support for business issues, organizations have been created around the globe to provide education, mentoring, and peer-to-peer support opportunities, as well as establish accountability models for women in business.

One such organization for business owners is the Women Presidents' Organization (WPO), founded by its president, Marsha Firestone, Ph.D., to provide peer-to-peer support groups so women presidents can meet regularly to help each other.

When asked to explain the purpose and success of her organization, she shared:

Mastermind: Bringing Out the Genius of the Group

The Mastermind concept at the core of the Women Presidents' Organization (WPO) business model is the peer advisory group. The objective is for women business owners to share the benefits of their expertise, experience, and education, what's working for them and what's not working, providing real-time and on-target feedback. Designed particularly for leaders of second-stage companies that have moved beyond the start-up phase and are focused on steady, sustainable growth, the fundamental premise of WPO's peer-to-peer learning tool focuses on sharing experiences instead of giving advice.

In chapters composed of approximately twenty accomplished women entrepreneurs, WPO members address their business concerns in a roundtable format and function as an informal board of directors for their businesses. Each chapter is driven by the four Cs of WPO: collaboration, confidentiality, commitment, and connections. There is no fixed curriculum. It is as much about giving as it is about getting.

The goal is to accelerate growth, implement next steps, and promote economic security. Members make a commitment to support each other and share their expertise. The group is composed of noncompetitive businesses, with a million-dollar-minimum revenue level. Everyone is a peer. They sit with a group of others who know what it's like to be in their shoes, facing many of the same issues, and benefiting from others who have "been there, done that." WPO chapter chairs are business owners themselves and trained in the roundtable process and work to bring the genius out of the group.

The process provides practical as well as intangible results. Women tend to lack confidence. Research shows that girls starting at age eleven begin to seize on the most self-critical thoughts they can come up with. WPO chapters work to rebuild this lack of confidence and validate their business strategies.

The WPO peer advisory groups provide the validation needed that the steps and strategies taken by women entrepreneurs are valuable. One of the most important outcomes is stress reduction by being afforded the opportunity to talk about an issue these business owners can't discuss with family or colleagues at work.

We understand the value of interacting with and learning from colleagues who face similar leadership and business problems. WPO members address financial concerns, organizational development, hiring and firing, and other issues.

Women presidents of multimillion-dollar companies are faced with the everyday challenges of running a business. It can be lonely at the top. Through intimate and powerful monthly chapter meetings, WPO members tackle a multitude of issues that have significant impact on professional and personal successes. It is the place where we connect, learn, and transform.

There are many organizations that provide education, mentoring, and networking opportunities to both professional women and women business owners. Your goal should be to locate a group that best suits your needs where you can connect with other women best suited to become part of your MASTERMIND. Just a few of these organizations are listed here with a brief description of their core focus.

The **National Association of Women Business Owners** (NAWBO) propels women entrepreneurs into economic, social, and political spheres of power worldwide by:

- Strengthening the wealth-creating capacity of our members and promoting economic development within the entrepreneurial community;
- Creating innovative and effective change in the business culture;
- Building strategic alliances, coalitions, and affiliations;
- Transforming public policy and influencing opinion makers.

In 1975, a group of a dozen like-minded businesswomen in the D.C. area gathered to share information and create an atmosphere of professional community to further and strengthen their entrepreneurial interests. Since then, NAWBO has risen to become the strong and unified voice of more than 10 million women-owned businesses across the country.

NAWBO created an affiliation with **Les Femmes Chefs d'Enterprises Mondiales (World Association of Women Entrepreneurs)**, which was founded in France in 1945 at the end of World War II by Yvonne Foinant. Offering both solidarity and friendship, it brings together like-minded women who share a common interest, entrepreneurship. Today, the FCEM network includes more than eighty countries from the five continents and is led by World president Laura Frati Gucci.

85 Broads is a global network of thirty thousand trailblazing women who are inspired, empowered, and connected worldwide. The "founding members" of 85 Broads were women who worked for Goldman Sachs at 85 Broad Street, the investment banking firm's former New York headquarters. Over the past decade, 85 Broads expanded its membership to include women who are alumnae and students of the world's leading colleges, universities, and graduate schools. Members are located in more than 130 countries around the world and work for thousands of for-profit companies and not-for-profit organizations. Sallie Krawcheck, former president of Bank of America Wealth Management, purchased 85 Broads from its founder, entrepreneur and former Goldman Sachs executive Janet Hanson. In an interview with *HuffPost Live*, Sallie shared her thoughts on success, saying, "The number one unwritten rule of success is networking. Having a network of people of the same gender is good for both genders. You should network with everyone, but there is something that's more comfortable for folks about asking that 'Hey, how about this question [with the same gender]?'"

Women's Information Network (WIN) provides women worldwide (152 countries) with online and on-land education and empowerment in their personal lives and in their businesses. The WIN invites all women, all ages, all cultures, and all religions to participate. Paula Fellingham, CEO of WIN, shares the mission statement: "The WIN mission is to strengthen women and families worldwide through education, enlightenment, and entrepreneurship in an effort to eradicate illiteracy, poverty, and hunger and increase the level of love, prosperity, and peace on earth. The WIN motto: 'We are women helping women live our best lives.'"

eWomenNetwork was founded by Sandra Yancey in 2000, from a room above the garage of her suburban Dallas, Texas, home. With limited entrepreneurial experience, Sandra bootstrapped her way to create one of the largest and most decorated business networking organizations in North America. Today, eWomenNetwork is a multimillion-dollar enterprise with 118 chapters in six countries that helps thousands of women grow their businesses. The organization produces more than a thousand women's business events each year, including one of the largest, the four-day International Women's Business Conference in North America. Sandra created the eWomenNetwork Foundation, which has awarded cash grants to ninety-four nonprofit organizations and scholarships to 132 emerging female leaders of tomorrow.

National Association for Female Executives (NAFE) is one of the country's largest organizations for women professionals and business owners, and provides resources—through education, networking, and public advocacy—to empower its members to achieve both career and personal success. Dr. Betty Spence has served as its president since 2001.

There are countless other organizations, too many to list here, that are available to you. Many are industry specific, while others, like the WPO, strive to diversify its members across different industries, creating a collaborative, not a competitive, environment.

In addition to these large organizations, there are professional women who provide mentoring and opportunities to guide women entrepreneurs in taking their businesses to the next level. When attending the California Women's Conference, the following women shared their thoughts on the importance of having a MASTERMIND.

Ali Brown, founder and CEO of Ali International LLC, has created a dynamic enterprise that is devoted to empowering women entrepreneurs around the world, and currently has more than sixty-five thousand members in her online and offline programs. When asked about the power of Masterminding, Ali was quick to acknowledge the power of Napoleon Hill's work and the role it played in shaping her success.

She shared: "Someone handed me a copy of *Think and Grow Rich* when I was in my twenties. I remember picking it up, looking at it, and saying, 'Why should I listen to this old, dead dude?' That's really what I was thinking. I remember putting the book away. A few years later, when I was out on my own and I launched my first business, I was moving and unpacking. I found the book again. I'm thinking, 'Ah, what if I just get rid of this?' Instead, I opened it up and it had a whole new meaning for me. The chapter that had the most influence on my life was the chapter on masterminding because I've been working by myself for so long and realized that I had to surround myself with successful people. We could share our challenges, our strategies for success. I could get the advice I needed. That principle changed my life."

"Two heads are better than one," and working together with other successful business owners to help you with your business brainstorming and challenges will help you develop ideas and answers faster.

Mari Smith, considered a leading social media expert and an evangelist for Facebook, was named by *Forbes* as one of the top ten social media influencers. Mari helps independent professionals, entrepreneurs, and business owners to accelerate their business profits using an integrated social marketing strategy, with particular focus on Facebook and Twitter.

In an interview she shared: "What Napoleon Hill teaches in *Think and Grow Rich* about who you surround yourself with and who supports you in that tight-knit group where you absolutely have everybody's back, made a profound difference to me. Fast-forward thirteen years and I like to joke, saying I'm an overnight success—ten years in the making. I am now running my own Masterminds and implementing a lot of what Napoleon Hill talks about.

"The importance of the millionaire mind-set—that we really do have control over our mind, that our thoughts become reality, and that who we are associating ourselves with and being influenced by—makes a huge difference to our success."

Novalena Betancourt, author of the *Total Female Package,* is a young woman dedicated to helping other women succeed. Novalena has also read *Think and Grow Rich* many times and embraces Hill's message about the need for creating your own Mastermind.

She shares, "You need to have the associations around you. You need to have a team in place and not just any team. They have to be the specific people who can execute on your vision and it has to be within their strengths. So, look at your communication tools, your strategies, and get to know yourself completely, so you can connect to people where you're engaged in each other, you're serving each other as resources, you're shopping together, and you're promoting each other. With a strong team behind your vision, anything is possible."

Wake Up Women. Karen Mayfield, the founder of Wake Up Women, shared, "Every experience I ever had prepared me for my universal assignment to Wake Up Women. Empowering women around the globe became a possibility when I first saw those words and I inherently knew that by waking up a woman, she would wake up the world around her! When you rise above your problems, you flow among your possibilities."

CHAPTER IN PRACTICE—IN MY LIFE

There is nothing better than working on a team where everyone is working toward the same common goal. The chemistry of the shared passion and commitment charges the air with energy, and ideas begin to flow as if effortlessly.

There is nothing worse than working on a team where members have hidden agendas and do not share the same common goal. The result is an environment charged with negative energy, and often a lot of wasted effort.

I have had the blessing of working on wonderful teams for most of my life, and the unfortunate experience of being on several teams that were not so wonderful.

Joining the WPO in the late 1990s was one of the greatest gifts I have given myself. To find a group of women whose common goals are to counsel each other, to celebrate each other's successes, and to serve as sounding boards providing needed support during the valleys of our careers, all while in a safe and confidential environment, is priceless.

Many of my closest friends today are women from my WPO chapter. We have literally grown up together in both our business and personal lives. We provide each other an important element of accountability. The bond that we have formed is both deep and precious to each of us.

In traveling the world speaking to women's groups, I am able to draw on the shared experiences of our group to make sure my message is timely, relevant, and meaningful. When referring to the power of Mastermind, I often refer to the equation $1 + 1 = 2$. As a result of the power of masterminding and brainstorming with a group of women committed to each other, I have rewritten the equation to be:

$1 + 1 = \textbf{11}!$

This best describes the benefit of a powerful MASTERMIND.

Natalie Ledwell started her company, Mind Movies, and quickly learned the positive, exponential power of using a Mastermind. She shared, "The power of one is something . . . but when you power that by 10, you create a whirlwind and a tidal wave that cannot be stopped. There are so many different networks that you can join to give you a hand and to help you so that your wonderful idea that can change the world will get that power of 10 and then you'll be able to create a tidal wave of change."

Napoleon Hill also writes about the powerful MASTERMIND between a man and a woman . . . and that the most important Mastermind is that between a husband and a wife, and it is most certainly true in my life.

I am so fortunate to have my husband, Michael, in my life. We are so very different in our thought processes, but when we put our heads together to solve a business issue, magic happens. In fact, we have many friends and clients who call us and simply say, "We need to come to your table." Our dining room table has given birth to many businesses, and helped many other businesses blast through plateaus on their way to greater success.

Michael and I also believe that mentoring others is an important part of Masterminding. We not only seek advice on our business issues, but strive to serve others seeking counsel on their business issues. In addition, we will involve younger members of our team so that they can learn from the Masterminding process, and bring their valuable perspective to the table as well.

Business is a team sport. Masterminding provides the opportunity to get new perspectives and leverage alternative expertise than what we have individually. But make sure you have the right people on your team!

THE SISTERHOOD MASTERMIND

Wisdom from women of success and significance on POWER OF THE MASTERMIND:

MARGARET MEAD (1901–1978)
AMERICAN CULTURAL ANTHROPOLOGIST

"Sister is probably the most competitive relationship within the family, but once the sisters are grown, it becomes the strongest relationship."

"Never doubt that a small group of thoughtful, committed citizens can change the world. Indeed, it is the only thing that ever has."

MIA HAMM
RETIRED AMERICAN PROFESSIONAL SOCCER PLAYER, MEMBER OF THE NATIONAL SOCCER HALL OF FAME

"I am a member of a team, and I rely on the team, I defer to it and sacrifice for it, because the team, not the individual, is the ultimate champion."

EMILY KIMBROUGH (1899–1989)
AMERICAN AUTHOR AND JOURNALIST

"Remember, we all stumble, every one of us. That's why it's a comfort to go hand in hand."

MELISSA ROSENBERG
AMERICAN SCREENWRITER AND COFOUNDER, LEAGUE OF
HOLLYWOOD WOMEN WRITERS

"It doesn't matter if you're the smartest person in the room: If you're not someone who people want to be around, you won't get far. Likewise for helping those in line behind you. I take seriously my role as a mentor to young female filmmakers—I make sure my time is tithed."

PHYLICIA RASHAD
TONY AWARD–WINNING AMERICAN ACTRESS, SINGER,
AND STAGE DIRECTOR

"Any time women come together with a collective intention, it's a powerful thing. Whether it's sitting down making a quilt, in a kitchen preparing a meal, in a club reading the same book, or around the table playing cards, or planning a birthday party, when women come together with a collective intention, magic happens."

DEBORAH BATEMAN
EXECUTIVE VICE PRESIDENT, DIRECTOR OF WEALTH STRATEGIES,
NATIONAL BANK OF ARIZONA

"The beauty of women helping women is that it is a complete circle. Women give in an open and loving manner—and in return, their gifts are many, including understanding the value we bring and discovering our purpose."

ASK YOURSELF

Use your journal as you go through this section to identify your action steps, trigger your "aha" moments, and create your plan for achieving success!

In your journal answer the following questions:

Are you currently involved in a Mastermind?
Is it structured to achieve a certain goal?
When was the last time you met?
What other groups do you belong to?
Should you consider joining a new organization to help drive you to the next level of success? Which organization sounds most appealing to you?
Will you make a commitment to attend a meeting within the next month?

Maybe you have decided to create your own Mastermind.

List a few people you think would be great members for your Mastermind.

Now that you've identified who is or should be in your Mastermind, identify what expertise they each have.

Does your Mastermind group represent women who are now where you would like to be? Are they individuals who represent a variety of skill sets?

Steps for Creating a New Mastermind

1. Get over yourself. A lot of people are afraid to admit they need help.
2. Get specific about what you want to achieve.
3. Give the group a name, it makes it more real.
4. Set meeting dates.
5. Will you meet in person, by telephone, or online?

6. Will there be any fees involved?
7. Invite the people to join who will commit to helping you achieve your goal.
8. Be respectful of their commitment. How can you reciprocate?
9. To show your appreciation, include some fun.
10. Listen but lead. Be the leader by reminding members of the meetings and being prepared, but allow your Mastermind members to contribute their ideas, while you listen.
11. Enjoy the synergy of energy, commitment, and excitement that participants bring to a Mastermind Group.

SISTERHOOD MASTERMIND OF WOMEN HEADS OF STATE

QUEEN ELIZABETH II
MONARCH REIGNING OVER THE UNITED KINGDOM AND FIFTEEN OTHER COMMONWEALTH REALMS

"I know of no single formula for success. But over the years I have observed that some attributes of leadership are universal and are often about finding ways of encouraging people to combine their efforts, their talents, their insights, their enthusiasm and their inspiration to work together."

"I have to be seen to be believed."

CRISTINA FERNÁNDEZ DE KIRCHNER
PRESIDENT OF ARGENTINA

"Our society needs women to be more numerous in decision-making positions and in entrepreneurial areas. We always have to pass a twofold test:

first to prove that, though women, we are no idiots, and second, the test anybody has to pass."

QUEEN MARGRETHE II
QUEEN OF DENMARK

"I can, of course, think what I want, just like everyone else. I simply have to refrain from saying everything I think."

ANGELA MERKEL
CHANCELLOR OF GERMANY

"The question is not whether we are able to change but whether we are changing fast enough."

"I am not here for women only, but also for women."

ELLEN JOHNSON SIRLEAF
PRESIDENT OF LIBERIA

"Every time I got into trouble it became a challenge for me to survive that, and every challenge became an opportunity for me to move higher and to take a better position and to take a leadership role. . . . That's been the story of a long life."

DILMA VANA ROUSSEFF
PRESIDENT OF BRAZIL

"I hope the fathers and mothers of little girls will look at them and say, 'Yes, women can.'"

"I believe that Brazil was prepared to elect a woman. Why? Because Brazilian women achieved that. I didn't come here by myself, by my own merits. We are a majority here in this country."

YINGLUCK SHINAWATRA

PRIME MINISTER OF THAILAND

"Perhaps I can bring a bit of a woman's touch to addressing this conflict [between parties of the South China Seas disputes], and focus more on what we can do together rather than what divides us."

PARK GEUN-HYE

PRESIDENT OF SOUTH KOREA

"South Korean society accepting a female president could be the start of a big change."

DALIA GRYBAUSKAITĖ

PRESIDENT OF LITHUANIA

On being elected the first woman president, "The taste of victory is the burden of responsibility."

KAMLA PERSAD-BISSESSAR

PRIME MINISTER OF THE REPUBLIC TRINIDAD AND TOBAGO

"I am grateful for the immense support from women and women's groups across the country and to the extent that this helps to break the barriers so many competent women face. I celebrate this victory on their behalf. But, the picture is much larger than any single group and those very women would be the first to acknowledge that."

SHEIKH HASINA

PRIME MINISTER OF BANGLADESH

"As a woman, I am obviously partial to good health of women. I believe healthy women bear and raise healthy children, thereby contributing to a healthy nation."

ATIFETE JAHJAGA
PRESIDENT OF KOSOVO

"My election as a woman head of state shows the willingness of Kosovo society and institutions to enhance and build a state based on true democratic principles. Democracy is not full until half of its population is equally represented at all levels of society. I will not stop until this principle is realized."

HELLE THORNING SCHMIDT
PRIME MINISTER OF DENMARK

"I try to think in a sisterly way throughout my entire day. The more power and influence I get, the more this is a responsibility that rests on my shoulders."

NKOSAZANA DLAMINI-ZUMA
CHAIRPERSON, COMMISSION OF THE AFRICAN UNION
(SOUTH AFRICA)

"The need for business incubators was raised to enable women and youth to be better trained and equipped with the necessary skills so as to graduate from micro enterprises to medium and larger enterprises with a view to satisfying both national and export demands and contribute to their respective countries' economies."

HELEN CLARK
ADMINISTRATOR, UNITED NATIONS DEVELOPMENT PROGRAMME
(UNDP), AND FORMER PRIME MINISTER OF NEW ZEALAND

"It's true that as a woman leader you attract probably a disproportionate amount of influence because there are so few of us. Think ahead. Have a plan. Leave space for yourself. Reevaluate. Reset your goals. . . . I think it's important to have goals, but they will change over time as circumstances change."

GOLDA MEIR (1898–1978)
PRIME MINISTER OF ISRAEL (1969–1974)

"Trust yourself. Create the kind of self that you will be happy to live with all your life. Make the most of yourself by fanning the tiny, inner sparks of possibility into flames of achievement."

"Whether women are better than men I cannot say—but I can say they are certainly no worse."

MARGARET THATCHER (1925–2013)
PRIME MINISTER OF THE UNITED KINGDOM (1979–1990)

"If you want something said, ask a man; if you want something done, ask a woman."

"It may be the cock that crows, but it is the hen that lays the eggs."

SISTERHOOD MASTERMIND OF WOMEN IN THE MEDIA

JILL ABRAMSON
EXECUTIVE EDITOR, *NEW YORK TIMES*

"I don't expect that I can ever raise all female boats, but I try to go out of my way, not to the exclusion of men, but I do take a particular interest in careers and work of many of the younger women at the Times *... and I'm ... open about it. If anyone has a problem with that, too bad."*

ARIANNA HUFFINGTON
PRESIDENT AND EDITOR IN CHIEF, HUFFINGTON POST
MEDIA GROUP

"The first revolution was women getting the vote, the second was getting an equal place at every level of society ... the third revolution is changing the world that men have designed. It's not sustainable. Sustainability is not just about the environment, it's personal sustainability. Ironically,

when we succeed at making these changes, not only are we going to have a lot of grateful men because they are paying too heavy a price, but we're going to have a lot more women at the top. Many women currently leave the workplace because they don't want to pay the price."

CHRISTIANE AMANPOUR
NEWS ANCHOR, ABC AND CNN

"Dear Girls of the World,

"There are more than 7 billion people in the world. Half of them are women and girls.

"Just imagine the whole world rising, as it will, when all women and girls are empowered.

"It has to start with education. All the number crunchers have it right on this one: education = empowerment, from here in the United States to Uruguay and Ulan Bator.... It's high time the rest of the world caught on. Go, girls! Power the world! We can do it."

MOIRA FORBES
PUBLISHER OF FORBESWOMAN

"Beyond our borders, having societies empower and unleash the brainpower of over half the world's population is a benefit to us all."

"Leaders must use both hard and soft power, but now more than ever, they must be able to connect with those around them. Their followers are now their stakeholders, so today's leaders have to encourage collaboration while making decisions that support their vision and priorities on a global stage."

DIANE SAWYER
NEWS ANCHOR, *ABC WORLD NEWS*

"But across the Capitol, a milestone in history. One after the other, women were sworn in as senators. For the first time ever, twenty U.S. senators

in all and they were lawyers, ranchers, a former governor. They are also mothers . . . and they said they fought to win tough races and they're not going to stop now. They are living, breathing history, climbing the stairs and sending a signal. They are twenty senators, Republican and Democrat, who say they have had it with gridlock and the way Congress works."

ELLEN DEGENERES
AMERICAN STAND-UP COMEDIAN AND TELEVISION HOST

"The worst thing for women to do is look at a magazine and see a sixteen- or a seventeen-year-old girl who is airbrushed to hell. It's not fair! To me, being beautiful is being comfortable in your own skin."

ANNA WINTOUR
EDITOR IN CHIEF, *VOGUE*

"When women are in positions of power, and they're featured in a women's magazine like Vogue *. . . they tend to be incredibly unfairly criticized. It's an incredibly old-fashioned approach. Just because you're in a position of power, and you look good and you enjoy fashion—does that mean you're an idiot, or that it's not seemly to be in a women's magazine? If a man is in GQ, they don't get the same kind of criticism."*

GRETA VAN SUSTEREN
FOX NEWS HOST

"Here is a 'dirty little secret' and advice to women in the workplace— some women are very generous to other women in the workplace, others want to slit your throat and try to undermine you. Young women need to find those women in the workplace who enjoy the success of other women—and get advice from them, get guidance, etc. It is fun to work together and enjoy others' success."

MEGYN KELLY
FOX NEWS HOST

"You can have it all but you're going to be very tired."

"But I really do want people to know I reject this thought, the suggestion that you have to choose between a top-notch career and a loving, meaningful family. Because I am living it . . . I have an amazing, amazing, loving, supportive, present husband. And I know that that's not always the case. But that makes it possible for me."

GAYLE KING
COANCHOR OF *CBS THIS MORNING* AND EDITOR AT LARGE
FOR *O* MAGAZINE

"Failure doesn't mean that you're not good. Rather, it can be a powerful opportunity to examine and reassess larger goals. Sometimes you fail for a reason. Use that to plot your next path. Quite often when one door closes, another one opens. And everything, even though you don't believe it at the time, works out the way it's supposed to, the good and the bad."

LESLEY JANE SEYMOUR
EDITOR IN CHIEF, *MORE* MAGAZINE

"Being a mom means I can do any high-powered job, period. Without the support system from my family (even if my daughter is constantly berating me as a typical twelve-year-old), I wouldn't be where I am now, since I rely on them for love and care. The job is a job, a great one, but having my true loves in my life at home—my kids and husband—means I can keep the job where it belongs, in its place."

ALISON ADLER MATZ
PUBLISHER OF *MORE* MAGAZINE

"You have to have passion—you have to believe, or else it shows. Aligning myself with really smart people—I would attribute a lot of my suc-

cess to that, just being a sponge, learning as much as I can [from them] every day."

PAT MITCHELL
FORMER PRESIDENT AND CEO OF PBS

"A world where girls are valued, because they must be, they have so much to contribute, and that's the economic opportunity that the world is missing. And then a world where a woman's voice really makes a difference. Because we have a different set of values, and if we speak them and live them, then the world will reflect that. And that's bound to be a more equitable and just place."

KATIE COURIC
JOURNALIST AND TALK-SHOW HOST

"Be fearless. Have the courage to take risks. Go where there are no guarantees. Get out of your comfort zone even if it means being uncomfortable. The road less traveled is sometimes fraught with barricades, bumps, and uncharted terrain. But it is on that road where your character is truly tested and has the courage to accept that you're not perfect, nothing is, and no one is—and that's OK."

KATHIE LEE GIFFORD
TELEVISION HOST, SINGER, AND ACTRESS

"My daddy . . . used to say, 'Honey, find something you love to do and then figure out a way to get paid for it.' He understood that where your true passion is, there your joy is also. And a joyful life is a truly successful life. Perhaps not by the world's standards, but whose life is it anyway?"

TINA BROWN
FOUNDER OF TINA BROWN LIVE MEDIA

"Was it always so hazardous for women in the public eye? . . . When a woman is the subject the vortex of venom reaches a spinning climax."

MIKKI TAYLOR

EDITOR AT LARGE, *ESSENCE*

"Many women live like it's a dress rehearsal. Ladies, the curtain is up and you're on."

LISA GERSH

FORMER CEO, MARTHA STEWART LIVING OMNIMEDIA

"When things are going really bad, make sure you put on your lipstick. People are watching you and they want to see that you are confident—especially in times of trouble."

CATHIE BLACK

FORMER CHAIRMAN AND PRESIDENT, HEARST MAGAZINES

"You can love your job, but your job will not love you back."

"Women are always angsting over things. Guys don't do that."

BARBARA WALTERS

AMERICAN BROADCAST JOURNALIST AND TELEVISION HOST

"If it's a woman, it's caustic; if it's a man, it's authoritative."

"Success can make you go one of two ways. It can make you a prima donna—or it can smooth the edges, take away the insecurities, let the nice things come out."

DR. JOSEPHINE GROSS

COFOUNDER AND EDITOR IN CHIEF, *NETWORKING TIMES*

"There is a special place in heaven for women who help other women. This 'heaven' is a place of shared dreams, collaboration, mentorship, and celebration of our global sisterhood."

"When women support each other, the rewards are transgenerational. Women empowering women makes families prosper and villages thrive, and the world becomes a better place."

MONICA SMILEY

EDITOR AND PUBLISHER, *ENTERPRISING WOMEN MAGAZINE*

"It is vital for women to have a seat at the table when important policy decisions that impact our businesses and our lives are debated."

SUSAN KANE

EDITOR IN CHIEF, *SUCCESS MAGAZINE* (IN AN INTERVIEW ON CBS)

"Sometimes you put your work first. Sometimes you put your children first."

"If we are happy we have a much greater impact on our children than if we are unhappy. If we are happy working we are going to be better mothers."

SISTERHOOD MASTERMIND OF WOMEN CEOS

DENISE MORRISON

CEO, CAMPBELL SOUP COMPANY

"Women need to take charge, they've got to recognize that they can't get there by themselves. They are going to need mentors and sponsors and build relationships and they have to give back to those relationships, as well. I use the term, networking is working ... Now is the time for women to be strategic about themselves."

VIRGINIA "GINNI" ROMETTY

CEO, IBM

"Don't be your 'first, worst' critic."

"Don't let others define you. You define yourself!"

MARILLYN A. HEWSON

CEO AND PRESIDENT, LOCKHEED MARTIN CORPORATION

"Women must be prepared to take on new and more challenging assignments ... and to pursue mentors ... to network with others to learn

from them. And, most importantly, to always perform at our best and focus on continuous learning."

DATO DR. JANNIE CHAN

COFOUNDER AND EXECUTIVE VICE CHAIRMAN, HOUR GLASS LTD.

"A woman's life is like a juggling act. We're constantly trying to balance different roles."

PATRICIA A. WOERTZ

PRESIDENT AND CEO, ARCHER DANIELS MIDLAND

"I had a very pragmatic upbringing. I'm not one to get stuck in doubt or to dwell on a dilemma. Instead, you make intelligent choices. You take reasonable risks. You calibrate, decide, and go forward with commitment."

ELLEN J. KULLMAN

CHAIRMAN AND CEO, DUPONT

"It's not about having a set time; both personal and professional lives are 24/7. It's more about making the right allocation to each one and recognizing it's going to be different every day. But you don't do these jobs unless you really love what you do."

MARISSA MAYER

CEO AND PRESIDENT, YAHOO!

"I always did something I was a little not ready to do. I think that's how you grow. When there's that moment of 'Wow, I'm not really sure I can do this,' and you push through those moments, that's when you have a breakthrough."

"You can't have everything you want, but you can have the things that really matter to you."

ROSALIND BREWER
PRESIDENT AND CEO, SAM'S CLUB

"I truly believe in treating people the way I want to be treated and that's with respect and honest intentions. Whenever I am true to this, success happens for me, the business and the company."

HEATHER BRESCH
CEO, MYLAN, INC.

"We need to better address the issues that hold women back from leadership roles. Part of the equation is certainly societal. However, the other half is what I think of as 'the ambition gap.' Women don't necessarily understand that it is possible to have the same level of ambition as men—they allow themselves to be held back by the obstacles, rather than empowered by the possibilities. Starting early in life and in school, we need to ensure women develop the confidence and capabilities to work in a team that will allow them to reach the heights of leadership."

URSULA M. BURNS
CHAIRMAN AND CEO, XEROX

"Most days, even back when Xerox was under siege, I could not wait to get to the office. I love my work. And you should too."

"I take each day one step at a time. I'm certainly proud of where I am, but I have much more to do to provide value for our company, our people, our customers, and our shareholders."

IRENE ROSENFELD
CEO AND CHAIRMAN, MONDELEZ INTERNATIONAL
(FORMERLY KRAFT)

"Our emerging workforce is not interested in command-and-control leadership. They don't want to do things because I said so; they want to do things because they want to do them."

PHEBE NOVAKOVIC

CHAIRMAN AND CEO, GENERAL DYNAMICS

"At our core, we are in business to earn a fair return for our shareholders. In doing so, we must use our company's assets wisely and we must deliver on our promises to our customers, our partners, and our people. These are the ethics that guide our conduct and decisions."

DONNA KARAN

FORMER CHAIRMAN, DONNA KARAN INTERNATIONAL, INC.

"Delete the negative; accentuate the positive!"

ILENE LANG

FORMER PRESIDENT AND CEO, CATALYST

"Influential, highly placed sponsors can supercharge a woman's or a man's career, providing access to assignments that help propel a protégé to the top of the list of promotions."

MARY BARRA

CEO, GENERAL MOTORS

"I am proud to represent the men and women of General Motors and to have this role; it is an honor and I am humbled by it. I just want to focus on leading the team."

ALEXA VON TOBEL

CEO, LEARNVEST

"When everyone zigs, zag. Be a risk-taker. I dropped out of Harvard Business School in the heart of the recession to launch LearnVest. Was it a crazy idea? Probably. But I was passionate about my mission and had a solid business plan in place. Diving in is a scary move, but the rewards make it all worthwhile."

"Get up, dress up, show up. It's important to be ready to go, whatever day you have ahead of you. Show up with a smile and a great attitude."

MARGERY KRAUS
FOUNDER AND CEO, APCO WORLDWIDE

"The keys to being successful in any profession, I think, are to know yourself very well and play to your strengths. Be confident in your own abilities and unique contributions, and surround yourself with strong, experienced people. Don't be timid. Don't be afraid to try new things. Work should be a continual learning experience. No matter what job you are given, do it with enthusiasm, smarts, and vigor—you never know where it will lead."

SISTERHOOD MASTERMIND
OF WOMEN EDUCATORS

ANA MONNAR
FOUNDER AND PRESIDENT, READERS ARE LEADERS USA

"To some, education is just a bore; to most, education is food for the brain and enrichment for the present and future."

SHIRLEY TILGHMAN
FORMER PRESIDENT, PRINCETON UNIVERSITY

"My goal has always been to do as good a job as I can, where I am at that moment. It's a tremendous coping skill."

JULIET V. GARCÍA
FIRST FEMALE HISPANIC TO BECOME PRESIDENT OF A UNIVERSITY, PRESIDENT, THE UNIVERSITY OF TEXAS AT BROWNSVILLE

"We're trying to send a very clear signal that the Latino human capital in this country simply needs access to the same opportunities that have been present for other people."

LAURA BUSH

FORMER FIRST LADY OF THE UNITED STATES

"A love of books, of holding a book, turning its pages, looking at its pictures, and living its fascinating stories goes hand in hand with a love of learning."

BEVERLY DANIEL TATUM

PRESIDENT, SPELMAN COLLEGE

"We are changing the world all the time, sometimes for the better, sometimes for the worse. We're not always conscious of the way we're changing the world, but each of us in our daily interactions is making an impact."

DONNA HENRY

CHANCELLOR, UNIVERSITY OF VIRGINIA—WISE

"As I look back on my life, I am convinced that my education had the greatest influence on my career. As a first-generation college student, the faculty who taught me and the friends that I made helped me to envision a future that was unimaginable. My mentors encouraged me to see my strengths and abilities, which ultimately led to the chancellorship at U.Va.-Wise."

JANET NAPOLITANO

PRESIDENT, UNIVERSITY OF CALIFORNIA, AND FORMER
SECRETARY OF HOMELAND SECURITY

"As we move deeper into the twenty-first century, the need for a quality public school system will become more of an economic issue and more of a civil rights issue. Because, as our economy relies more on brains and less on brawn, the only way everyone can secure all the blessings of liberty is to receive a quality education."

CONDOLEEZZA RICE
FORMER PROVOST, STANFORD UNIVERSITY, AND FORMER
SECRETARY OF STATE

"The essence of America—that which really unites us—is not ethnicity, or nationality or religion—it is an idea—and what an idea it is: That you can come from humble circumstances and do great things. That it doesn't matter where you came from but where you are going."

SUN-UK KIM
PRESIDENT, EWHA WOMANS UNIVERSITY, REPUBLIC OF KOREA

"Ewha stands at a crucial turning point, faced with new challenges. We are determined to turn these challenges into new opportunities that will open the door to exciting new changes, to build an institution that is equipped for world-class education and research; that seeks future paradigms rooted in new values of femininity; that leads fearlessly into an adventurous future of experimentation and challenge; that strives to define and execute new social responsibilities of the university for our times."

DREW FAUST
PRESIDENT, HARVARD UNIVERSITY

"We educate women, first, because it is fair—a level field as we aspire to include women as full and equal participants in society. We educate women also because it is smart—women are one-half of our human resources, and we increasingly see the beneficial effects of educated women in all realms of life and in all parts of the world. Finally, we educate women because it is transformative. Education doesn't just boost incomes and economies, it elevates us, defusing differences, opening common ground, and making the most of all our human capacities."

DAWN DEKLE

PRESIDENT, AMERICAN UNIVERSITY OF IRAQ

"To see female students walking across the stage at graduation, knowing what the Taliban had done to women's education. It was one of the best days of my professional life."

SISTERHOOD MASTERMIND OF WOMEN LEADERS IN NETWORK MARKETING

The following women have created financial success for themselves and their families while becoming leaders and mentors to millions of other women within the network marketing industry. They come from close to thirty different companies and from around the world. The network marketing industry provides a low-cost way to start your own business, with proven systems and invested mentors. In considering network marketing it is important to research the company, its revenue model, and its training in deciding which company may be right for you.

CAMILITA P. NUTTALL

"Starting later or eventually is too late. There's no better time than the present."

JANINE AVILA

"I can't imagine where I would be today had I not read Think and Grow Rich *and integrated the principles into my business and life. As a busy single mother of seven, I was spinning my wheels, determined, and passionate, but without the 'Organized Planning' described in the book, and wasting time and resources until I studied and understood the value of 'Being decisive in nature.'* Think and Grow Rich *is a gift I continue to give to myself and others."*

YOUNGHEE CHUNG

"I can feel it 110 percent when I'm in sales. I can see the growth, not only financially but mentally. It's hard to be successful in society, but I get to help those who are really dedicated."

MEGAN WOLFENDEN

"Women have more choices than ever before and with that comes responsibility. To keep us on track with our lives we need to keep learning and developing and constantly ask the right questions. All obstacles can be overcome and huge accomplishments can be yours with time, patience, and consistently acting on the right principles for success."

MARJORIE FINE

"You will get back what you put in. I think women are finding that to be true. There are phenomenal women leaders in this industry and you will see them step up and take leadership roles."

SHARON WEINSTEIN

"The opportunity to pay it forward by helping others to help themselves and to enhance their health and their lives is a privilege."

TAUREA AVANT

"It's not about you. It's about that young woman who is watching you!"

SYLVIA CHUKWUEMEKA

"I love to show individuals how to get out of the rat race and onto the fast track and how to work smart instead of simply working hard without compromising existing commitments."

LISA M. WILBER

"I went from living in a trailer in a trailer park, driving a Yugo, and eating macaroni to earning a six-figure annual income. It all started the day I finally took 100 percent responsibility for my actions and my outcomes."

SHELBY FORD

"When you have a positive experience with a product, it's natural to share it with family, friends, and neighbors. But when a product truly changes your life, you can't help sharing it with everyone you know."

BELYNDA LEE

"Success is a creative act. It is also the best route to fulfillment, and totality. So while you are chasing success, start with doing things that make you feel complete even if it is out of the norm. There is nothing wrong with being a unique elite performer. On your way to success, you may have opinions put onto you—ignore them and feed your hunger. Stay focused in igniting your greatest gift. Because once you have success, it will awaken joy, and that itself is significance when you have both."

DANETTE KROLL

"I've never doubted my ability to succeed, but others have. Thank goodness I get to control my thoughts, therefore my actions. I went from wanting to make a little money to striving to make a huge difference. It's noble how the two go hand in hand. As a dear friend once said, 'You don't have to be perfect to be powerful,' and you don't have to be perfect to make a difference."

SUSAN SLY

"At the end of any day, there is nothing more fulfilling than the knowledge that in some small way we have uplifted the life of a sister/mother/ daughter/niece/girlfriend. When we link arms with our sisters we amplify our power and there is nothing that we cannot accomplish. If you help enough women get what they want, you will ultimately get what you want. It only takes a small handful of committed women to create massive results."

GAYLE NORTHINGTON

"My passion in life is to help women of all ages become empowered to do more, become more, and to have more. Coaching women of all ages to be able to really do this business is my mission. Network marketing is the ultimate level playing field."

ONYX COALE

"I wanted my girls to see that if you consistently and persistently work at anything you wanted, you could have it in this life. No matter where you are in the world, women especially hunger for something better for their families."

SARAH FAIRLESS ROBBINS

"If it's to be, it's up to me! I can do anything for a short time to produce long-term rewards for my family and our future. You can too. Be relentless, have a 'do whatever it takes' attitude!"

GLORIA MAYFIELD BANKS

"Your attitude is everything. Find the joy in what you are doing and work hard to succeed in it."

EVA CHENG

"Never take for granted that people will understand your business model. You need to be in aggressive communication mode all the time."

CAROLYNE RODRIGUES

"I am passionate about health and empowering women to take control of their future and their families. The profession of network marketing has no glass ceilings, allowing women to dream, to be who they know they can be, and to build a legacy for themselves and their families. Through consistent daily action and investing in my personal growth, I have become a million-dollar earner in my company and now show others how to do the same."

JULES PRICE

"One of the most fulfilling aspects of this profession is that you can make a truly positive difference by helping women shift their mind-set in how they interpret challenges, face setbacks, and even redefine their belief in their own talents or abilities."

KIMMY EVERETT

"I challenge you to be a part of the solution. Ask yourself what you can give versus what you can get, how many others can you help, and you will receive an abundance of riches."

STACY JAMES

"Success in a woman's life is not the result of a specific brand of education. It is most often the result of a soul that has become inspired, a heart that was ready to believe, a mind positioned to grasp a vision of what is possible, and a body that is eager to take flight."

EILEEN WILLIAMS

"*I wanted to have it all. I wanted children and an exciting career. Learning how to build a network set me free. Now my passion is to empower other women to create a life for themselves and their families. Women can and will change the world!*"

JUNO WANG

"*Successful female entrepreneurs should take pride in and showcase our characteristics that are unique to women. We should be warm and personable and optimize our clear vision and excellent planning skills. Our maternal traits give us strength and perspective. We can persevere and adapt. We excel in not only leading people, but also helping people grow.*"

DANA COLLINS

"*The things you affirm and give energy to are the things you are creating. Success is created with intention, through thoughts, words, and actions.*"

"*There is no such thing as idle words; your words are like stamps on an envelope sending your thoughts out to create your life.*"

ANN FEINSTEIN

"*It is important to find purpose in our life by giving back, even if we are just holding on by our fingertips. Start small but start. For when we are willing to enrich the lives of others, we are enriched and become part of the transformational journey.*"

LOREN ROBIN

"*DREAM BIG . . . I mean REALLY BIG and on purpose! Women move mountains when aligned with something greater than ourselves. The*" most amazing people reveal themselves and great things start showing up from every direction to support us on our path. What's even better is we become those amazing people that show up the same way for others. This is when magic happens."

KATHY COOVER

"What I love about this profession is it allows women to shine and grow to their full potential. Women have the ability to nurture and help others succeed and in the process become more successful. It is really all about freedom and the ability to live your life serving others. Remember, what you think about will come about, so believe in yourself and go for it."

TARA WILSON

"I've worked since age twelve, and I love working hard. I feel blessed that I have discovered how to harness that into something significant that I am passionate about. I'm even more excited to be able to inspire, motivate, and teach other women to take massive action toward their passion and live the life they deserve!"

JANINE FINNEY AND LORY MUIRHEAD, MOTHER AND DAUGHTER

"This industry has given us the gift of a lifetime—the ability to plan our work around our life rather than our life around our work. And now we want to share that gift."

FAINA BALK

"Male accomplishment is launched by the man's own self, while a woman is driven by her concern for others. It's nature. To succeed in business, a woman should follow her nature instead of fighting it. My female business slogan: money shall come to those who passionately do everything for the well-being of their beloved ones."

HILDE RISMYHR SAELE

"If you want to be a world shaker and history maker, the best way is to empower women to think and grow rich."

PAIGE RIFFLE

"Being in the right place at the right time is not enough. Being in the right place at the right time and taking action is the key."

MARION CULHANE

"Get very clear about your goals and dream. Commit to them 100 percent. Ask powerful questions within that will direct and focus your mind and subconscious toward realizing your dream. Stay focused and take steps every day that move you closer to realizing your intent. Allow the magic to unfold in ways you might never have imagined. Appreciate and give thanks for every step and person along the way."

SARA MARBLE

"It is my hope and dream that women around the world will see the amazing opportunity that network marketing offers. Doors to their future will be opened and they will be living the life of their dreams as women entrepreneurs—successful, powerful, inspiring, and making a difference in the lives of all those around them."

JACKIE ULMER

"One of my favorite principles of Think and Grow Rich is that of the Mastermind. Women are powerful as collaborators and when we come together to support each other, and a common goal, look out! We know how to listen, ask great questions, offer ideas when needed (and wanted), and support and uplift each other. This important success step is showcased brilliantly when women come together!"

The Mystery of Sex Transmutation

The Emotion of Sex Brings into Being a State of Mind

■

Men reach their sexual peak at eighteen.
Women reach theirs at thirty-five. Do you get
the feeling that God is playing a practical joke?
—RITA RUDNER

THIS CHAPTER GETS A LOT OF ATTENTION. FOR SOME, THE TOPIC of sex transmutation is a bit confusing. What does that mean? Other women look at it as very chauvinistic and therefore question how I would make sense of it for inclusion in *Think and Grow Rich for Women*. To them I ask:

- Have you ever chosen a certain outfit because it makes you more sexually appealing?
- Have you ever looked at someone out of the corner of your eye?
- Have you ever flirted with or teased someone?
- When you shake someone's hand do you lightly touch their shoulder or hand with your other hand, creating more intimacy?
- Have you ever said no, but with a smile?
- Do you look at yourself when you pass a mirror?

If you answered yes to any of these questions, you understand the power of sexual attraction. Hill noted, "Sex desire is the most powerful of human desires." Sex transmutation simply means transferring sexual energy from sexual expression into expression of a different sort, such as increased imagination, courage, or keenness of thought. He shares the following simple examples of how someone's personal magnetism is an expression of sex energy.

1. The handshake. The touch of the hand indicates instantly the presence of magnetism, or the lack of it.
2. The tone of voice. Magnetism, or sex energy, is the factor with which the voice may be colored, or made musical or charming.
3. Posture and carriage of the body. Highly sexed people move briskly, and with grace and ease.
4. The vibrations of thought. Highly sexed people mix the emotion of sex with their thoughts, or may do so at will, and in that way, may influence those around them.
5. Body adornment. People who are highly sexed are usually very careful about their personal appearance. They usually select clothing of a style becoming to their personality, physique, complexion, etc.

Certainly these are all examples that apply equally to men and women. How do you feel when you shake another woman's hand and she offers you her limp fingers to shake rather than a full firm handshake? Does your voice change based on whether you are speaking to a child, spouse, or business associate?

Have you ever been in a business meeting or at a party, when someone comes in who exudes a palpable sense of self-confidence and positive energy? Her charisma, or magnetic personality, instinctively draws people to her. Some people just seem to have "it" while others do not. However, Hill believes you can improve your own magnetic personality by reviewing his list of the twenty-one elements that are important for achieving a Magnetic Personality.

1. Good showmanship: Understand and apply the art of catering to the masses.
2. Harmony within self: Be in control of your own mind.
3. Definiteness of purpose: Be definite in developing relationships of harmony with others.
4. Appropriateness of clothing: First impressions are lasting.
5. Posture and carriage of the body: Alertness in posture indicates alertness of the brain.
6. Voice: The tone, volume, pitch, and emotional coloring of one's voice are important factors of a pleasing personality.
7. Sincerity of purpose: Builds confidence of others.
8. Choice of language: Avoid slang and profanity.
9. Poise: Poise comes with self-confidence and self-control.
10. A keen sense of humor: One of the most essential qualities.
11. Unselfishness: No one is attracted to a selfish person.
12. Facial expression: It shows your moods and thoughts.
13. Positive thoughts: Vibrations of thoughts are picked up by other people, maintain pleasing thoughts.
14. Enthusiasm: Essential in all forms of salesmanship.
15. A sound body: Poor health does not attract people.
16. Imagination: Alertness of imagination is essential.
17. Tact: Lack of tact is usually expressed through loose conversation and boldness of expression.
18. Versatility: General knowledge of the important subjects of current interest and deeper problems of life.
19. The art of being a good listener: Listen attentively, do not break in and take the conversation away from others.
20. The art of forceful speech: Have something to say that is worth listening to and say it with all the enthusiasm at your command.

21. Personal magnetism: Controlled sex energy. Major asset of every great leader and every great salesman.

Developing and employing a magnetic personality will most certainly assist in your efforts to become successful in life. Reverend Karen Russo, who earned her M.B.A. from Columbia University and is an ordained minister with the Centers for Spiritual Living, has worked with thousands of people helping them integrate universal spiritual principles with practical financial strategies and she had taken a close look at Hill's philosophy on sexual energy and the role it plays in creating success. She shares:

MYSTERY OF SEX TRANSMUTATION

Napoleon Hill posed the problem that the sex urge in men is so strong that they will risk life and reputation to indulge their physical sex desires, at the risk of losing their character, family, profession, and more. Hill's assertion is that when this powerful energy is redirected, professional and financial success is enhanced. Napoleon Hill studied thousands of married, white, privileged men in the early 1900s.

While success principles are universal, some of the dynamics of sexual expression can expand to include the issues women face today. A transformed approach to sexual energy can include men and women, gay and straight, single and partnered, celibate and sexually active, and more!

SEXUAL ENERGY FUELS SUCCESS

Hill identified uncontrollable sex urges as an "irresistible force," which risk diminishing a man's power. He suggested an empowered and, at the time, provocative solution to this problem. He points out that the desire for sex, love, and romance is inborn and natural, and that the sex desire is connected to spiritual urges. The intensity, power, and primacy of sex, love, and romance are energies. When we value those natural and inborn urges we prosper.

In today's world, applying, directing, and making sacred our sexual, romantic, passionate natures is a success strategy that enriches mind, body, and spirit, in addition to our paychecks, pocketbooks, and portfolios.

Sexual energy can create financial fuel for women as well as men. Madonna is known for continuously reinventing both her music and her image as a philanthropist and icon, and has received acclaim as a role model for businesswomen in media. She has been able to build a global brand that has stood the test of time. She has also been criticized for her overt sexuality, but she is a woman who, well before her time, was able to appreciate, value, and express her sexual energy, and obviously her feminine passion and play.

When asked about her sexual energy, Madonna responded, "Everyone probably thinks that I'm a raving nymphomaniac, that I have an insatiable sexual appetite, when the truth is I'd rather read a book."

UNFULFILLED PASSIONS DRAIN RESOURCES

As a spiritual mentor to thousands of women across the globe from all different socioeconomic, business, and professional backgrounds over the last decades, I've discovered that a woman risks diminishing her *worth* when she feels unfulfilled in sex, love, and romance. The consequences of the resulting low self-esteem are numerous: eating disorders, alcohol abuse, binge spending, sexual promiscuity, and social withdrawal. Women with an ambivalent experience of their sexuality don't feel good about themselves.

An estimated 90 percent of all women want to change at least one aspect of their physical appearance, and only 2 percent think they are beautiful. [http://www.confidencecoalition.org/statistics-women]

For many women, the challenge in love, romance, and sexual passion is lack of fulfillment or expression. Yearning for what she doesn't have drains a woman's vital energy. She loses mental, emotional, and psychic resources when wondering, "Why hasn't he called?" and "Does he love me?" She ignores her own needs and depletes time and energy that could be invested in more profitable, fulfilling pursuits.

Hill asserts that men need to discover the willpower to not be controlled by their needs. For women, it's very different, almost the opposite. A woman needs to learn to care for herself and give her inner and outer self the attention that she is yearning for. The sex, love, and romance energy is transmuted in a healthy, vital, physically, mentally, spiritually, and financially rich life.

TIME, ENERGY, AND ATTENTION TO FINANCIAL AND PHYSICAL FITNESS

Spiritual practice is the primary way for women to feel worthy and connected. Ironically, a woman who is developing a spiritually and financially rich life must do more than just engage in spiritual practices. She also needs to get into financial action. Time, energy, and attention must be spent developing orderly and effective money habits.

Self-love in money starts with basic financial literacy. All women need to be involved with how money flows in and out of their families, professions, and lives. Whether or not you are the primary earner in a family, you must understand how money, taxes, and investments are flowing and affecting you and your partner.

To be able to provide for, care, and respect the self through being self-sustaining is vitally important. Including a healthy and vibrant body to ensure pleasure, play, and satisfaction in our lives enhances a woman's capacity to earn, appreciate, receive, keep, and manage money.

CREATIVE ENERGIES WORKING TOGETHER

Napoleon Hill talks about the creative imagination and how geniuses create by harnessing sex, love, and music as an outlet to stimulate and open the mind to receiving inspiration from the infinite intelligence. This is a beautiful example of how all humans create and how masculine and feminine energies come together.

When it comes to understanding creative energies working together, all people have within them masculine and feminine qualities of wealth creation. The masculine qualities of wealth are created through action, much of which is the basis of *Think and Grow Rich*— purpose, focus, and clarity. The feminine aspects create wealth through awareness; the ability to feel that we have the thing we desire. The feminine qualities are grace, receptivity, satisfaction, and most important, an infinite capacity for gratitude.

Mother Teresa is well known as a humble Catholic nun, a spiritual teacher, and guide. She possessed those precious feminine attributes of grace, receptivity, piety, and modesty. She was a deep lover of Jesus and someone who maintained a deep spiritual practice. She had a heart of compassion for helping, healing, and working with the poor. Mother Teresa was also a fund-raiser extraordinaire. She raised billions to fund her charities in India with a savvy and effectiveness that are world-renowned. She took the energy of love and passion, and the creative energies of masculine and feminine, and placed them together into a beautiful, inspiring life.

It's vital for women to nurture and cultivate wealth through feminine awareness, and also to access, as appropriate, wealth through masculine action practices. With both awareness and action, women feel worthy and well. If you are single, commit to creating a rich life of pleasure, worth, and wealth for yourself. If you're partnered, in a family or in a business, include the passion and connectedness of those relationships as you create wealth.

The more passion and pleasure in your life, the more profitable your life will be.

Karen Russo reminds us that we all have masculine and feminine traits related to wealth, financial and spiritual, creation. From purpose, focus, and clarity to grace, receptivity, satisfaction, and gratitude, women are well equipped with all of these attributes and will not only create wealth for themselves, but through their gratitude bring financial and spiritual wealth to their families, associates, and communities.

CHAPTER IN PRACTICE—IN MY LIFE

I started my career in the late seventies, when very few women held executive or management positions. Having been raised by parents who taught me that I could achieve anything I set my mind on, I was startled to find a less than welcoming attitude toward women in the workplace. The term "sexual discrimination" had not yet been identified, and my fellow female associates and I found that we would often have to work harder and smarter than our male counterparts in order to stay in step with them for promotions. It was just the reality of our careers. Many of us even wore pantsuits and ties and our hair in buns to hide our femininity. It was truly absurd.

So when I think about sex transmutation, I remember those times when we were trying so hard to "look" like men and smile. There was a "turning point" day when four of us were celebrating passing the CPA exam, and decided it was time to shed our cocoons and become ourselves. We had our hair styled and went shopping for business suits—with skirts! We were having our own "coming out" party, and it was a blast.

For any woman younger than fifty this story may sound silly, but it was very real. It was a turning point for us, and for the women we mentored coming up behind us, to be authentic, to be CPAs and *women*.

Even though Hill published *Think and Grow Rich* in 1937, during a male-dominated time in business, he recognized the power of the emotion of sex. He warned, "The emotion of sex is a virtue ONLY when used intelligently, and with discrimination. It may be misused, and often is, to such an extent that it debases, instead of enriches, both body and mind."

There are countless examples in business, in media and in movies, where sex has been misused and created disastrous results. The mere subject of sex and sexual energy is intimidating and uncomfortable for many people to discuss.

Hill, however, made another distinction that I believe is very important for the future of business. He pointed out that "Love is spiritual while sex is biological. Love, is without question, life's greatest experience. It brings one into communion with Infinite Intelligence. When mixed with the emotions of romance and sex, it may lead one far up the ladder of creative effort. The emotions of love, sex, and romance, are sides of the eternal triangle of achievement-building genius. Nature creates genii through no other force."

I believe that men see love as spiritual and sex as biological and have a much easier time separating the two than women do. Hence, I am sure the term "sexual conquests" was coined by a man. Men have an intense competitive nature that served them well during the Industrial Age.

Women, on the other hand, see love and sex as intricately woven together and are constantly creating the romance component to complete the triangle. When we have all three—love, sex, and romance—we possess the eternal triangle of achievement-building genius that Hill identifies. When motivated by all three, work is not burdensome but a labor of love.

As the business environment moves from one of intense competition to an environment of cooperation and collaboration, women's ability and capacity for love will help them rise to the occasion and flourish.

I am happy to see that we are experiencing another tipping point for women today, where more than 50 percent of college graduates are women, where two out of every three new businesses are being started by women, and more than half of the workforce is now women.

It is the Age of the Woman and our influence will continue to grow. I am not a feminist, but I am a champion for women achieving the success they deserve.

A woman-led business world will be in very capable hands!

THE SISTERHOOD MASTERMIND

Wisdom from women of success and significance on the MYSTERY OF SEX TRANSMUTATION:

MAYA ANGELOU
BORN MARGUERITE ANN JOHNSON, AMERICAN AUTHOR AND POET

"I've learned that people will forget what you said, people will forget what you did, but people will never forget how you made them feel."

COCO CHANEL (1883–1971)
FRENCH FASHION DESIGNER AND FOUNDER OF THE CHANEL BRAND

"Dress badly, and people will notice the dress. Dress well and people will notice you."

AUDREY HEPBURN (1929–1993)
BRITISH ACTRESS, FASHION ICON, AND HUMANITARIAN

"There is more to sex appeal than just measurements. I don't need a bedroom to prove my womanliness. I can convey just as much sex appeal picking apples off a tree or standing in the rain."

SOPHIA LOREN

ITALY'S MOST RENOWNED AND HONORED ACTRESS

"I think the quality of sexiness comes from within. It is something that is in you or it isn't and it really doesn't have much to do with breasts or thighs or the pout of your lips."

ROSEANNE BARR

AMERICAN ACTRESS, COMEDIAN, WRITER, TELEVISION PRODUCER, AND DIRECTOR

"The thing women have yet to learn is nobody gives you power. You just take it."

ELIZABETH GILBERT

AUTHOR OF *EAT, PRAY, LOVE*

"I met an old lady once, almost a hundred years old, and she told me, 'There are only two questions that human beings have ever fought over, all through history. "How much do you love me?" and "Who's in charge?"'"

KRISTIN CASHORE

AMERICAN FANTASY AUTHOR

"How absurd it was that in all seven kingdoms, the weakest and most vulnerable of people—girls, women—went unarmed and were taught nothing of fighting, while the strong were trained to the highest reaches of their skill."

ASK YOURSELF

Use your journal as you go through this section to identify your action steps, trigger your "aha" moments, and create your plan for achieving success!

Making changes or transitioning from a position of unawareness or insecurity to being in control of sex energy may be uncomfortable for some. If after reading this chapter you are still unsure of how to get started, consider finding a role model or creating a Mastermind group specifically for this purpose. Who do you know in your life who has been successful at SEX TRANSMUTATION and developing success in her own life?

**Review Hill's Twenty-One Steps to Improve
Your Magnetic Personality:**

1. Good showmanship: Understand and apply the art of catering to the masses.
2. Harmony within self: Be in control of your own mind.
3. Definiteness of purpose: Be definite in developing relationships of harmony with others.
4. Appropriateness of clothing: First impressions are lasting.
5. Posture and carriage of the body: Alertness in posture indicates alertness of the brain.
6. Voice: The tone, volume, pitch, and emotional coloring of one's voice are important factors of a pleasing personality.
7. Sincerity of purpose: Builds confidence of others.
8. Choice of language: Avoid slang and profanity.
9. Poise: Poise comes with self-confidence and self-control.
10. A keen sense of humor: One of the most essential qualities.
11. Unselfishness: No one is attracted to a selfish person.

12. Facial expression: It shows your moods and thoughts.
13. Positive thoughts: Vibrations of thoughts are picked up by other people, maintain pleasing thoughts.
14. Enthusiasm: Essential in all forms of salesmanship.
15. A sound body: Poor health does not attract people.
16. Imagination: Alertness of imagination is essential.
17. Tact: Lack of tact is usually expressed through loose conversation and boldness of expression.
18. Versatility: General knowledge of the important subjects of current interest and deeper problems of life.
19. The art of being a good listener: Listen attentively, do not break in and take the conversation away from others.
20. The art of forceful speech: Have something to say that is worth listening to and say it with all the enthusiasm at your command.
21. Personal magnetism: Controlled sex energy. Major asset of every great leader and every great salesman.

Select three of the twenty-one steps that you want to improve upon over the next thirty days and commit to working on them.

If you aren't sure how to begin making changes, ask your mentor. Be sure to give yourself the opportunity to "practice" personal adjustments. While there is a significant mental and emotional aspect to sex transmutation, we convey our sex energy through our actions.

Spend some quiet time reflecting over your life.

When have you felt most confident? Describe that time.

When have you felt the least confident? Describe that time.

Now go back to both of these times and reflect on the other aspects of life at the time.

Were you employed?

Were you financially secure?

Were you healthy physically?

How was your love life?

Which of the twenty-one elements were lacking when you
were least confident?

Identify which areas of your life today share similarity to when
you were least confident.

What changes can you make beginning today in order to
improve upon these areas of your life?

Now reflect on your financial knowledge and health.

Schedule a financial review of your family, business, or
portfolio.

Create a plan for improving your financial health, and
employ it.

AND schedule a pleasurable, playful experience for yourself in
the coming weeks.

The Subconscious Mind

The Connecting Link

■

We cannot always control our thoughts, but
we can control our words, and repetition
impresses the subconscious, and we are
then master of the situation.
—JANE FONDA

HAVE YOU EVER OVERREACTED TO SOMETHING, OR SOMEONE—
and then asked yourself, "Where did that reaction come from? Why
did I say, or do, what I did?"

Have you ever arrived somewhere, and not remembered driving
there?

Have you ever awakened in the middle of the night, with a great
idea, or remembered something you couldn't remember the night
before?

These are all examples of when your subconscious was in control,
and your conscious mind was at rest. The subconscious is always
working, 24/7, day and night, but works best when you are not alert;
for instance, while you are sleeping, driving, or meditating. You cannot entirely control your subconscious mind, but you can influence it
by what plans, desires, or goals you feed it. If those plans, desires, or
goals are emotional, they become even more influential.

Your conscious mind can serve as a gatekeeper, by controlling what thoughts it "serves up" to your subconscious. This is why the chapters on AUTOSUGGESTION and creating your own personal mission statement are so critically important. Hill's thirteen principles provide the methods with which you can reach, and therefore consciously influence, your subconscious mind.

For instance, if you are constantly worried about money and your thoughts are those of fear and poverty, those negative thoughts will dominate your subconscious mind. However, if through practicing these thirteen principles you transform your thoughts to abundance and creating success, your subconscious will focus its attention on the positive outcome. Thus the saying "What you think about, you bring about," and Hill's key statement: "What your mind can conceive and believe, it can achieve."

Hill also cautions that positive and negative emotions cannot occupy your mind at the same time. One or the other will take control and dominate. It is up to you to ensure that positive emotions get the upper hand in influencing your subconscious.

By creating the habit of rejecting negative emotions and thoughts, and focusing only on positive emotions and thoughts, you will see positive transformation in your life. Before long, you will see that negative thoughts literally bounce off your positively charged conscious and subconscious mind. When the two minds are aligned you have gained control over your subconscious mind.

Let's review the seven major positive and negative emotions outlined by Napoleon Hill:

THE SEVEN MAJOR POSITIVE EMOTIONS

The emotion of DESIRE

The emotion of FAITH

The emotion of LOVE

The emotion of SEX

The emotion of ENTHUSIASM

The emotion of ROMANCE
The emotion of HOPE

THE SEVEN MAJOR NEGATIVE EMOTIONS
The emotion of FEAR
The emotion of JEALOUSY
The emotion of HATRED
The emotion of REVENGE
The emotion of GREED
The emotion of SUPERSTITION
The emotion of ANGER

Focusing only on positive emotions and thoughts so that you will see positive transformation in your life is the basis of the Law of Attraction, a fundamental principle that Napoleon Hill taught years before it was popularized by Rhonda Byrne in her book and movie, *The Secret*. She brought together an impressive group of contemporary thought leaders and personal development gurus to share their insights into the importance of positive thinking. Both the movie and the book were wildly successful around the globe.

The Secret, in her words is, "thought = creation. If these thoughts are attached to powerful emotions (good or bad) that speeds the creation . . . Your life is in your hands. No matter where you are now, no matter what has happened in your life, you can begin to consciously choose your thoughts, and you can change your life. There is no such thing as a hopeless situation. Every single circumstance of your life can change!"

Lisa Nichols was one of the stars of *The Secret* and shared her insight: "Think about your feelings. You have good feelings and you have bad feelings. And you know the difference between the two because one makes you feel good, and the other makes you feel bad. It's the depression, it's the guilt, it's the resentment, the anger. It's those feelings. They don't make you feel empowered. Those are the bad feelings.

"The flip side to that is that you have good emotions, good feelings. And you know when they come because they make you feel good. Excitement, joy, gratitude, love—imagine if we could feel that way every day. When you celebrate the good feelings, you'll draw to yourself more good feelings and things that make you feel good. Your thoughts and your feelings create your life. It will always be that way. Guaranteed."

Marci Shimoff, who was also part of *The Secret*, simplifies the message to this: "Go for the sense of inner joy, of inner peace, of inner vision first and then all the other things from the outside appear."

But what happens when you recognize that you need to make a change, but don't know how?

Donna Root is a corporate cultural management consultant for C-suite executives and has devoted the last fifteen years to understanding the mechanisms that make people, leaders, and organizations more effective and powerful. Her thorough analysis of the subconscious mind provides us with a unique six-step plan that will allow you to take control of your subconscious mind, take control of your future, and create the success you so richly deserve.

The subconscious mind is like a computer with multiple components running at the same time. It takes in information from the five senses, as well as information sent out into the field of consciousness from multiple streams of consciousness that are unseen but real. The subconscious mind stores the data, organizing and filing the data it takes in.

Your subconscious mind will in fact create by default rather than by design if you allow it to simply run without guidance or input. A significant amount of what we create in life comes from the unexamined patterns, beliefs, programs, and habits that we run from the subconscious mind.

The subconscious mind will draw on what is stored and what it has experienced in previous situations, what we have believed is real in our lives to *create* in our three-dimensional reality. If you have a desire that differs from what you believe, you will always bring into reality what you believe, not what you desire. This is what I call an opposing force paradox because your subconscious mind will draw from what it knows and that knowing comes from belief.

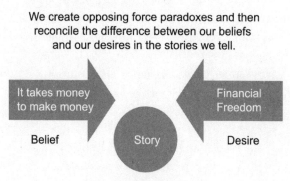

We create opposing force paradoxes and then reconcile the difference between our beliefs and our desires in the stories we tell.

It takes money to make money

Financial Freedom

Belief   Story   Desire

Opposing Force Paradox

We will always create what we think we know and we draw this from the storage unit of our subconscious mind. Note that the mind and consciousness are not the same. Mind is the computer that accepts, stores, and retrieves files, while consciousness is the all-knowing and connected aspect of each individual to the universe and Universal Intelligence.

These patterns and beliefs once brought to the conscious mind for examination *can be retrained and dismissed*. It is imperative to be aware of the subconscious thought patterns that run through our minds. There are two types of thoughts that have a profound impact on our ability to be on-purpose in our lives. There are thoughts that run through our mind like streakers. They simply pass through our minds, but we do not "charge" them with emotion. We simply notice them as they pass.

There are also those thoughts that become creative thoughts in our lives. Any thought that we charge with emotion expands. All charged thought expands whether it is positive or negative, good or bad, helpful or hurtful. Expansion is always happening in our mind.

All charged thought has the potential to create. This is why many religious texts tell us to guard our thoughts and to not have vain repetition in our prayers or meditation. It is also why we need to always examine what emotions we are attaching to thought.

We cannot serve two masters, even in our minds. Where there is no supply through charged thought, there will be no demand or reflection in your life.

So our thoughts must be retrained.
We cannot serve two masters.

Stress ~ Anxiety ~ Fear ~ Worry Anger ~ Poverty

Peace ~ Harmony ~ Cooperation ~ Joy ~ Prosperity

For where there is no demand there
will be no evidence of supply.

The subconscious mind will pull from its database whatever you dare to store as your truth and will then create that as your reality.

There is a six-step process of transforming and programming subconscious thought. Step 1 is simply to be aware and to recognize the thoughts you charge. Step 2 is to redefine the reality of those thoughts. If they are not thoughts that are serving you well, they should be released. This releasing is what is spoken of in the scriptures of 1 John 4:18: "There is no fear in love: but perfect love casteth out fear: because fear hath torment. He (She) that feareth not is made perfect in love." The use of the word "casteth" is a wonderful visual term. It denotes that we have the ability and the responsibility to "catch and release" those charged thoughts that are not fostering our highest growth and development, which is Step 3 of the transformation process. Step 4 is the understanding and use of the imagination and understanding of what we truly desire to create, Step 5 is the replacing of old thought with *purposeful charged thought and emotion,* and Step 6 is the *practicing of purposeful charged thought.*

It is in the practicing of intentional charged thought that new creation and new realities magically take form in our lives.

The 6 Rs of Transformation

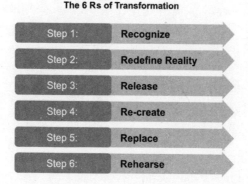

Step 1:	Recognize
Step 2:	Redefine Reality
Step 3:	Release
Step 4:	Re-create
Step 5:	Replace
Step 6:	Rehearse

When we practice the six Rs of transformation, and create intentional files for our subconscious minds to pull from, we begin to have true personal integrity. True personal integrity is when our thoughts, beliefs, emotions, desires, and behaviors are aligned. That alignment can be stored as *real* into our subconscious minds to be a creative force from which our realities play out.

BELIEVE + EMOTIONS + THOUGHTS + DESIRES + BEHAVIORS = ALIGNMENT

With disciplined thought we have the ability to decide the programming from which our subconscious minds will draw data, animate it, and bring it into our individual realities.

Many individuals fall short of creating wealth, health, abundance, and prosperity in their lives because they do not practice using the imagination as a source of reality or they imagine too far outside of their current reality.

It is advisable to begin storing in your subconscious mind things you can accept as true even if they seem like baby steps to great imagination. It is through this process that you will create evidence of those small accepted truths and as you fine-tune and refine this process your logical mind will be able to fully disregard any logical limit to creating anything in your world.

Let's repeat Donna's closing words: "creating anything in your world!" I challenge you to check what is happening in your mind right now. Do you doubt that you can create anything in your world, therefore allowing that negative thought to impact your subconscious? Or do you applaud the thought and have faith that you can create anything in your world, making way for your subconscious to support the successful realization of your goals? If you are unsure of what "baby steps" you can take, try daily affirmations. They are a great way to start the habit of positive self-talk and to feed your subconscious with positivity as well.

Can you think of people whose negativity has played out in negative ways? Or others who seem to have "great luck," always happy and successful? The next story shares how you can transform your life by focusing on maintaining positive beliefs and thoughts.

D. C. Cordova is the CEO of Excellerated Business Schools and Money & You, global organizations that have more than ninety-five thousand graduates all over the world. She shares how, when she discovered the power of her thoughts, and that she could actually control her thoughts, her life changed instantly—and determined the course of her career.

When I was in my early twenties, someone recommended the *Think and Grow Rich* book.

I remember thinking, "Wow! There may be hope that I can have a life of fulfillment, success, and contribution." I was "moving up the ladder" in the legal field—from being an assistant legal secretary to interpreter to official court reporter. My end game plan was to become an attorney. I was following a very traditional career path but knew in my heart that it was not what I was meant to do.

As destiny would have it, my life took a different path when I learned the importance of the "right" kind of education. As a Latina having accomplished the American Dream, I know my success had a lot to do with the values that were taught to me by my mother, auntie, grandmother, and amazing family members. But before I could truly realize success, I had to learn how to overcome other strong beliefs and thoughts in my subconscious that limited my ability to see the possibility of true success in my life. These beliefs and thoughts were learned in traditional schools; in fact, I believe

I was literally brainwashed in traditional schools. In addition, I had experienced a lot of loss in my life—my beloved, miscarriages, and friends, which had impacted my thoughts and behaviors in negative ways.

Think and Grow Rich taught me that our subconscious mind affects our thoughts, behaviors, feelings, and our actions! It empowered me. If I couldn't have control over my circumstances or my past, at least I could have control of my consciousness. It gave me a glimpse that I could have a life that could work for me, with much less fear, anxiety, and stress.

It was by reading books like *Think and Grow Rich,* focusing on my own personal development, and joining Mastermind groups that supported me, that I was able to start putting my attention on clearing my subconscious of detrimental beliefs.

In the process I discovered how the left and right brains impact learning differently. I learned that using experiential games can unlock what's really happening in our subconscious—and reveal how much it affects the (little and big) decisions that shape our lives. Through these experiential tools, you can find, uncover, reexamine those old lessons, and create new positive learning opportunities.

As CEO of Excellerated Business Schools and Money & You I have been able to share this knowledge with people around the globe.

By unlocking the power of your subconscious, you can retrain it through positive thoughts and actions to help you realize your goals.

CHAPTER IN PRACTICE—IN MY LIFE

I had quite the love-hate relationship with my subconscious mind for most of my life. Having been raised by a military father and excelling in school, it became my firm belief that I could consciously control the outcomes of my life if I was just smart enough. Any problem could be solved with logic and hard work. Tears were definitely a sign of weakness, so I trained my subconscious to believe that emotion was bad.

This training may have helped me succeed in a man's world professionally, but it also set me up for many years of beating myself up, trying to consciously control any signs of weakness or emotion. My outward veneer of strength and control covered years of pent-up emotion and anger at myself for having feelings that I had taught myself showed weakness.

Today, I know it had little to do with my father but everything to do with me wanting to please my father. I wanted to be perfect so he would be proud of me.

And being far from perfect, this led me to be in a perpetual state of guilt and shame. My self-esteem was constantly under attack—by me. I had high self-esteem when it came to my ability to perform in school or professionally, but low self-esteem personally. This guilt and shame was intensified by a lifetime of religious training, which taught me mixed messages about God. One minister would teach me to fear God, while another would teach me to have faith in God.

So when I read *Think and Grow Rich* at the age of nineteen, the most powerful part of the chapter on the Subconscious Mind was Hill's discussion on prayer because it talked about Faith vs. Fear.

You must have noticed that most people resort to prayer ONLY after everything else has FAILED! or else they pray by a ritual of meaningless words. And, because it is a fact that most people who pray, do so ONLY AFTER EVERYTHING ELSE HAS FAILED, they go to prayer with their minds filled with FEAR and DOUBT, *which are the emotions the subconscious mind acts upon,* and passes on to Infinite Intelligence. Likewise, that is the emotion which Infinite Intelligence receives, and ACTS UPON.

The subconscious mind is the intermediary, which translates one's prayers into terms which Infinite Intelligence can recognize, presents the message, and brings back the answer in the form of a definite plan or idea for procuring the object of the prayer. Faith is the only known agency which will give your thoughts a spiritual nature, FAITH and FEAR make poor bedfellows. *Where one is found, the other cannot exist.*

The book helped me confirm that God is a loving God and strengthened my faith.

My faith has seen me through a lot of ups and downs in my life, and while I may not get the answer to all cries of "Why?" during the down times, I trust that God has a greater plan for my life.

I still have an ongoing battle between my conscious and subconscious mind, however. I catch myself allowing that wall to separate my professional life from my personal life. Instead of practicing "catch and release" as Donna suggested, I found myself "catching, releasing, and then grabbing back" my fears and concerns.

This usually happens even when I have little to no control over what is happening. I called this my own personal rototiller, eating me up inside emotionally. Whether it is worrying about teenagers out too late at night, or over a friend making bad choices in her life, I would take it on and make myself sick with worry.

When I discovered the definition of worry that reads "To worry is to pray for what you do NOT want," a lightbulb came on for me. It is magical. When I catch myself with my rototiller in action I remind myself of the definition and it is like throwing cold water on my face. Then I force myself to reframe my thoughts into what I DO want to happen.

I truly believe, however, that my own experience with this issue has provided a lot of the passion that I have for helping people, especially young people, today.

So many people, including very young people, are striving for perfection, and are experiencing similar types of self-sabotage, allowing it to manifest in negative ways and interfere with their long-term goals. The problem with perfectionism and being the winner at everything you do is that it creates an imaginary and unattainable goal. There is always someone faster, better, and more perfect.

So the belief that you need to be the best needs to be replaced with *do* your best.

My work is focused on teaching people, young and old, that they are each in the driver's seat of their own lives. That every choice they make will either drive them to succeed or not! As long as they do their best in making good choices, they are on the right path.

THE SISTERHOOD MASTERMIND

Wisdom from women of success and significance on the SUBCON-SCIOUS MIND:

FLORENCE SCOVEL SHINN (1871–1940)
AMERICAN ARTIST AND BOOK ILLUSTRATOR WHO BECAME A
SPIRITUAL TEACHER AND AUTHOR OF *YOUR WORD IS YOUR WAND*

"You will be a failure, until you impress the subconscious with the conviction you are a success. This is done by making an affirmation which 'clicks.'"

FAY WELDON
ENGLISH AUTHOR, ESSAYIST, AND PLAYWRIGHT WHOSE WORK HAS
BEEN ASSOCIATED WITH FEMINISM

"Only one thing registers on the subconscious mind: repetitive application—practice. What you practice is what you manifest."

FLORENCE WELCH
ENGLISH MUSICIAN, SINGER, AND SONGWRITER

"I've always been able to just concoct a melody quite easily—it's just kind of instinct, really. You've got to channel your subconscious."

HILARY MANTEL
ENGLISH WRITER TWICE AWARDED THE BOOKER PRIZE

"Imagination only comes when you privilege the subconscious, when you make delay and procrastination work for you."

HELEN MIRREN
ACADEMY AWARD–WINNING ENGLISH ACTRESS

"Painters hate having to explain what their work is about. They always say, 'It's whatever you want it to be'—because I think that's their inten-

tion, to connect with each person's subconscious, and not to try and dictate."

ELLEN GOODMAN
PULITZER PRIZE–WINNING SYNDICATED COLUMNIST

"*Traditions are the guideposts driven deep in our subconscious minds. The most powerful ones are those we can't even describe, aren't even aware of.*"

MELISSA AUF DER MAUR
CANADIAN MUSICIAN, SINGER-SONGWRITER, ACTRESS,
AND PHOTOGRAPHER

"*As soon as I became old enough to make my dreams my reality, I became a firm believer that the subconscious and the world outside of our flesh and blood is essentially the truth.*"

MARY GALE HINRICHSEN, PH.D.
CHRISTIAN COUNSELOR

"*Once our subconscious mind gets hold of an idea, it will automatically facilitate it to become a reality. So we must correctly think about what is accurate. We are enough, we are worthy, and we can achieve what our heart desires. As long as we consciously think about our goals, get excited emotionally, and take steps in that direction.*"

"*The Bible teaches about this principle. It states we are to think about what we are grateful for, what is true, honest, just, and praiseworthy. Philippians 4:8. Each time we think we are not good enough, or not worthy, we are dishonest with ourselves. We must not place limits on ourselves because of our sex, age, or education.*"

CANDACE PERT, PH.D. (1946–2013)

AMERICAN NEUROSCIENTIST AND PHARMACOLOGIST

"Your brain is not in charge."

NAN AKASHA

CEO, AKASHA INTERNATIONAL

"Success and true transformation and true impact never feel easy or safe or comfortable—that's the whole point. NEW is not familiar, and if you let your subconscious convince you that you made a mistake or you can't do it . . . nothing new will happen."

The subconscious mind is a powerful yet intangible force, as this chapter has shown. In an effort to further explain how you can take control of your thoughts, Hill dedicated the next chapter to the brain, the twelfth step to riches, which he referred to as "a broadcasting and receiving station for thought." It moves us from the intangible subconscious mind to the physical brain so that we can better understand the process of thought.

ASK YOURSELF

Use your journal as you go through this section to identify your action steps, trigger your "aha" moments, and create your plan for achieving success!

This chapter asks you to do a lot of soul-searching. In your personal journal, write down the Seven Major Positive Emotions and the Seven Major Negative Emotions. Then for each write the first life experience that comes to mind where you have experienced that emotion. Don't overthink the exercise; it may just tap into your subconscious.

The Seven Major Positive Emotions

The emotion of DESIRE
The emotion of FAITH
The emotion of LOVE
The emotion of SEX
The emotion of ENTHUSIASM
The emotion of ROMANCE
The emotion of HOPE

The Seven Major Negative Emotions

The emotion of FEAR
The emotion of JEALOUSY
The emotion of HATRED
The emotion of REVENGE
The emotion of GREED
The emotion of SUPERSTITION
The emotion of ANGER

Now write down your parents' philosophy about:

Religion
Sex

Money
Politics

For each, think of what "belief" you may have today that came from your childhood?

Is there a belief that is not serving you positively today? Write it down.

Now practice Donna's six Rs process by referring back to the text for each to replace that belief that is not serving you with a new belief that will create positive thoughts.

Recognize
Redefine reality
Release
Re-create
Replace
Rehearse

Many people are not aware that they are self-sabotaging, so it may be good to review this exercise with a close friend where you can help each other with the first step, and "recognize" that belief that needs to be released and replaced.

Some Things You May Want to Consider:

- Catch yourself when you are about to judge yourself.
- Change thoughts of your self-worth to thoughts of your best efforts.
- Make a point of seeing failure or mistakes as learning opportunities, and don't allow them to define you.
- Learn to be good to yourself by allowing yourself to have

your own feelings, both good and bad, without judging yourself.

• Have compassion for others as they express their own emotions.

• Replace "be the best" with "*do* your best."

The Brain

A Broadcasting and
Receiving Station for Thought

·

When your entire brain is active, that means
you are taking everything in through all
sense perception. Your entire memory bank
and your instincts are in play, so you make
much quicker and more intelligent choices.
—MARTHA BECK

NOW THAT WE HAVE TRIGGERED THE IMPORTANCE OF YOUR subconscious, let's take a look at its physical protector, your BRAIN. So much of our discussion is about what is happening inside the brain that it is important to look at the actual vessel itself.

Hill spends a lot of time talking about the "sending station" function of the brain, which is our subconscious mind. Then he talks about our Creative Imagination and autosuggestion as the other two ways to trigger your mind and the importance of starting with DESIRE.

Perhaps Hill's message teaches that this "other self" is more powerful than the physical self we see when we look in the mirror. While we know little about the mechanism of thought, we may know even less about the physical brain "and its vast network of intricate machinery through which the power of thought is translated into its material equivalent." One hundred years after Hill began researching the principles of success and how the brain works, science has given us a greater understanding of the brain—but we have learned that it is even more complex than he could have imagined.

THE ANATOMY OF THE BRAIN

Hill estimated in 1938 that there were from 10 billion to 14 billion nerve cells in the human cerebral cortex, and that they were arranged in definite patterns. For the last several decades, scientists had believed and reported that the human brain as a whole contained close to 100 billion neurons. The female neuroscientist Suzana Heculano-Houzel, from Brazil, however, has recently discovered that the number for the total brain is closer to 86 billion neurons, with the cerebral cortex having 16.3 billion (as compared to Hill's 10 to 14 billion), the cerebellum housing 69 billion, and the balance in the rest of the brain. Let's take a closer look at the physical brain:

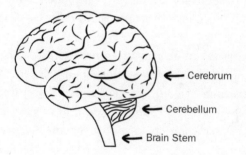

The biggest part of the brain is the **cerebrum**, and the cerebral cortex is its outer layer, called the gray matter. The cerebrum also contains white matter, which serves you by connecting the gray matter. The cerebrum makes up 85 percent of the brain's weight. Its function is to remember, problem solve, think, and feel. It also controls movement in your voluntary muscles. It has two halves. The right half helps you think about abstract things like music, colors, and shapes, while the left half is more analytical, helping you with math, logic, and speech.

The right half of the cerebrum controls the left side of your body, and the left half controls the right side.

The **cerebellum** means "little brain" in Latin and is at the back of the brain, below the cerebrum. It's a lot smaller than the cerebrum at only one-eighth its size, but contains more neurons than the rest of the brain. It is a very important part of the brain because it controls balance, movement, and coordination. It is also believed that the cerebellum is involved in cognitive functions like attention and language, and it may regulate your fear and pleasure responses.

The **limbic system** connects the lower and higher brain functions. It regulates emotion and memory, including motivation, mood, and sensations of pain and pleasure.

The **brain stem** connects the cerebrum to the spinal cord. It is underneath the limbic system and is responsible for basic vital life functions such as breathing, heartbeat, and blood pressure.

The **reptilian brain** includes the cerebellum and brain stem. It regulates vital functions like breathing, heart rate, and your "flight or fight" response.

These physical brain structures work together to help carry out the role of cognition, or understanding. Brain cells communicate with each other through an electrochemical process. Every time you think, learn, or communicate, a neuron (brain cell) in your brain sends a nerve impulse that connects to another neuron through something called a synapse.

So is there a difference between our brain and our mind? Opinions vary on this topic, but most agree that the mind is invisible, yet it processes incoming data and information, accessing long-term memory, creating short-term memory, and using conscious attention.

In more simple terms, the brain is the physical part of our body that coordinates our movements, thoughts, and feelings, while our mind refers to our intangible understanding of these things, or our thought process.

MALE VS. FEMALE BRAINS

Recent studies have found that there are distinct physical differences between male and female brains, which may have a direct impact on and clarify how we think differently. It may even help explain why men and women tend to approach business and life differently.

I asked Dr. Pam Peeke to share her thoughts on modern research related to our brain and how women and men differ. Pam is a medical doctor, a Fellow of the American College of Physicians, and received her master's degree in public health. She is also the author of *Body for Life for Women* and *The Hunger Fix* and has studied women and their brains extensively. She shared:

> Women are hardwired to collaborate, empathize, create lasting relationships, and communicate the mission statements that form the basis of sustainable success. Here's an interesting fact: Female brains are typically 8 to 10 percent smaller than male brains, but they are of equal intelligence. The reason, researchers have found, is that the feminine brain works more efficiently with less mass.
>
> Recent neuroimaging studies of the brain have demonstrated that, in comparison to men, women's brains are more active in seventy out of eighty areas tested. This means that the feminine brain is often activated a notch or so above its male counterpart. This can lead a woman to tend toward deeper engagement in life's activities.
>
> There's no mystery as to why women are such terrific caregivers. The supercharged feminine activation of the limbic or emotional system helps a woman create strong bonds and relationships.
>
> Women have a larger deep limbic system than men do, keeping them in touch with their own feelings as well as the

feelings of the people around them. Women are also faster at identifying emotions, as they encode facial differences and vocal intonations. But women are also better at controlling emotions. Sections of the brain used to control anger and aggression are larger in women than in men. In other words, women are more likely to hit the pause button than sprint from quiet to rage.

Compared to males, female brains have almost ten times as much white matter, the stuff that helps to facilitate connections throughout the brain. When men listen to a novel being read, one cerebral hemisphere is activated, while in women, both hemispheres light up. Men's left hemisphere predominance results in their solving problems from a task-oriented perspective, while women's combined use of both hemispheres leads to a heightened focus on feelings during communication and problem solving. The prefrontal cortex, which houses the brain's executive function, is bigger in volume and more organized in women.

As well, women process language in both hemispheres as opposed to men's reliance on their dominant hemisphere. This helps to explain why women's language skills far surpass men's throughout their life. This skill can be used to establish relationships, to collaborate, as well as plan and strategize. Optimal executive function also promotes creativity and vigilance, as well as the ability to rein in impulsivity, impatience, and irritability. Clearly this continues to be a significant survival skill, as women tend and befriend, creating the necessary deep bonds needed to navigate life's stresses.

While men are more likely to be task-oriented, less communicative, and operate in isolation, women focus on creating solutions that work for a group, enhancing communication, and demonstrating empathy.

Pam's analysis is eye opening and is critically important to understand when we discuss the business world being at a tipping point for women and their influence on the economy and how business will be conducted in the future. Her analysis is validated by the work of Helen E. Fisher, Ph.D., an American biological anthropologist and human behavior researcher and a professor at Rutgers University, who has contrasted women as using "web thinking" to men who use what she calls "step thinking."

As she describes it:

Women tend to generalize, to synthesize, to take a broader, more holistic, more contextual perspective of any issue. I coined a term for this broad, contextual, feminine way of reasoning: *web thinking*.

Men are more likely to focus their attention on one thing at a time. They tend to compartmentalize relevant material, discard what they regard as extraneous data, and analyze information in a more linear, causal path. I call this male pattern of cogitation *step thinking*.

Both web thinking and step thinking are still valuable, but in the contemporary business community, buzzwords include "depth of vision," "breadth of vision," and "systems thinking." In this highly complex marketplace, a contextual view is a distinct asset. Women are built to employ this perspective.

Women's web thinking provides them with other natural leadership qualities. According to social scientists and business analysts, women are better able to tolerate ambiguity—a trait that most likely stems from their ability to hold several things simultaneously in mind. If I had to sum up the modern business environment in one word, I would call it "ambiguous." Women are well endowed for this indefinite business climate.

Women's web thinking also enables them to exercise more intuition—and intuition plays a productive, if often unrecognized, role. Also related to web thinking is long-term planning—the ability to assess multiple, complex scenarios and plot a long-term course in managerial decision making. Women's brain architecture for web thinking has endowed them with another natural talent—mental flexibility. Mental flexibility is an essential trait of leadership in our dynamic global economy.[29]

As I read Pam's and Helen's analyses, it gave me great hope for the future of women and the opportunities for women to assume more and even greater leadership roles. Why? Because the business world is evolving to where women's strengths will be in great demand, and as a result women will respond and lead.

Globalization will continue to require greater communication skills, as will the world of social networking and social media. The health-care industry and issues related to global poverty and the environment are all gaining momentum, and women are perfectly suited to excel in these and other areas that will require leadership and creative problem solving.

THE POWER OF OUR THOUGHTS

The topic of empathy is extremely important, especially for women. While it can be a tremendous asset, as shared by Pam, it can also become a detriment to women. Empathy is defined as the ability to understand and share someone else's experiences and emotions, to "feel" their feelings. So while it is important to be empathetic, it is equally important to be able to control your own thoughts so that you do not become overwhelmed or obsessed by the other person's feelings.

Let's review our "thoughts" and our awareness of those thoughts.

The National Science Foundation has statistics that estimate we have between twelve thousand and sixty thousand thoughts per day, depending on things like our creativity, problem-solving skills, and our career. Other research reveals that as many as 95 to 98 percent of those thoughts are exactly the same thoughts we had the day before and even more significantly, 80 percent of our thoughts are typically negative. These 98 percent, as well as the negative thoughts, are automatic and take place in our subconscious. This is proof positive that we need to understand the power of our subconscious mind as discussed in the previous chapter.

This gives much greater impact to the saying "What you think about, you bring about!"

THE IMPACT OF NEGATIVE THOUGHT

The fact that 80 percent of our thoughts are negative is startling, to say the least! Compound that with our ability to be empathetic, which means other people's negative thoughts become contagious and can add to our own negative thoughts!

Jutta Joormann, Ph.D., an associate professor at the University of Miami, has studied this field extensively and talks about people who have negative thoughts from which they can't recover. In her words, "They basically get stuck in a mind-set where they relive what happened to them over and over again. Even though they think, 'Oh, it's not helpful, I should stop thinking about this, I should get on with my life'—they can't stop doing it."[30]

This never-ending cycle of negative thoughts causes mental and physical stress and will impact your physical well-being and health. In fact, the Centers for Disease Control and Prevention (CDC) has established a significant link between stress and its physical consequences. Stress can make us fat, cause disease and other illnesses, and can even lead to death. The CDC has linked stress to six of the leading causes of death: heart disease, cancer, lung ailments, accidents, cirrhosis of the liver, and suicide.

This mind/body connection is defined as *psychoneuroimmunology* in medical terms. Jennifer Hawthorne, coauthor of *Chicken Soup for the Woman's Soul* and *Chicken Soup for the Mother's Soul*, draws this simple comparison: "If you're tired physically, it's hard to think clearly. On the other hand, if you've been using your mind doing mental work all day, you're likely to feel the effects physically, too. Negative thoughts are particularly draining. Thoughts containing words like 'never,' 'should,' and 'can't,' complaints, whining, or thoughts that diminish our own or another's sense of self-worth deplete the body by producing corresponding chemicals that weaken the physiology. No wonder we're exhausted at the end of the day!"[31]

IMPACT OF HORMONE IMBALANCE

A discussion of the mind/body connection for women cannot be complete without taking time to discuss the role that hormones play in our lives and physical health. We all recognize that hormone changes occur throughout our lives and are a natural part of aging. Women, however, experience much more dramatic hormonal changes during menopause, in contrast to men, whose hormonal changes occur more gradually. This is an important topic to understand especially for professional women at the height of their career, who are suddenly faced with the impact of hormonal imbalance. Such imbalances, whether caused by menopause, hormonal changes, or other hormonal or physiological changes can cause "brain fog" and memory loss as well as extreme depression, mood swings, anxiety, and agitation.

Unfortunately, few women truly understand the dramatic impact that hormone imbalances have on their quality of life. Michelle King Robson experienced the devastating impact. Her medical condition was misdiagnosed many times in her search for answers to her health. She had a devastating hysterectomy at an early age and suffered years of bad health and mental anguish before discovering the importance of properly balanced hormones. In her words, "I got sick, I got well, and then I got mad."

Michelle turned her anger into action. She started her company, EmpowHER, to make sure no other woman would suffer as she had. The site gives women health resources, community, and support to improve their health and wellness.

In order to feel well emotionally and physically, it is important that our brain chemistry be in balance. Let's review how our brain is impacted by the following hormones and brain neurotransmitters that are responsible for stabilizing our moods:

Serotonin is a contributor to feelings of well-being and happiness;
Dopamine is most responsible for alertness;
Norepinephrine is the hormone and neurotransmitter most responsible for concentration.

You want these brain chemicals to remain in balance and work together. If they are, you will feel much more calm and in control.

Here is an example of when your changing hormone cycle can disrupt that balance and lead to disastrous results:

Estrogen fluctuations can impact your levels of **serotonin**. Without enough serotonin in your brain, you may experience depression, anxiety, and irritability. However, low **serotonin** levels will impact your ovaries and their production of **estrogen**. When estrogen levels are out of whack, either too low or too high, your moods can swing wildly. You may vacillate from extreme rage to extreme depression.

Sound like a catch-22? It most certainly is. This brain chemistry complication can create an ongoing cycle of depression that is hard to overcome unless you understand what caused it in the first place. Michelle shared:

I see a lot of women who start to drink alcohol to help them cope and to make them feel better, which actually deepens their depression. It makes them less productive in the workplace. It's a very slippery slope. Also, sleeplessness can cause brain fog because one is not getting enough sleep, and we know a lot of these issues are hormone/stress related.

This is why it is important to have resources like Michelle's website EmpowHER. Her mission is to drive innovation and change in patient experience, health-care delivery, and development and approval of health-improving, life-changing medicine, treatments, and procedures for women around the world. She wants every woman to become an advocate for her own health and achieve optimal health.

When you don't feel well, it is very difficult to do well.

You may find dramatic positive results if you seek out the proper medical support in making sure your hormones are truly in balance.

But let's not forget the impact your physical health has on your mental health. If you in fact are having physical health issues, more than likely it is increasing the number of negative thoughts being churned out by both your conscious and subconscious mind.

While you work on improving your physical health, it is just as important to work on your mental health. You have the ability to choose to flood your mind with positive thoughts and rid it of negative thoughts. Here are some suggestions that may help you along the way.

IMPROVE YOUR THOUGHTS, IMPROVE YOUR HEALTH

One study recently published in *Psychological Science* shares an easy technique to rid yourself of negative thoughts:

Just write your negative thoughts down and throw them away.

The study, funded by the U.S. National Science Foundation and the Spanish Ministerio de Ciencia e Innovación, asked people to write a thought about themselves (e.g., perceived body image) and then examined the lasting impact of their written thoughts. The results were very enlightening. Those participants who actually threw away or deleted their written thoughts about themselves were able to get over them and no longer be influenced by their written response.

In contrast, those participants who kept their written thoughts and did not throw them away continued to be influenced by their written negative thoughts.

The scientists' conclusion was that the physical act of getting rid of the thought in written form seems to allow your mind to move on to other things.

Could it be that simple?

Some of us may need to take a closer look at other ways as well, in order to decrease our negative thoughts and increase our positive thoughts. The first step is to identify and learn to "catch" your negative thoughts. Some of the following habits may expose a tendency to think negatively.

Overdramatizing—Also called catastrophic thinking. You can't find a parking place in the morning, so you decide the rest of your day is ruined.

Perfectionism—You finish a project at work and it is well received, but you realize you forgot to share one part of it. Instead of being happy that what you did present was well received, you beat yourself up about the one part you forgot to share. You magnify the negative instead of the positive.

Personalizing—When something bad occurs, you automatically find a way to blame yourself.

Judgmental—You tend to see things as right or wrong, black or white. You are quick to label as such instead of being open to other possibilities.

Now that you can more readily identify your negative thoughts, let's focus on ways to convert them into positive thoughts. Like any habit, it will take time and practice, but will yield a lifetime of positive results. Review the following eight steps to improve the positive energy in your life.

Ask yourself, "What do I typically think negatively about?" If you are truly honest with yourself, you may come up with several areas in your life. It may be work related, family related, or how you perceive yourself. Choose one area to focus on first.

1. Exercise at least three times a week, or increase your existing level of exercise.
2. Eat a healthy diet to provide good nutrition to your body and mind.
3. Set aside a time each day to reflect on what negative thoughts you have had that day. Think of how you can turn a negative thought into a positive one. For instance, instead of saying, "It's too hard," say to yourself, "Let's give it a shot!"
4. Add humor to your life. Studies have proven that humor helps reduce stress and adds optimism to your life.
5. Create a positive environment. Add light, happy art, and positive sayings to your work and home environments.
6. Spend time with positive people. Reduce the time you have to spend with negative people.
7. Engage in positive self-talk.

As you begin practicing these methods, you will see tangible results. You will find yourself smiling more, more confident, and optimistic about the future. In addition, you will be more in tune, more empathetic with others around you and therefore create a better environment for your subconscious mind to be in tune with Infinite Intelligence.

COMBINING POSITIVE
THOUGHT AND EMPATHY

Have you ever known who was calling you before you picked up the phone?

Have you ever found yourself thinking about someone, to look up only to see them looking back at you? Or if you are not in the same room, your phone rings and it is them?

This is telepathy, and we have all experienced it. It is the ability to communicate without words or body language. Often this communication is between people close to each other but it can also happen between people separated by a great distance.

In the original *Think and Grow Rich*, Napoleon Hill highlights the importance of telepathy and its role in the successful application of the MASTERMIND principle. He referred to the close working relationship he had with two of his colleagues, and how they would stimulate their minds to find solutions to problems presented to them.

He described the process: "The procedure is very simple. We sit down at a conference table, clearly state the nature of the problem we have under consideration, then begin discussing it. Each contributes whatever thoughts that may occur. The strange thing about this method of mind stimulation is that it places each participant in communication with unknown sources of knowledge definitely outside his own experience."

By tapping into these unknown sources of knowledge, you can expand your own thinking and receive wisdom from Infinite Intelligence. Hill believed that this would facilitate your sixth sense, which is described in the next chapter, in helping you create material reality from your Definite Purpose.

CHAPTER IN PRACTICE—IN MY LIFE

I learned a great deal about the brain, and the differences between men and women, in writing this chapter that I wish I had known years ago.

Our natural abilities to empathize and collaborate as women position us well to succeed in the future as businesses move from the competitive, dog-eat-dog world to a more collaborative and cooperative business environment.

There are a couple of additional issues, however, that I need to address from my experience over the years. When we talk about negativity, it can come at you directly, or it can sneak up on you, as if in stealth mode.

For instance, let's review the subjects of gossip, sarcasm, and unhappy employees. Gossip and sarcasm can start as innocent chitchat between friends or coworkers but turn into deadly hurtful poison. Likewise, one unhappy employee can use his or her unhappiness to create a toxic workplace environment for everyone.

We have all gossiped or been sarcastic, and most likely we have all been hurt by gossip or sarcasm directed at us.

Over the years, I have learned some simple tactics to help me minimize gossip and sarcasm and steer clear of unhappy employees or coworkers, such as:

1. Keeping myself busy doing something constructive.
2. Simply avoiding the person who tends to gossip, be sarcastic, or is unhappy.
3. When exposed, making it a habit to walk away. Even if I just listen, I am still participating in and spreading negativity.
4. Being careful what I share with others about my own life; it may come back to haunt me.
5. If I'm uncomfortable, I find someone trained to help me and then sharing my feelings, rather than keeping them bottled up.
6. Countering the negativity with something positive.

By practicing these six steps, you can minimize your exposure to the negativity associated with gossip, sarcasm, and unhappy coworkers or employees.

My friend Donna Root helped me create a process when I found myself stewing over something troubling in my life. I called it my own personal "rototiller" in a previous chapter.

She told me that when I feel consumed with a negative thought I should do the following:

1. Imagine myself driving a car.
2. Stop long enough to identify the individual thought.
3. Visualize the thought as separate and distinct from "me."
4. Place the thought into the passenger seat of my car.
5. Ask it, "What am I supposed to learn from you?"
6. If there is a lesson to learn, learn it.
7. If not, tell the thought that it is powerless.
8. Go about your life—in control of your thoughts.

And when all else fails, I turn on the sounds of Motown and start dancing!

THE SISTERHOOD MASTERMIND

Wisdom from women of success and significance on the BRAIN:

ERMA BOMBECK (1927–1996)
AMERICAN HUMORIST, COLUMNIST, AND AUTHOR

"I have a theory about the human mind. A brain is a lot like a computer. It will only take so many facts, and then it will go on overload and blow up."

MAYA ANGELOU

AMERICAN AUTHOR AND POET

"The idea is to write it so that people hear it and it slides through the brain and goes straight to the heart."

ANNIE BESANT (1847–1933)

BRITISH SOCIALIST AND WOMEN'S RIGHTS ACTIVIST

"As the heat of the coal differs from the coal itself, so do memory, perception, judgment, emotion, and will differ from the brain, which is the instrument of thought."

"We learn much during our sleep, and the knowledge thus gained slowly filters into the physical brain, and is occasionally impressed upon it as a vivid and illuminative dream."

FARRAH FAWCETT (1947–2009)

AMERICAN ACTRESS AND ARTIST

"God gave women intuition and femininity. Used properly, the combination easily jumbles the brain of any man I've ever met."

BARBARA DE ANGELIS

AMERICAN RELATIONSHIP CONSULTANT, LECTURER, AND AUTHOR

"A man's brain has a more difficult time shifting from thinking to feeling than a woman's brain does."

SUSAN BLACKMORE

ENGLISH FREELANCE WRITER, LECTURER, AND BROADCASTER

"In proportion to our body mass, our brain is three times as large as that of our nearest relatives. This huge organ is dangerous and painful to give birth to, expensive to build and, in a resting human, uses about 20 percent of the body's energy even though it is just 2 percent of the body's weight. There must be some reason for all this evolutionary expense."

SUSANNAH CAHALAN

AMERICAN REPORTER AND AUTHOR OF *BRAIN ON FIRE*

"The mind is like a circuit of Christmas tree lights. When the brain works well, all of the lights twinkle brilliantly, and it's adaptable enough that, often, even if one bulb goes out, the rest will still shine on. But depending on where the damage is, sometimes that one blown bulb can make the whole strand go dark."

MARILYN FERGUSON (1938–2008)

AMERICAN AUTHOR, EDITOR, AND PUBLIC SPEAKER

"The brain's calculations do not require our conscious effort, only our attention and our openness to let the information through. Although the brain absorbs universes of information, little is admitted into normal consciousness."

MARIANNE WILLIAMSON

SPIRITUAL TEACHER, AUTHOR, AND LECTURER

"You may believe that you are responsible for what you do, but not for what you think. The truth is that you are responsible for what you think, because it is only at this level that you can exercise choice. What you do comes from what you think."

KATIE KACVINSKY

AMERICAN AUTHOR OF TEEN AND YOUNG ADULT FICTION

"Thoughts are circular, they don't take you anywhere. They don't have feet—they can't gain any ground. They can trap you if you don't eventually stand up and make a move."

DREW BARRYMORE

AMERICAN ACTRESS AND FILM DIRECTOR

"I personally battled with my own body image for years. I used to tell myself, You can't wear anything sleeveless or strapless. All of a sudden I

was like, *What if I just didn't send such negative messages to my brain and said, Wear it and enjoy it? Now I'm more comfortable in clothes than ever."*

MARILU HENNER
AMERICAN ACTRESS, PRODUCER, AND AUTHOR

"Research has shown that even small amounts of processed food alter the chemical balance in our brain and cause negative mood swings along with noticeable dips in energy."

"Healthful whole foods improve our brain function as well."

In the next chapter Hill brings us to his last principle, or the apex of the *Think and Grow Rich* philosophy, the Sixth Sense, the Door to the Temple of Wisdom. The Sixth Sense is inspired by and triggers our Creative Imagination when all the other principles come together.

ASK YOURSELF

Use your journal as you go through this section to identify your action steps, trigger your "aha" moments, and create your plan for achieving success!

After reading about your subconscious and your brain and how they work together, take some time to meditate on what you read and how it applies to your own life.

Think of some of your positive traits and record them in your journal.

Now think of some things you would like to change about yourself and record them.

Answer the following questions:

- Do you tend to overdramatize?
- Are you a perfectionist?
- Do you make everything personal?
- Are you judgmental?
- Do you tend to gossip?
- Are you sarcastic?

Choose one negative trait that you would like to conquer and convert it into a positive trait. Record it in your journal and commit to working on that trait first. Practice catching yourself when you start thinking about it.

Now, review the seven methods to improve the positive energy in your life from page 238. Select at least one of them that you will commit to employing for the next month.

At the end of the month, record your experience in your personal journal. Then choose another one to focus on.

Remember to think of something positive each night before you go to sleep.

Sweet dreams!

The Sixth Sense

The Door to the Temple of Wisdom

■

*Trust your hunches . . . Hunches are usually based
on facts filed away just below the conscious level.*
—DR. JOYCE BROTHERS

HAVE YOU EVER TAKEN AN IMMEDIATE DISLIKE TO SOMEONE AS soon as you met them because you just "know" that they can't be trusted?

Have you ever gotten a chill and had the hairs stand up on the back of your neck, and realized your intuition was sending you a 911 call?

Have you ever made a decision against the advice of your business associates, or family and friends, because you just "knew" it was right?

Have you ever awakened with a "great new idea"?

These hunches, gut feelings, flashes of "knowing," taps on the shoulders, or inspirations are most likely your SIXTH SENSE at work. The SIXTH SENSE is your subconscious mind, referred to as Creative Imagination in earlier chapters. Hill called it the door to the temple of wisdom, because he describes how it connects you to Infinite Intelligence and becomes the "receiving set through which ideas, plans and thoughts flash into the mind."

You may only fully engage your SIXTH SENSE after you master the first twelve principles of success. As Hill explains it, it is the combining of the mental and spiritual realms, and allows you to contact what he refers to as the Universal Mind. As you develop your SIXTH SENSE you will realize that it serves as your "guardian angel," opening the door to the Temple of Wisdom just at the right time.

It helps transform your BURNING DESIRES into organized plans and turn those plans into their concrete, or material, reality. Once you understand the process, and put it to practice, you will transform your knowledge into UNDERSTANDING. This understanding is helped along when you recognize and tap into your SIXTH SENSE. It will lift you to a higher level of understanding and mental awareness.

The word "intuition" comes from the Latin work *intuir*, which means "knowledge from within."

The *Merriam-Webster's Collegiate Dictionary* defines "intuition" as "a natural ability or power that makes it possible to know something without any proof or evidence: a feeling that guides a person to act a certain way without fully understanding why."

Donna Root highlights that we all have a SIXTH SENSE, but not all of us listen to it. She posits: "Although we are all born with a SIXTH SENSE, much of the population has previously placed a low value on the illogical gift of knowing the unknowable. I believe women throughout history have had the great wisdom in not having to explain logically what they 'know in their gut' to be real and true although illogical. 'Women's intuition' is the capacity to forge ahead using an intuitive knowledge without having to have a logical explanation. The ability to continue to enhance this sense is in fact a matter of discipline."

"This ability to create from and be totally in tune with this SIXTH SENSE is a conscious way of living in the world, and as women I believe it is easier for us to expand and magnify these SIXTH SENSE gifts. We are living in a great time where science has discarded some myths previously embedded in our culture and thinking. Today we know we are living in a totally connected universe and that we can reach higher in consciousness then our current state of consciousness allows."

This higher state of consciousness is where we receive guidance, receive the higher level of understanding, and connect with Infinite Intelligence.

You may ask, is this an occasional connection? Or is it available to us anytime?

Shakti Gawain taught us to listen to our intuition and to rely on it as a guiding light more than twenty-five years ago in her book *Living in the Light*. In an interview with B. J. Gallagher of the *Huffington Post*, she reiterated its importance: "It's so *practical* to connect to that source of guidance on a day-to-day, hour-by-hour basis. Your intuition will tell you where you need to go; it will connect you with people you should meet; it will guide you toward work that is meaningful for you—work that brings you joy, work that feels right for you. Listening to your internal guidance system will lead to a rich, fulfilled, happy life. That's been my experience, and millions of folks can attest to it in their own lives as well.[32]

In addition to being our guiding light, our intuition also serves as our protector and our safety net by sending warning signs if something is out of whack. Once again, we need to be aware of and prepared to listen to those warning signs.

Judith Orloff, M.D., a board-certified psychiatrist and an assistant clinical professor of psychiatry at UCLA, as well as a best-selling author, validates the important role our intuition plays in keeping us safe. She defines intuition as a "potent form of inner wisdom, not mediated by the intellect. Accessible to us all, it's a still, small voice inside—an unflinching truth teller committed to our well-being. You may experience intuition as a gut feeling, hunch, a physical sensation, a snapshot-like flash, or a dream. Always a friend, it keeps a watchful eye on our bodies, letting us know if something is out of sync."[33]

IS IT INTUITION OR EMOTION?

It is important to recognize that emotion can often seem like intuition, and therefore it can be easy to confuse the two. Intuitively knowing that you should not do something or take an action is not the same thing as being scared to do it. It may seem, however, like fear is what is telling you to walk away.

The key difference between emotion and intuition or SIXTH SENSE is that the latter is based on knowledge—it may be unexplainable knowledge, but knowledge nonetheless. Emotions such as resentment, anger, and even happiness can cloud a situation with untruth and therefore block intuition from communicating with you.

Fear, in particular, is very effective in blocking your intuition. Because this emotion operates from the false assumption that the world is a dangerous and fearful place, it can only offer false guidance. In fact, guidance you receive from fear will result in increased energy being spent on "having control" rather than discovering ways to support your definite purpose and ultimate desire.

When we think our intuition is in the "caution" mode sending us warning signs, it is very important to make sure that it truly is our intuition and that we are not being confused by our emotion of fear. Fear causes a feeling of powerlessness to change your circumstances related to some impending issue, while intuition gives you the power to change your circumstances for the better and nudges you in the right direction. Dr. Orloff provides the following distinctions between experiencing intuition versus an irrational fear:

- A reliable intuition conveys information neutrally, unemotionally.
- A reliable intuition feels right in your gut.
- A reliable intuition has a compassionate, affirming tone.
- A reliable intuition gives crisp, clear impressions that are "seen" first, then felt.

- A reliable intuition conveys a detached sensation, similar to being in a theater watching a movie.
- An irrational fear is highly emotionally charged.
- An irrational fear has cruel, demeaning, or delusional content (either toward yourself or toward others, perhaps both).
- An irrational fear conveys no gut-centered confirmation or on-target feeling.
- An irrational fear reflects past psychological wounds that have not been healed. An irrational fear diminishes being centered and having sound perspective.[34]

Can you think of a time when you thought you were responding to your intuition, only to realize later that you were reacting to fear? In the future, in order to help yourself determine whether you are being guided by intuition or controlled by emotion, take the time to ask yourself the following questions.

1. Am I having a physical reaction? If so, your subconscious may be manifesting in a physical way. Intuition feels "right" in your gut, fear creates negative feelings in your gut.
2. Can I say with ultimate conviction that I "just know" that something is true, correct, or necessary? This is your SIXTH SENSE tapping you on the shoulder. Intuition is your instinct combined with your knowledge and cognitive ability.
3. Does your certainty toward a viewpoint last only momentarily and then your self-talk tries to convince you that you are wrong? If there is a strong emotion tied to this experience, you may be receiving false guidance by that emotion.
4. Are you experiencing emotion that is tied to a previous experience? If so, you may need to quiet your logical mind and sit with the emotion long enough to allow your intuition to break through it.

5. Do you allow your emotion, or desire for being "in control," to influence your decision making, and then label it as intuition? You are blocking your intuition. If you let go of needing to be "in control" you may feel intuition start flowing freely.

6. Are your thoughts dealing with the present, or the future? Intuition typically deals with what is happening in the present, right now, while fear deals with possible negative outcomes in the future.

ARE YOU IN CONTROL?

Being "in control" is a huge issue for many women. When you are in a state of fear, you are actually giving up control to something that may or may not happen in the future. (We are talking here about imaginary fear—not a very real fear like escaping a burning building.) However, even when it is their intuition speaking to them, many women tend to dismiss it and not benefit from their intuition.

More than likely this chapter has reminded you of several times where your intuition, or SIXTH SENSE, protected you or gave you that "aha" moment. But ask yourself if you have been the innocent receiver of the messages it sends, or have you employed it and used it as a tool to tap into Infinite Intelligence in order to gain the higher level of understanding?

How do you engage and develop your intuition, or SIXTH SENSE?

First, ask yourself if you accept the existence of your SIXTH SENSE. Your openness to receiving guidance is absolutely essential, as Hill referred to your intuition as the guardian angel at the gate of the Temple of Wisdom.

Create the best environment to allow your body and mind to become still, eliminate the chatter, so that you are better able to receive guidance.

Are your thoughts positive or negative? Positive thoughts open your mind, while negative thoughts will most certainly close your mind.

Learn to ask questions, and become receptive to receiving the answer from Infinite Intelligence.

Ask for guidance before you go to sleep at night and pay attention to your dreams.

In writing this book, I was trying to find examples to share with you, when I came across a blog post called "The MOST Important Time of Day for Entrepreneurs," by Ali Brown, literally posted five days before I started looking. It was intuition at work. I asked for assistance and "happened upon" her site. In part, she wrote:

Let me share a secret with you: I NEVER get true clarity, great ideas, or brilliant answers while sitting at my desk or while working on my computer. They ALWAYS generate when I give myself space and silence.

In order for me to receive what I call my "Divine Downloads"—the answers or "aha" moments—I need to clear some RAM in my brain. Just like on your computer, if you have twenty applications open and running, they will use up all your energy. You won't get what you need. A **reboot** is needed! So clearing your head and opening up for answers is the key.

When you are in this meditative state, you open your heart and your mind and truly connect with your spiritual nature. Call it what you will, but for me it's connecting to Spirit. It's surrendering your mind in order to connect with something deeper.

Quiet time allows you to hear answers. You just write down a question, and listen, and see what comes up. At first, you think you're just making it up. But then, you realize later that what came to you was a FLOW of ideas.

The point is to get into the HABIT of connecting with Spirit. Once you master the art of being quiet, you can start to hear the whispers of the Divine—the voices that have been trying to reach you all along.[35]

So not only is creating the environment important (the quiet time Ali discusses), but equally important is the need for us to "ask" for the guidance.

And Beverly Sallee credits learning to ask for guidance from her SIXTH SENSE as an integral part of her success in building an international network of business owners. She shares:

A woman often says, "I just had a feeling."

Men sometimes laugh and ask for a factual basis for it.

Napoleon Hill called it "creative imagination" or "hunches."

As an important part of developing my sixth sense, I have learned to practice "prayerful listening." James 1:5 of the Bible says: "If any of you lack Wisdom let him ask of God who gives to all men liberally and doesn't scold you for asking."

In building my business in India, I often spent long days in counseling with new network owners. I asked for wisdom before each appointment. They would remark, "How did you know to ask that?" or "Who told you that about us?" I replied, "I ask God for wisdom." As a result of my prayerful listening, my business in India grew very fast.

As a result of this business success, I have been able to provide many orphans schooling and medical care in India.

It pays to ask for guidance.

Intuition is the mechanism by which implicit knowledge is made available during an instance of decision making. Trust in your knowledge, ask for guidance, and allow your intuition to steer you in the right direction!

CHAPTER IN PRACTICE—IN MY LIFE

My intuition, or my sixth sense, has always been strong, but I haven't always listened to it. In fact, most of my life, I ignored it. I remember so many times in school where the first answer that came to mind on a test was the right one, but I rationalized why another answer must be the right one and then chose the wrong answer. Needless to say, I should have learned quickly—but I didn't.

As I have shared in earlier chapters, my upbringing centered on working hard and doing well in school. My family was intellectual, rational, and any sign of emotion was considered a sign of weakness. So I learned that most things are right or wrong, black or white, and that being logical and rational was rewarded. As a result, I did very well in school. But in that type of environment, you tend to become skeptical about anything that isn't black or white. If you can't prove something, then it doesn't exist.

As a result, I became quite serious and focused on my future. I forgot to "be present."

Little children start out very intuitive. They create all kinds of imaginary environments and friends, maybe as a result of both their imagination and intuition. Little children at play appear to float through the air, enjoying just "being." As we get older, however, we are taught to listen to directions. That some greater authority (teacher, parent, well-meaning adult) knows better than we do. As a result, we start looking around to see what everyone else is doing, looking for guidance from others, doubting our own ability to make decisions. We start doubting our own inner wisdom and therefore our intuition.

Napoleon Hill talks about the "fear of criticism" as one of the six ghostly fears that will be discussed in the next chapter. I see this as one of the greatest problems with society today. People judge themselves through the eyes of others, on how other people think of them, instead of building their own self-confidence and self-worth. I am particularly sensitive to this fear of criticism because I have always battled it myself. I have always wanted to please everyone else, making sure I have done my absolute best, and done the "right" thing, even when it wasn't the "right" thing for me, or even when I didn't want to do it in the first place.

Can you relate?

I have shared several turning points in my life, where I successfully listened to my intuition and never regretted it. My life's motto of "Why not?" came to me through my sixth sense when I asked for guidance. Today, I am more aware than ever that a higher power is at work, and I strive to create the environment to be more receptive at all times.

I still catch myself not "being present" sometimes. I try to blame it on how hectic my life has become and how many responsibilities I have. My life is filled with so many wonderful opportunities, and I try to do them all! By being focused on "doing, accomplishing, and making things happen," I found that I had lost touch with the value of just "being." In fact, the "busy-ness and doing-ness" was my excuse for not being present. Today, I am working on learning to say no more, learning how to reduce the "chatter" in my life, and focusing on my stop-doing list, so that I will have more time for me to just "be."

I have been blessed with fabulous guardian angels all my life. My intuition has guided me into fabulous experiences, and saved me from potential setbacks over and over. By allowing myself to learn how to "be" more often, I am feeling a kind of peace I never imagined possible.

THE SISTERHOOD MASTERMIND

Wisdom from women of success and significance on the SIXTH SENSE:

FLORENCE SCOVEL SHINN (1871–1940)
AMERICAN ARTIST AND BOOK ILLUSTRATOR WHO BECAME A
SPIRITUAL TEACHER

"Intuition is a spiritual faculty and does not explain, but simply points the way."

"I am always under direct inspiration. I know just what to do and give instant obedience to my intuitive leads."

MARILYN MONROE (1926–1962)
BORN NORMA JEAN MORTENSON; AMERICAN ACTRESS, MODEL,
AND SINGER

"A woman knows by intuition, or instinct, what is best for herself."

GISELE BÜNDCHEN
BRAZILIAN FASHION MODEL, U.N. GOODWILL AMBASSADOR

"The more you trust your intuition, the more empowered you become, the stronger you become, and the happier you become."

JEAN SHINODA BOLEN
PSYCHIATRIST AND AUTHOR ON SPIRITUALITY

"Insights from myth, dreams, and intuitions, from glimpses of an invisible reality, and from perennial human wisdom provide us with hints and guesses about the meaning of life and what we are here for. Prayer, observance, discipline, thought, and action are the means through which we grow and find meaning."

MINNA ANTRIM (1861–1950)
AMERICAN WRITER, FAMOUS FOR QUOTE "EXPERIENCE IS A GREAT TEACHER, BUT SHE SENDS IN TERRIFIC BILLS."

"Intuition is truly a feminine quality, but women should not mistake rash conclusions for this gift."

BETTY WILLIAMS
IRISH CORECIPIENT OF THE NOBEL PEACE PRIZE, 1976

"Compassion is more important than intellect in calling forth the love that the work of peace needs, and intuition can often be a far more powerful searchlight than cold reason."

MADAME DE GIRARDIN (1804–1855)
FRENCH AUTHOR WITH PEN NAME VICOMTE DELAUNAY

"Instinct is the nose of the mind."

ANNE WILSON SCHAEF
AUTHOR AND FEMINIST, HOLDS A PH.D. IN CLINICAL PSYCHOLOGY

"Trusting our intuition often saves us from disaster."

ASK YOURSELF

Use your journal as you go through this section to identify your action steps, trigger your "aha" moments, and create your plan for achieving success!

In your journal, record three or four times in your life when your intuition, or SIXTH SENSE, either gave you an "aha" moment or protected you. Think of a time when you got goose bumps, a knot in your stomach, or butterflies in your stomach—more than likely it was your intuition speaking to you.

Can you think of times when you ignored your intuition, or SIXTH SENSE? What was the outcome?

Review the steps for engaging and developing your intuition, or SIXTH SENSE, as provided earlier in the chapter, and be honest with yourself. Do you employ these techniques?

- First, ask yourself if you accept the existence of your SIXTH SENSE. Your openness to receiving guidance is absolutely essential, as Hill referred to your intuition as the guardian angel at the gate of the Temple of Wisdom.
- Create the best environment to allow your body and mind to become still and eliminate the chatter, so that you are better able to receive guidance.
- Are your thoughts positive, or negative? Positive thoughts open your mind, while negative thoughts will most certainly close your mind.
- Learn to ask questions, and become receptive to receiving the answer from Infinite Intelligence.
- In addition, ask for guidance before you go to sleep at night and pay attention to your dreams.

Ask yourself the following questions:

Do you pay attention when your body is tired?

Do you pay attention to other people's body language when you meet them?

Do you find yourself crossing your arms when you are in an uncomfortable situation?

Do you avoid people who are negative?

Do you consider yourself serious?

Do you consider yourself spontaneous?

Do you ask a higher power for guidance?

Do you pay attention to your dreams?

For the next month, keep a journal and record the times when you recognize your intuition, or SIXTH SENSE, is at work. You will become more aware of it, and as a result you will become more open to it.

Keep your journal beside your bed. Before you go to sleep, ask a question to a higher power, or Infinite Intelligence. For instance, "How do I challenge myself to get to the next level?" Then pay close attention to your dreams, and record them as soon as you wake up, even if they don't make sense at the time.

Your guardian angel is at work.

How to Outwit the
Six Ghosts of Fear

Take Inventory of Yourself as You Read
This Chapter, and Find Out How Many of
the "Ghosts" Are Standing in Your Way

We gain strength, and courage, and confidence
by each experience in which we really stop
to look fear in the face . . . we must do
that which we think we cannot.

—ELEANOR ROOSEVELT

NAPOLEON HILL SPENT MORE THAN TWENTY YEARS OF HIS LIFE studying more than five hundred of the most successful men of his time, as well as thousands of people who considered themselves failures, from which he developed the philosophy of success he shares in *Think and Grow Rich*. Just as he was ready to publish, he realized that even though many people "know" what they need to do in order to become successful, they just DON'T DO IT!

Can you think of someone you know to whom this applies? Someone who holds herself back from fear or other self-limiting beliefs? Can you think of a time when your own fear paralyzed you and kept you from moving forward?

So Hill added the last chapter of the book, "How to Outwit the Six Ghosts of Fear," to help people overcome their own self-limiting beliefs. He called them ghosts because they only exist in your mind. These ghosts create INDECISION, DOUBT, and FEAR. Hill knew that the influence of fear is so impactful that, after completing *Think and Grow Rich*, he went on to write *Outwitting the Devil* as the sequel to specifically address the influence of fear and negativity and how to overcome them.

Let's review the Six Ghosts of Fear, the symptoms Hill outlined that may help you recognize each one, and some sage advice I found from successful women on how to blast through them.

THE SIX BASIC FEARS
The fear of POVERTY
The fear of CRITICISM at the bottom of most of one's worries
The fear of ILL HEALTH
The fear of LOSS OF LOVE OF SOMEONE
The fear of OLD AGE
The fear of DEATH

THE FEAR OF POVERTY

You are either a master of your money or a slave to it.

The Fear of Poverty is, without doubt, the most destructive of the six basic fears. It is the most difficult to master.

There is no doubt that women have a tremendous amount of fear about money. According to the 2013 Women, Money & Power study from insurer Allianz Life, nearly half of all American women fear becoming a "bag lady." This includes 27 percent of women earning more than $200,000 per year who, even with that level of income, still fear becoming a "bag lady."

Why do so many women delegate their financial security to a spouse or partner?

Why do so many women spend more than they earn and become mired in debt?

ELEANOR ROOSEVELT (1884–1962)
FIRST LADY OF THE UNITED STATES (1933–1945)

"Do what you feel in your heart to be right—for you'll be criticized anyway. You'll be damned if you do, and damned if you don't."

"No one can make you feel inferior without your consent."

DIANA ROSS
AMERICAN SINGER, MUSIC ARTIST, AND ACTRESS

"Criticism, even when you try to ignore it, can hurt. I have cried over many articles written about me, but I move on and I don't hold on to that."

MARY KAY ASH (1918–2001)
AMERICAN BUSINESSWOMAN, FOUNDER OF MARY KAY COSMETICS

"Sandwich every bit of criticism between two layers of praise."

THE FEAR OF ILL HEALTH

We are constantly being bombarded with issues about health and the latest remedies. You probably have dear friends and/or family members dealing with severe health issues. But have you taken the time to think about your own health? Are you taking care of the most precious asset you have—your mind and body?

Many women tend to put everyone and everything else before themselves. I know that I have sacrificed my own health many times, because I put priority on things I needed to get done instead of getting the proper exercise and rest. Can you relate?

Eventually we see the negative physical results of ignoring our own health, and we start to worry about our own health problems. Our minds are also very powerful receivers. From the last several years of economic uncertainty, to all the media talk about health issues and our need to provide for our later years of certain bad health, we have been, and continue to be, bombarded with negative messages that can trigger our fears and impact us negatively in many physical ways. Every form of negative thinking may cause ill health.

SYMPTOMS OF THE FEAR OF ILL HEALTH

AUTOSUGGESTION—Looking for, and expecting to find, the symptoms of all kinds of disease. Trying home remedies.

HYPOCHONDRIA—The habit of talking of illness, concentrating the mind upon disease, and expecting its appearance. Negative thinking.

LACK OF EXERCISE—Interferes with proper physical exercise, and results in being overweight.

SUSCEPTIBILITY—Breaks down Nature's body resistance and creates a favorable condition for any form of disease.

SELF-CODDLING—Seeks sympathy, using imaginary illness as the lure.

INTEMPERANCE—Using alcohol or drugs to "treat" pains instead of eliminating their cause.

The battle against fear of ill health is won by taking care of ourselves! A woman who is active, healthy, and in tune with her body will feel confident in knowing she is being proactive in creating a life of sustained well-being. Keeping a positive mental attitude is also very important to maintaining good health.

SISTERHOOD MASTERMIND

Wisdom from women of success and significance on FEAR OF ILL HEALTH:

NAOMI JUDD
AMERICAN COUNTRY MUSIC SINGER, SONGWRITER
"Your body hears everything your mind says."

ELIZA GAYNOR MINDEN

DESIGNER OF THE GAYNOR MINDEN POINTE BALLET SHOE

"Respect your body. Eat well. Dance forever."

DOROTHY PARKER (1893–1967)

AMERICAN POET, SHORT STORY WRITER, AND CRITIC

"Money cannot buy health, but I'd settle for a diamond-studded wheel-chair."

KARYN CALABRESE

ENTREPRENEUR AND POPULAR HOLISTIC HEALTH EXPERT

"If you don't take care of this, the most magnificent machine that you will ever be given, where are you going to live?"

THE FEAR OF LOSS OF LOVE

This fear can be the most painful of all. Hill warned, "Careful analysis has shown that women are more susceptible to this fear than men."

I think this fear goes hand in hand with the fear of criticism. When we lose someone we love through their choice, not ours, we often judge ourselves very harshly. We torment ourselves by blaming ourselves with negative thoughts like, "What did I do wrong? If only I had done more for him. If only I was skinnier, prettier."

The fear of loss of love is most likely tied to confidence as well. A woman who immediately blames herself for a failed personal relationship will most likely suffer from low self-esteem or self-confidence in some form or another. The following statistics shared by the Confidence Coalition of the Kappa Delta Sorority clearly show this lack of confidence in women:

- Ninety percent of all women want to change at least one aspect of their physical appearance.
- Only 2 percent of women think they are beautiful.

SYMPTOMS OVER FEAR OF LOSS OF LOVE

JEALOUSY—Being suspicious of friends and loved ones without any reasonable evidence.

FAULT FINDING—Finding fault with friends, relatives, business associates, and loved ones.

GAMBLING—Gambling, stealing, cheating, and otherwise taking hazardous chances to provide money for loved ones, with the belief that love can be bought.

Dealing with loss of love is not easy. A woman who is empowered to be strong, has conviction in her values, and is financially independent will, however, suffer less of the fear of loss of love than one who looks to others to create her happiness and self-worth.

SISTERHOOD MASTERMIND

Wisdom from women of success and significance on FEAR OF LOSS OF LOVE:

MARIANNE WILLIAMSON
AMERICAN AUTHOR

"Love is what we were born with. Fear is what we learned here."

SONIA JOHNSON
AMERICAN FEMINIST AND WRITER

"What we have most to fear is failure of the heart."

HELEN KELLER (1880–1968)
AMERICAN AUTHOR, POLITICAL ACTIVIST, AND LECTURER

"What we have once enjoyed we can never lose. All that we love deeply becomes a part of us."

cesses of transition, or change, but it cannot be destroyed. Death is a mere transition."

SYMPTOMS OF THE FEAR OF DEATH

THINKING—About dying instead of making the most of LIFE.
CAUSES—Ill health, poverty, lack of appropriate occupation, disappointment over love, insanity, and religious fanaticism.

The greatest advice for getting past the fear of death is to make the most of each and every day. If you have a BURNING DESIRE FOR ACHIEVEMENT, and back it up with useful service to others, your focus will be on living a life of significance, and leave no room for the fear of death.

SISTERHOOD MASTERMIND

Wisdom from women of success and significance on FEAR OF DEATH:

MAYA YING LIN
AMERICAN ARCHITECTURAL DESIGNER AND ARTIST

"If we can't face death, we'll never overcome it.
You have to look it straight in the eye.
Then you can turn around and walk back out into the light."

HELEN KELLER (1880–1968)
AMERICAN AUTHOR, POLITICAL ACTIVIST, AND LECTURER

"Death is no more than passing from one room into another. But there's a difference for me, you know. Because in that other room I shall be able to see."

KATHARINE HEPBURN (1907–2003)
AMERICAN ACTRESS OF FILM, STAGE, AND TELEVISION
"Death will be a great relief. No more interviews."

J. K. ROWLING
BRITISH AUTHOR OF THE HARRY POTTER FANTASY SERIES
"To the well-organized mind, death is but the next great adventure."

WORRY AND FEAR— THE ENEMIES OF HAPPINESS

"Worry is a state of mind based on fear. It works slowly, but persistently. It is insidious and subtle. Step by step it 'digs itself in' until it paralyzes one's reasoning faculty, destroys self-confidence and initiative. Worry is a form of sustained fear caused by indecision therefore it is a state of mind which can be controlled." This is timeless and powerful advice from Napoleon Hill.

Earlier I shared the definition of worry that helped change my life:

To worry is to pray for what you do NOT want.

Whenever I find myself in the downward spiral caused by worry, I stop and repeat this definition to myself over and over until I calm myself down.

And more wisdom from Hill: "You are the master of your own earthly destiny just as surely as you have the power to control your own thoughts. You may influence, direct, and eventually control your own environment making your life what you want it to be—or, you may neglect to exercise the privilege which is yours, to make your life to order, thus casting yourself upon the broad sea of 'Circumstance' where you will be tossed hither and yon, like a ship on the waves of the ocean."

When you decide that nothing positive comes from worry, and in fact its price is more than you are willing to pay, you will find peace of mind, and a calmness that will bring you happiness.

SISTERHOOD MASTERMIND

Wisdom from women of success and significance on WORRY and FEAR:

CAMERON DIAZ
AMERICAN ACTRESS

"What we women need to do, instead of worrying about what we don't have, is just love what we do have."

EMMA GRAY
EDITOR FOR THE *HUFFPOST*—WOMEN

"Over the years I have learned little tricks and coping mechanisms for handling my anxiety: put both feet on the ground, breathe in and out of your nose, take a walk, be aware of destructive thought patterns and actively work to change them. I have come to know my anxiety like a close 'frenemy,' and the more I talk about her, the more I find that other women relate. When we've reached a point where 23 percent of American women are all struggling with the same demons, it's time to start talking about them and confronting them—collectively."

ALICE WALKER
AMERICAN AUTHOR OF *THE COLOR PURPLE*, WINNER OF THE PULITZER PRIZE AND THE NATIONAL BOOK AWARD

"I have learned not to worry about love; but to honor its coming with all my heart."

MARIA SHARAPOVA

WORLD-RANKED RUSSIAN TENNIS PLAYER

"I don't worry about what my opponent is doing."

MARTHA BECK

AMERICAN SOCIOLOGIST, THERAPIST, LIFE COACH,
AND BEST-SELLING AUTHOR

"Instead of fretting about getting everything done, why not simply accept that being alive means having things to do? Then drop into full engagement with whatever you're doing, and let the worry go."

THE DEVIL'S WORKSHOP— THE SEVENTH BASIC EVIL

As Hill was wrapping up his discussion of the Six Basic Fears, he added a Seventh Basic Evil, which is the Susceptibility to Negative Influences. He warns: "IT IS MORE DEEPLY SEATED AND MORE OFTEN FATAL THAN ALL OF THE SIX FEARS."

While the ability to overcome the six basic fears lies in your mind and the ability to control your thoughts, the seventh basic evil can best be controlled by your actions as well as your willpower to not allow other people's negativity to permeate your spirit and bring you down.

For a moment, visualize yourself at the funeral of a six-year-old child who was tragically killed in an accident. Do you feel your own emotions? Do you feel the heaviness around you, caused by just thinking of such a sad event?

Now, in contrast, visualize yourself at a party with all of your friends celebrating your achieving a huge WIN in your business. You are dancing to the sounds of Motown and laughing with the people you cherish. Do you feel your emotions now? Do you feel the lightness around you, caused by just thinking of such a happy event?

While these examples are relatively obvious, we deal with this type of emotional roller coaster every day. Have you ever gotten a call from a dear friend in a crisis and felt your own emotions immediately drawn down to her level of sadness? It is human nature. If you can train yourself to protect yourself from negative influences, however, you can instead bring your friend up to a higher level of happiness.

You can become a beacon of light, and create your own environment of positivity.

SISTERHOOD MASTERMIND

Wisdom from women of success and significance on NEGATIVE INFLUENCES:

HEIDI KLUM

GERMAN-AMERICAN MODEL, BUSINESSWOMAN, AND FASHION DESIGNER

"I think it's important to get your surroundings as well as yourself into a positive state—meaning surround yourself with positive people, not the kind who are negative and jealous of everything you do."

SOPHIA BUSH

AMERICAN ACTRESS

"I have walked away from friendships when I've realized that someone smiles to someone's face and talks about them the minute they walk out of a room. I have no room in my life for that kind of negative energy anymore."

PEACE PILGRIM (1908–1981)

AMERICAN NONDENOMINATIONAL SPIRITUAL TEACHER AND PEACE ACTIVIST

"If you realized how powerful your thoughts are, you would never think a negative thought."

JACQUELINE KENNEDY (1929–1994)
WIFE OF THE THIRTY-FIFTH PRESIDENT OF THE UNITED STATES,
JOHN F. KENNEDY

"We should all do something to right the wrongs that we see and not just complain about them."

HODA KOTB
AMERICAN TELEVISION NEWS ANCHOR AND COHOST OF *TODAY*

"When I first came to NBC, I thought it was going to be swimming with the sharks, all men for themselves, be careful and all that. I have to tell you, I learned that you can be kind and a hard worker and move up. You don't have to play dirty or do things that you think happen at big corporations."

MARSHA PETRIE SUE
AUTHOR AND PUBLIC SPEAKER

"Every day is a new beginning. Treat it that way. Stay away from what might have been, and look at what can be."

MARY MANIN MORRISSEY
AMERICAN SPIRITUAL TEACHER

"Even though you may want to move forward in your life, you may have one foot on the brakes. In order to be free, we must learn how to let go. Release the hurt. Release the fear. Refuse to entertain your old pain. The energy it takes to hang on to the past is holding you back from a new life. What is it you would let go of today?"

ASK YOURSELF

Use your journal as you go through this section to identify your action steps, trigger your "aha" moments, and create your plan for achieving success!

Take some time to think about your parents, and how they dealt with the Six Fears. Record your thoughts in your personal journal. Just by reviewing how your parents dealt with each fear, you may discover the source of some of your own fears.

The fear of POVERTY
The fear of CRITICISM at the bottom of most of one's worries
The fear of ILL HEALTH
The fear of LOSS OF LOVE OF SOMEONE
The fear of OLD AGE
The fear of DEATH

Now review what you wrote about your parents and how they dealt with fear. Turn your focus on your spouse or partner and then record how they deal with each of the Six Fears.

Now, with the knowledge of how your parents and your spouse or partner deal with fear, think about how their fears have impacted you in each of the six areas.

Finally, take some time to record what your thoughts are about each fear, how and when you have experienced each one, and one thing you will commit to do to minimize each of them in the future.

Then take some time to remember occasions when you were paralyzed by fear. Record them and how they impacted you physically and emotionally.

Now, can you remember any occasions when fear motivated you to do something?

Fear can either paralyze us or motivate us. Let's strive to answer fear in the future with motivation to succeed.

The Devil's Workshop—The Seventh Basic Evil

Record a time when you were influenced by a negative environment. (Remember the example of a child's funeral.)

Now record a time when you felt yourself influenced by a positive environment. (Remember the example of the party celebrating a WIN.)

Commit to become more aware of the way your environment influences you, and to use your positive mental attitude to help make your environment positive as well.

One Big Life

*The hardest thing to find in life is balance—especially
the more success you have, the more you look to
the other side of the gate. What do I need to stay
grounded, in touch, in love, connected, emotionally
balanced? Look within yourself.*

—CELINE DION

THIS BOOK HAS PURPOSEFULLY FOLLOWED THE CHAPTER OUT-
line of the original book, *Think and Grow Rich*, and addressed each of
Napoleon Hill's "13 proven steps to riches" through the eyes of women,
for women. While I believe the specific steps to riches and success
are the same for both men and women, I believe as women we fundamentally approach those principles with different beliefs, different
attitudes, and different strengths and weaknesses.

As I came to the end of writing *Think and Grow Rich for Women*,
I felt compelled to add a closing chapter that specifically addresses
an ongoing concern for almost every woman wanting to create a life
of success and significance.

Have you ever struggled with competing priorities in your life?
Have you ever been at work and felt guilty that you were not with your
spouse or children?

Have you ever been with your children and felt guilty about not get-
    ting your work done?

At the end of the day do you feel guilty about what you didn't get done
    at home or work, instead of feeling great about what you did ac-
    complish?

This chapter addresses the propaganda that surrounds women,
convincing them that they need to achieve and maintain "balance" in
their lives and filling them with guilt and worry when they don't feel
like they are "in balance" with their work and family lives. The result
is that many women find themselves in a constant state of guilt and
worry.

Just hearing someone complain about not having balance in her
life drives me nuts. Are you wondering why I have that reaction?

The very *Merriam-Webster's Collegiate Dictionary* definition of
the word identifies the problem as "the ability *to remain in a position
without losing control* or falling."

When do women ever "remain in a position"?

Let's demonstrate by doing a little exercise. Stand up with your
feet shoulder-width apart. Let your arms dangle at your sides, keeping
them motionless. Now close your eyes and be still, be balanced.

I ask you. How relative is the position you are now in to your daily
life? You are in balance, and you are not moving!

As women, we never stand still. We are in constant motion. In
addition to always moving we are continually making choices on how
we are spending our time, with whom we are spending it, all while we
are thinking about the ten other things we have waiting on our to-do
list. Some call this multitasking, others call it "out of balance."

Then we are bombarded with messages telling us that we should
be balanced, or that anyone with balance can "have it all."

And what is our reaction? Instant guilt or feelings of failure is the
answer if we are feeling anything other than perfectly balanced (and
I tend to throw things as well).

personally and professionally. I was still a newlywed and although I was rewriting my professional destiny, I still envisioned myself having kids relatively young. For as long as I could remember, I had known for certain that I was put on earth to be a mom. I never worried about how to manage the demands of a rising career with the responsibilities of being a parent. As far as I was concerned, I could not achieve my greatest success without having both as part of my life.

From one day to the next, I find myself as a caretaker, a tutor, a coach, an advocate, a confidante, and like most mothers, could not possibly condense the experience of parenthood into a series of words on a page. I have found many interesting parallels between being a parent and pursuing a life of professional success and influence, however. Leading by example, communication, and relationship management are essential skills for success as both a parent and a businesswoman. Organization and problem-solving skills and having the ability to draw out the strengths in others are equally important. Being able to navigate uncertainty and pivot in order to find the right resources and partners are part of both gigs as well. The uncompromising passion and love I have as a parent is complimented by the commitment and dedication I have to my business. This overlap makes it difficult to compartmentalize the professional and personal aspects of life.

As a partner at Pay Your Family First, our pursuit of daily opportunities and educational requirements around financial literacy has given me the ability to build a career promoting a cause that will positively impact the lives of my own children. The passion I have for one part of my life bleeds over into the other. As rewarding as this is, it also complicates the issue of trying to achieve balance between the two. In fact, I had not been a mom for very long and was still very early in my career when I sought out mentorship on how to do it. When I asked Sharon Lechter how to go about achieving balance, the insight I received could not have been more valuable.

What Sharon enlightened for me over lunch was the awareness I needed to release the burden of achieving work/life balance. Her guidance was that rather than focusing on how much time was spent on professional endeavors versus personal life, I should consider that achieving balance may be the wrong goal. All we can do is make the best choices we can, guided by our values, priorities, and ambitions. These choices are not always easy. But being present in the moment after making those decisions is the key. After thinking about the long-running guilt trip I had been on (and still find myself retracing some days) in connection with trying to find balance, it was a refreshing and relieving point of view.

The culture at Pay Your Family First is a testament to this philosophy. When I am with my children helping them with homework, reading to them, or even having playtime, that is what I am focusing on. My computer is sleeping and my phone is on silent. I volunteer in both of my children's classrooms every month, chair school events and programs, and help with fund-raisers. I work full-time, and then some, but still make the choices necessary to be an active part of my children's lives—during school and at home.

These choices may result in trade-offs with late nights, early mornings, or weekends when I catch up on my workload. My husband, children, and other family members know that I need the flexibility to make business a priority during these odd times in order to be fully present as a mom during my sons' school and sports activities. Not everyone will understand or relate to the willingness to make these trade-offs. Even today I am not always able to make them without hesitation. But I answer any doubt with the conviction that tainly, as you seek to transform your life, you may see some of the weaknesses create obstacles for you. You may not agree with all of them, but for the moment assume the following to be accurate.

WEAKNESSES

Women tend not to be as aggressive.
Women tend to be less confident.
Women tend to feel more personally responsible.
Women tend to put themselves last.

STRENGTHS

Women make great collaborators.
Women have greater empathy than men.
Women can tend to see the long-term vision better.
Women tend to be champions for others.

What if women chose to use their strengths to overcome their apparent weaknesses? Instead of trying to become more aggressive and focused on our personal advancement, why not choose a different strategy that works with our strengths? If women are much better fighters for others than they are for themselves, then let women come together and instead of fighting WITH each other, let them fight FOR each other.

Their weaknesses would disappear and their strengths would be magnified by the collective Mastermind of Women:

Women would use their empathy to become aggressive champions for OTHER women.

Women would use their collaborative skills to bolster each other's confidence.

Women, as a group, would take responsibility for the long-term vision, and achieve it together.

If women would stop fighting and pointing fingers at each other, and instead focus on celebrating each other and lifting up each other, miraculous things could and would start happening.

As we focus on our successes and helping each other, our generosity to each other will spill benefits around the globe.

As philanthropist Melinda Gates has said, "If you are successful, it is because somewhere, sometime, someone gave you a life or an idea that started you in the right direction. Remember also that you are indebted to life until you help some less fortunate person, just as you were helped."

By focusing on helping others, our generosity of spirit will spread positive energy wherever we go and will reap long-term benefits. Let's remember the old saying "a rising tide lifts all boats." Your goodwill will create a legacy for good and a lifetime of success and significance. You will have become a mentor, a cheerleader for others, a support system as well as a leader for other women, and a shining example of someone who successfully created One Big Life.

May you be blessed with success in all aspects of your ONE BIG LIFE!

Thank you.

Sharon Lechter

Afterword

THE MEN WHO ARE
TRUE CHAMPIONS FOR WOMEN

In writing *Think and Grow Rich for Women*, I purposely quoted only
Napoleon Hill and no other men. It was my goal to address Hill's principles of success through the eyes of women. It is important to know
that women cannot achieve true success without understanding how
important it is that they work together with men who can support
them and mentor them along the way. There are many incredible men
who are champions for women. They not only recognize the hugely
important role that women play in our economy, but applaud and help
pave the way for women to reach their utmost potential as leaders and
true success stories in their own rights.

I have asked some very special men who have not only influenced
me in my professional journey but have been true champions, and
ready mentors, for other women to share their thoughts about the importance of *Think and Grow Rich for Women*.

FROM THE NAPOLEON HILL FOUNDATION

One may ask why is a book for women being written more than seventy-five years after Napoleon Hill wrote *Think and Grow Rich*, arguably the most influential self-help book ever published?

At the beginning of the century, only a few women attended college and today women greatly exceed the number of men enrolled. Women's role in society has greatly increased and women often face challenges that men have not encountered.

Sharon Lechter, with her experience as an author (she coauthored fourteen Rich Dad Poor Dad books) and her background in the financial industry, gives her insight to help women today who want to expand their place in the economy. As a member of the President's Financial Literacy Advisory Council, a CPA, and an advocate of financial literacy, she is in an ideal environment to give timely advice.

Sharon shares her wisdom and the wisdom of women from diverse positions in life, from business executives to the presidency of a major university, to enable the reader to learn and be inspired to reach their God-given potential!

Sharon goes about her work with a passion, one of the reasons that her previous books have been bestsellers. *Think and Grow Rich for Women* is simply a book that needed to be written for today's woman to help her grow and serve others.

Don Green, CEO of the Napoleon Hill Foundation

FROM DR. CHARLES JOHNSON

Napoleon Hill was a man of great vision and remarkable perception.

He had an amazing ability to take massive concepts and mold them into facts that we all could understand and utilize for our betterment.

What Napoleon Hill lacked was the skill that required attention to detail. Two women provided those skills, without which he might never have had the enormous impact on our world and our lives that he did.

It was his stepmother who recognized this latent potential of her misdirected stepson. Without her guidance, Napoleon might well have continued his wayward life and become nothing more than a back-woods riffraff and delinquent (and never have realized the journalistic potential we have come to know and appreciate). It was she who talked him into giving up his pistol in exchange for a typewriter.

The other woman was a sweet but strong "old maid," my aunt, who was the de facto CEO of a large publishing firm in a tiny South Carolina town.

Annie Lou, who became Nap's wife, was endowed with great organizational skills and business acumen, which she used to direct Napoleon's writing skills and brilliance. (As an aside, it was Annie Lou who encouraged Napoleon to support my passion to attend medical school.)

It seems fitting that Sharon Lechter can now lend her well-defined knowledge and understanding of Napoleon's success principles to help women shatter any vestiges of the glass ceiling.

Charles Johnson, M.D., Napoleon Hill's nephew

FROM THE HILL FAMILY

In the 1940s, Rosa Lee Beeland made the last attempt to provide *Think and Grow Rich* with a feminine perspective. Her book *How to Attract Men and Money* failed to do either. The book did have merit but its title did not resonate well with post–World War II American women who had started to aspire to more than just a good marriage. Furthermore, the book's thinking and presentation was vintage Napoleon Hill with little feminine perspective until the "Dear Abby" chapters at the back of the book.

It was therefore with some reservation that I set about reading the manuscript for Sharon Lechter's *Think and Grow Rich for Women*. I felt that this book needed to be written; I just didn't think anyone could do it justice. I have been a fan of Sharon's work since reading the *Rich Dad Poor Dad* series; I should have known better.

Sharon did much more than just add a feminine perspective to my grandfather's monumental work; she rewrote it. Her new edition is now contemporary for the twenty-first century and reflects personal-development thinking by women that has evolved over the past seventy-five years. I was delighted by this new book. It adds value and breadth to Napoleon Hill's life work.

I believe that *Think and Grow Rich for Women* is the right book and written at the right time to bring Napoleon Hill's science of personal achievement to millions of women. It is destined to become a classic for all women with the desire to realize their potential.

Dr. James Blair (JB) Hill, Napoleon Hill's grandson

FROM TODAY'S THOUGHT LEADERS

Without question, one of the most inspirational and important books in my library is Napoleon Hill's *Think and Grow Rich*. I read it as a young entrepreneur, looking for guidance and reassurance. It had such an impact on my life and career that I have recommended it to thousands of readers of my own books as a must-read.

But it truly was a "man's world" when I first became acquainted with Hill's masterpiece during the 1960s. Fortunately for women, Sharon Lechter recognized that Napoleon Hill's steps to success apply across the board, understanding that women simply approach those steps differently.

With her grasp of the evolving roles of women in leadership and the workplace, Sharon has shared insights from more than a hundred successful women who demonstrate how these thirteen principles have helped them turn obstacles into opportunities.

To be sure, I will recommend this work to my daughters, granddaughters, and women of any age who are looking for inspiration as they make their mark on the world.

Harvey Mackay, author of the New York Times *#1 bestseller* Swim with the Sharks Without Being Eaten Alive

I began reading *Think and Grow Rich* in 1961. It has helped me earn millions of dollars and build a business that operates all over the world. I believe that I am one of the few people alive who has read from this book every day for over fifty years. When you consider that Napoleon Hill wrote in masculine gender and for the most part only interviewed men, you must agree it is quite incredible that no one has ever prepared this information for women before now. . . . Sharon Lechter deserves a medal for writing *Think and Grow Rich for Women*.

Think about it, and you will agree it is amazing that it has taken this long for someone to take the initiative to do what Sharon is doing. I have thousands of books in my library and when I'm asked for the top four or five books that I have read, *Think and Grow Rich* is always at the top of the list. This book is going to impact the lives of millions of women all over the world and rightly so, as the principles that both Napoleon Hill and Sharon write about are universal and will work for everyone everywhere. Any woman who makes the content of this book a part of her way of thinking, a part of her way of life, will accomplish every objective that comes to her mind.

When *Think and Grow Rich* was first placed in my hands, the gentleman who gave it to me said that the author of this book spent his entire life researching the lives of five hundred of the world's most successful individuals. It would be a prudent move on your part if you spent the rest of your life attempting to understand and apply what Napoleon Hill has written. In conclusion, permit me to suggest that you spend the rest of your life in an attempt to understand and apply what Sharon has written since she has spent the majority of her life in the same pursuit as Napoleon Hill.

Bob Proctor, chairman, the Proctor Gallagher Institute, author of You Were Born Rich, *and featured in* The Secret

■

Every woman intrinsically desires abundance, achievement, happiness, and health for herself and her family. She wants a future worthy of her that fulfills her God-given destiny. She wants to grow, expand, feel fully alive, and serve greatly with love. As Mary Kay Ash, founder and catalyst of Mary Kay Cosmetics told me once: "Every woman would rather be so excited and active doing great things that she would rather wear out than rust out." Historically, women were denied these basic human rights.

Times have changed. Thinking has changed.

As Dickens wrote in *A Tale of Two Cities*: "It was the best of times and the worst of times . . ." It's the worst of times if you let yourself get beat up by the nightly news and prognosticators of doom and gloom. It's the best of times, as you read deeply, absorb, and comprehend the timeless truths contained in this book. When you partake of this wonderful work that mingles the timeless success principles of Napoleon Hill with the practical and beautiful insights of Sharon Lechter and the other great women in this book, you become an even better you than you were before.

Dr. Napoleon Hill helped write us out of the Depression and stimulated this change to liberate women with his classic *Think and Grow Rich*. It opened the minds of all readers—male and female. With its hundreds of millions of readers and fans, I have met individuals around the world that personally told me their fortunes were launched, magnified, and multiplied by repetitive readings of *Think and Grow Rich*. It works for everyone who works it. I am proud to say it has helped me make millions in seven enterprise endeavors—including having sold more than 500,000,000 (that's a half billion) Chicken Soup for the Soul books, as its cocreator/author with Jack Canfield. After twenty years, our book still has rocking sales, is expanding into more products like *Chicken Soup for the Soul—Dog Food*, and a soon-to-be released major motion picture by Alcon. I am so thankful for the original book and now am even more elated that my beloved wife, Crystal Dwyer Hansen, is a contributor to this new volume.

Now, thanks to the effervescent brilliance of Sharon Lechter and her clear visionary leadership to rewrite this classic specifically for women, I predict that the women of the world are about to positively change and improve their life and lifestyles immensely. Women readers will truly discover and energize their full potential in business and in life. In this book women will have a philosophical touchstone to help them manifest their highest dreams, loftiest desires, and work together in mastermind groups to make 100 percent of humanity economically, physically, and socially successful.

The world can work, if women can take more of the leadership role they're destined for. Knowing and applying these life-changing principles helps make that happen.

My vision for Sharon's masterpiece is that more than one billion women read it in this decade to end poverty. I understand it is a big goal—basically one-eighth of our total world population—but I am a big thinker and desirous of the best for women. Women on a mission to share this with other women are unstoppable. Our friend Nobel Prize winner Dr. Mohammed Yunus says: "Poverty belongs in only one place—a museum." So, let's end poverty and with this book let's together create unlimited abundance, joy, and readers soul fulfillment as they manifest their secretly held desires for immense good.

Mark Victor Hansen, cocreator of Chicken Soup for the Soul *and* One Minute Millionaire

■

In 1908, Napoleon Hill was charged with the unique opportunity of meeting with that era's thought leaders to discover the actionable steps and thoughts needed to create a life of sustained abundance.

Fast-forward more than a hundred years and we find Sharon Lechter carrying the torch for a modern movement of today.

As I am sure you would agree, this book has distilled amazing insights, ideas, and direction to create a life that most will only dream.

The question is, what will we do with such knowledge?

Just as an unplayed piano makes no sound, non-applied wisdom gains few results.

Within your hands you have a literal map for anything you may desire from life.

Let today become the catalyst you've been waiting for to discover your personal treasure trove for success.

Question: Where could your life be tomorrow by applying what you know today?

Use this book as your guide, and before you know it—you may just separate yourself from the 99 percent who dream of success to that top 1 percent who actually achieves it.

Congratulations in advance—you are a champion!

Greg S. Reid, best-selling author of Stickability, *coauthor of* Think and Grow Rich: Three Feet from Gold, *filmmaker, and motivational speaker*

■

FULL PARTNERSHIP FOR WOMEN: Sharon Lechter and I have each spent the past forty years traveling to global locations no one can pronounce in any language, as well as federal and state capitals. We have lectured and educated leaders at the top of nations, to leaders in obscure tribal villages, advocating full partnership for women, as women are still thought of in many nations as no more than "shoes" that a man also owns, or collateral damage because the woman fell in love with someone outside her family's station or tribe. More than 2 billion women cannot own property, vote, or enjoy anything close to "full partnership" either inside the home or outside the home life. For two billion women reside in a life of involuntary incarceration and male bondage, lacking any voice or possibility to pursue their own dreams. Together Sharon and I work tirelessly for these women and for the unborn baby girls to follow us.

Uncle Nappy—having grown up on Napoleon Hill's LAP—"he" would endorse to his billion readers *Think and Grow Rich for Women* by Sharon Lechter—and so do I. Every reader of *The Secret, Think and Grow Rich,* or *Chicken Soup for the Soul* must read *Think and Grow Rich for Women* and give away copies to everyone. Free two billion women from their prison without walls. Provide them with the information and tools that will empower them to change their paradigms, to create economic freedom for themselves and the women who follow.

Berny Dohrmann, founder, CEO Space International, and best-selling author

■

For centuries now, women in households have been the cornerstone of stability. In the past one hundred years, women have become innovators in top industry companies around the world. In the future, women will become the world leaders, instilling global peace and prosperity for mankind. Sharon Lechter's new book, *Think and Grow Rich for Women,* is a must-read game changer!

Sharon Lechter is a best-selling author, industry icon, amazing mother, and ultra-successful entrepreneur. Her greatest asset is her ability to bring out the best in everyone who enters into her presence. With her new book, *Think and Grow Rich for Women,* her beautiful spirit will now touch millions worldwide. I could not think of a better combination for this message than Sharon Lechter and the Napoleon Hill Foundation. The timing is divine!

Sharon Lechter is taking the bold step to introduce the world to the critical message needed in today's global economy—to inspire women to step outside of their comfort zone and become brilliant world business leaders. The words in this book will change the thoughts of millions of women, to forever know it is okay to become your very best in business.

The message of Napoleon Hill has personally impacted my life to become everything that I am today. I launched Powerteam International to become the world's leader in success education for entrepreneurs. My faithful vision for Sharon Lechter is to help her take her message to five hundred million women worldwide.

Sharon Lechter has consistently elevated others with her presence. Now that vision will live on forever in the words of this masterpiece. It is so exciting to know the legacy of Napoleon Hill's message will be taken to an even higher level through the *Think and Grow Rich for Women* movement.

I urge you to share this book with everyone you know. The stories will inspire your heart and move you to become your very best in everything you do!

Bill Walsh, America's small-business expert and author of
The Obvious

Just a hundred years ago, it was very normal for a young man to find a job as an apprentice while his sister stayed home taking care of her household duties, as a young girl should. It was perfectly normal and accepted by most who saw this as a woman's role in society and family settings. While young men grew their knowledge, skills, and confidence, many women were held back from becoming all they could become in order to fit into society's expectation and dogma of the era.

Well, times have changed and now there are many women who have broken the mold and shattered the notion that a woman's place is in the kitchen raising her children while she waits for her husband to bring home the money to take care of her family.

Sharon Lechter is one of those women who has learned how to step into her power and utilize all of her God-given abilities to shatter the financial glass ceiling and find balance between family, finances, and success.

While one hundred years ago it was normal for young men to find their mentors and teachers, Sharon is a new breed of woman who is mentoring and empowering women to find their inner and outer power to achieve the life success and balance they are fully capable of achieving.

Think and Grow Rich for Women will show every woman example after example that it is not your circumstances or your resources that control your destiny. It is your attitude, mind-set, and resourcefulness that will.

Take this book and study it. Reading it will motivate you, while studying it will empower and inspire you. Pay close attention to how each of the women featured has overcome her own limitations to achieve a life of purpose, meaning, and success.

It's now your time to release whatever has held you back from living the biggest and best version of your life, so that you feel fulfilled, in control, and empowered to achieve all your goals and dreams.

John Assaraf, CEO of PraxisNow, featured in The Secret, *and* New York Times *best-selling author of* The Answer *and* Having It All

Each woman, and every person, has a deep-down desire to fulfill their full potential for health, happiness, and abundance.

Sharon Lechter, one of the most respected and esteemed authorities in the world, has now provided for women the most powerful and practical system for success ever discovered.

There has never been a better time for women than today. Their special gifts in every area are enriching and transforming our society.

With this remarkable book, each woman, each reader receives a proven formula that she can apply immediately to accomplish more, sooner, than she may have ever dreamed possible.

The great discovery is that you become what you think about— most of the time. With Napoleon Hill's 13 Principles as explained by Sharon Lechter, you learn how to think the very best way possible, liberating your full potential for extraordinary living.

Brian Tracy, professional speaker, author, success expert and CEO of Brian Tracy International[TM]

■

I am so honored and blessed by these wonderful men. They truly are champions to me and to all the women who seek their counsel and mentorship. But I would be remiss not to mention the two most important men in my life. Without their love and support, I would not be the woman I am today. First, my father, who told me that I could do, and excel at, anything I wanted to do. His entrepreneurial spirit and endeavors allowed me to grow up in an environment that had no "glass ceilings," where business endeavors that served a need or solved a problem for society were rewarded with success . . . regardless of the gender of the owner.

And then there is my husband of thirty-three years, Michael, the man who has been by my side and championed me and my work without question or disbelief. He has been my mentor, my counsel (legal and otherwise), my sounding board for all my ideas, my coach, and most of all, my cheerleader. He is truly my partner in love and life.

I hope that you have champions in your life who are there to catch you when you fall, open doors for you along the way, and cheer for you with every success.

Acknowledgments

This book would not have been possible without the lifetime endeavor of Napoleon Hill and his brilliance in writing the quintessential book on success, *Think and Grow Rich*. Its message is as valid today as it was when it was originally published in 1937. I want to thank Don Green, the CEO of the Napoleon Hill Foundation, and its board of directors for the incredible privilege of granting me the opportunity to honor Hill's work and to share its impact for women through the eyes of successful women.

I thank Napoleon Hill's grandchildren, Terry Hill Gocke and Dr. James Blair Hill, whose support of *Think and Grow Rich for Women* and its message means the world to me. And to Dr. Charlie Johnson, who called Napoleon Hill "Uncle Nap" and considered him the father figure he never had, for believing in me and for his tremendous support of my work with the Foundation.

I want to acknowledge women around the globe who have been

trailblazers creating success not only for themselves but opening the path for other women to follow them. Within the pages of *Think and Grow Rich for Women* you will find insights and wisdom from more than three hundred women. I want to particularly thank the women who dedicated their time to write their own personal stories so that you might not only find hope and encouragement, but realize that we all need to help each other along the way. They are Margie Aliprandi, DC Cordova, Suzi Dafnis, Rita Davenport, Dina Dwyer, Yvonne Fedderson, Paula Fellingham, Marsha Firestone, Crystal Dwyer Hansen, Mary Gale Hinrichson, Donna Johnson, Loral Langemeier, Sara O'Meara, Michelle Patterson, Dr. Pamela Peeke, Michelle Robson, Donna Root, Karen Russo, Beverly Sallee, Kimberly Schulte, Adriana Trigiani, and Judith Williamson.

While Napoleon Hill is the only man quoted in the body of the book, I want to thank the men who have impacted my life and the lives of millions of people around the world and shared their support for *Think and Grow Rich for Women* in the afterword to the book—John Assaraf, Berny Dohrmann, Don Green, Mark Victor Hansen, Dr. James Blair Hill, Dr. Charlie Johnson, Harvey Mackay, Bob Proctor, Greg S. Reid, Brian Tracy, and Bill Walsh.

I give a special thank you to Margie Aliprandi, who not only shared her own story but reached out and helped gather wisdom from women leaders from across her industry of direct selling. These women are proof positive that you can create success with the right definite purpose, the right initiative, and the right team supporting you.

On a more personal note, I thank our team members at Pay Your Family First and the Napoleon Hill Foundation for their never-ending support: Angela Totman, Kristin Thomas, Kyle Davidsen, Michael Lechter, Robert T. Johnson Jr., and Annedia Sturgill. In addition, I appreciate the encouragement and assistance from Allyn and Greg S. Reid, Bill Gladstone, Catherine Spyres, Greg Tobin, and Cevin Bryerman. And to all the women whom I admire and have had the pleasure of knowing, including my sisters of Women Presidents Organization, who helped me realize that this book was needed to help other women seeking success, and especially to my dear friend Elaine Ralls, whose philosophy of "One Big Life" was the inspiration for my final message in the book.

I thank the entire team at the Tarcher imprint of the Penguin Group for their faith and excitement for the book: to George Joel Fotinos for your encouragement and advocacy, to Gabrielle Moss for your enthusiastic response to the first manuscript, to Brianna Yamashita and Kevin Howell for your exciting marketing ideas, and to the rest of their team who have helped make *Think and Grow Rich for Women* a great success and available to women around the world.

And to my loving family who has "loved me through the process" for all the books I have had the honor of writing. Especially to Michael, my partner in love and life . . . thank you for being you!

Sharon Lechter

Notes

1. http://thenextweb.com/socialmedia/2012/01/24/the-top-30-stats
   -you-need-to-know-when-marketing-to-women/
   http://www.wlp.givingto.vt.edu/wealth/
2. http://www.she-conomy.com/facts-on-women
   http://thenextweb.com/socialmedia/2012/01/24/the-top-30-stats
   -you-need-to-know-when-marketing-to-women/
3. http://www.she-conomy.com/facts-on-women
4. http://www.nielsen.com/us/en/newswire/2013/u-s--women-
   control-the-purse-strings.html
5. http://thenextweb.com/socialmedia/2012/01/24/the-top-30-stats
   -you-need-to-know-when-marketing-to-women/
6. http://hbr.org/web/special-collections/insight/marketing-that-
   works/the-female-economy
7. Boston College Center on Wealth Philanthropy 2011

8. http://www.catalyst.org/knowledge/women-ceos-fortune-1000
9. http://www.catalyst.org/knowledge/statistical-overview-women
   -workplace
10. http://www.catalyst.org/media/companies-more-women-board
    -directors-experience-higher-financial-performance-according
    -latest
11. www.catalyst.org/knowledge/women-boards
12. http://www.catalyst.org/knowledge/womens-earnings-and-income
13. Ibid.
14. Ibid.
15. Ibid.
16. http://www.deloitte.com/assets/Dcom-Greece/dttl_ps_
    genderdividend_130111.pdf
17. http://www.womenlegislators.org/women-legislator-facts.php;
    www.guide2womenleaders.com
18. http://www.forbes.com/sites/moiraforbes/2013/03/06/women-and
    -the-new-definition-of-career-success/
19. http://www.huffingtonpost.com/2013/07/03/what-success-means
    -to-women_n_3536190.html
20. As quoted in the article Wangari Maathai: "You Strike the
    Woman . . ." by Priscilla Sears; published in the quarterly *In
    Context* #28 (Spring 1991).
21. http://news.harvard.edu/gazette/story/2013/05/winfreys-
    commencement-address/
22. Ibid.
23. Ibid.
24. Ibid.
25. http://www.huffingtonpost.com/tory-burch/empowering-women
    -through-_b_2957017.html
26. http://samasource.org/company/our-founder/#sthash.ImgXulmz
    .dpuf.
27. Women Matter Report, McKinsey & Company, 2013
28. http://www.upi.com/Business_News/2013/06/18/Survey-Most

-women-business-leaders-are-team-players/UPI-82881371588799/#ixzz2fv2khlSO

29. http://www.helenfisher.com/downloads/articles/07leadership.pdf
30. http://www.psychologicalscience.org/index.php/news/releases/
    depression-and-negative-thoughts.html
31. http://www.jenniferhawthorne.com/articles/change_your_
    thoughts.html
32. http://www.huffingtonpost.com/bj-gallagher/shakti-gawain-is
    -still-li_b_1840718.html
33. http://www.drjudithorloff.com/_blog/Dr_Judith_Orloff's_Blog/
    post/Do_You_Trust_Your_Inner_Voice
34. http://www.wikihow.com/Tell-the-Difference-Between-Fear-and
    -Intuition
35. http://www.alibrown.com/blog/2013/09/26/%E2%80%9Cthe
    -most-important-time-of-day-for-entrepreneurs%E2%80%9D
    -by-ali-brown/
36. http://www.dailymail.co.uk/femail/article-1342075/The-guilty
    -time-generation-How-96-women-feel-ashamed-day.html.

The Purpose of the Napoleon Hill Foundation Is to . . .

- Advance the concept of private enterprise offered under the American System
- Teach individuals by formula how they can rise from humble beginnings to positions of leadership in their chosen professions
- Assist young men and women to set goals for their own lives and careers
- Emphasize the importance of honesty, morality, and integrity as the cornerstone of Americanism
- Aid in the development of individuals to help them reach their own potential
- Overcome the self-imposed limitations of fear, doubt, and procrastination

- Help people rise from poverty, physical handicaps, and other disadvantages to high positions, wealth, and to acquire the true riches of life
- Motivate individuals to motivate themselves to high achievements

THE NAPOLEON HILL FOUNDATION

www.naphill.org

www.thinkandgrowrichforwomen.com

*A not-for-profit educational institution dedicated to
making the world a better place in which to live.*

Next Steps

Think and Grow Rich for Women shares the 13 Steps to Success for women through the eyes and experience of women who have created lives of success and significance. Now it is your turn! Sharon Lechter and her partners have developed an arsenal of resources to jump-start your journey to personal and professional fulfillment. Take action today by visiting www.sharonlechter.com/women to get started!

THINK AND GROW RICH FOR WOMEN WORKBOOK

Download this interactive resource, which includes all of the pivotal questions asked in *Think and Grow Rich for Women* and enables you to document your journey and memorialize your process as you pursue that One Big Life that you deserve. Download the workbook today using promo code GUIDEME at www.sharonlechter/women.

AUTHOR'S BOOK SALON

Join Sharon Lechter's Book Salon, where she guides you through *Think and Grow Rich for Women* chapter by chapter, addressing your questions and coaching you through the Success Principles. This series of online webinars and videos will share the steps that you can take now and the things you should stop doing today. Commit to your future today and learn from a master advisor and entrepreneur at sharonlechter.com/women.

TRAIN YOUR BRAIN FOR SUCCESS

AUTOSUGGESTION

Take the mystery out of Autosuggestion with online resources and training tools. Your personal trainer for the mind, this program helps you remove the mental obstacles that may be preventing you from overcoming fear, achieving your goals, growing your business, and making more money. With these programs, you have the tools and guidance needed to effectively employ Autosuggestion in your own life—creating the subconscious platform from which to build your foundation for success!

CREATE YOUR OWN MASTERMIND

Are the right people surrounding you to accelerate your path to success? Create or expand your own Mastermind group, attracting successful minds and spirits that will inspire and encourage you as you set goals, create plans for achievement, and work through the obstacles that may stand in your way. Your Mastermind group will give you the power of many, the experience of others, and one of the most powerful resources on your journey to success. Learn how you can create your own Mastermind!

COACHING PROGRAMS

In keeping with Hill's Mastermind principle, the One Big Life coaching program positions you to leverage the experience, expertise, and insights of women who have defined their life's purpose and successfully pursue this purpose through use of Hill's 13 Principles.

ONE-ON-ONE MENTORING

Are you looking for that catalyst to propel you down your path to success and significance? You can leverage the wisdom and strategies that Sharon Lechter has used to lead two of the largest brands on the planet while staying true to her personal mission and being of service to global communities.

Through Sharon's one-on-one mentoring program, you will learn directly from the expert entrepreneur, money mastery advocate, businesswoman, philanthropist, and mother. Sharon dedicates herself to identifying and supporting your true purpose while accelerating your progress on your journey to success.

YOUR FREE GIFT

In your search for answers, are you sure you are asking the right question?

Our free gift to you . . . *The Real Question—The Story of Why Not?*

Sharon Lechter reveals the one question that may be more important than any other . . . to opening doors, uncovering possibilities, and establishing the framework for becoming your best you. This one question has been a key factor in Sharon's own success. It offers a new perspective when faced with challenges and the vision to turn obstacles into opportunities.

Visit www.sharonlechter.com/women and check it out using promo code ANSWERTHIS for a *free* download of the most important question you will ever ask yourself.

WE WANT TO HEAR YOUR STORY!

Visit www.sharonlechter.com/women to share your inspiration, your challenges, your triumphs, and how you pursue your definite purpose each day. Whether you are just starting or well on your way to your One Big Life, there is a community of women waiting to support you, be lifted up by you, and to guide you down the path to living a life of success and significance.

Your story may be just the message that inspires another woman to take action today!

THE FUTURE IS YOUR CHOICE!

Visit www.sharonlechter.com/women to create your personalized blueprint.

WOMEN REFERENCED BY CHAPTER

Last Name	First Name	Chapter
Abramson	Jill	9
Adams	Abigail	6
Akasha	Nan	14
Al Qasimi	Sheikha Lubna	7
Aliprandi	Margie	7
Altschul	Randi	5
Amanpour	Christiane	9
Anderson	Marian	5
Anderson	Mary	5
Annis	Barbara	1
Angelou	Maya	1, 4, 10, 12
Antrim	Minna	13
Ash	Mary Kay	1, 6, 14
Auf der Maur	Melissa	11
Avant	Taurea	9
Avila	Janine	9
Bacall	Lauren	5
Balk	Faina	9
Banks	Gloria Mayfield	9
Bardot	Brigitte	14
Barr	Roseanne	10
Barra	Mary	9
Barrett	Barbara	4
Barrymore	Drew	12
Bateman	Deborah	9
Beck	Martha	12, 14
Besant	Annie	12
Betancourt	Novalena	9
Black	Cathie	9

Blakely	Sara	1
Blackmore	Susan	12
Bojaxhiu	Anjezë Gonxhe (Mother Teresa)	1, 10
Bolen	Jean Shinoda	13
Bombeck	Erma	12
Bresch	Heather	9
Brewer	Jan	3
Brewer	Rosalind	9
Brothers	Dr. Joyce	13
Brown	Ali	9, 13
Brown	Brené	6
Brown	Tina	9
Bündchen	Gisele	13
Burch	Tory	1
Burns	Ursula M.	9
Burt	Clarissa	7
Bush	Laura	9
Bush	Sophia	14
Byrne	Rhonda	11
Cacciatore	Tess	2
Cahalan	Susannah	12
Calabrese	Karyn	14
Cashore	Kristin	10
Chan	Jannie	9
Chanel	Coco	10
Chatzky	Jean	14, 15
Chavez	Anna Marie	6
Cheng	Eva	9
Chu	Chin-Ning	8
Chua	Amy	15
Chua	Yvonne	1
Chukwuemeka	Sylvia	9

Chung	Young Hee	9
Ciccone	Madonna	10
Clark	Helen	9
Coale	Onyx	9
Collins	Dana	9
Connelly	Anna	5
Coover	Kathy	9
Cordova	DC	11
Couric	Katie	9
Crowley	Katherine	9
Culhane	Marion	9
Curie	Marie	5
Dafnis	Suzi	4
Davenport	Rita	2, 14
Davis	Bette	14
De Angelis	Barbara	3, 12
de Kirchner	Cristina Fernandez	9
DeGeneres	Ellen	9
de Girardin	Delphine	13
Dekle	Dawn	9
Devers	Gail	2
Diaz	Cameron	14
Dickinson	Emily	2, 5, 14
Dion	Celine	15
Dlamini-Zuma	Nkosazana	9
Dole	Elizabeth	6
Donovan	Marion	5
Dove	Rita	5
Drexler	Peggy	1
Dwyer	Dina	3
Earhart	Amelia	7, 8
Edelman	Marian Wright	8
Elster	Kathy	9

Everett	Kimmy	9
Faust	Drew	9
Fawcett	Farrah	12
Fedderson	Yvonne	2
Feinstein	Ann	9
Fellingham	Paula	8, 9
Ferguson	Marilyn	12
Fine	Marjorie	9
Finney	Janine	9
Fiorina	Carly	7
Firestone	Marsha	9
Fisher	Helen E.	12
Foinant	Yvonne	9
Fonda	Jane	11
Forbes	Moira	9
Ford	Shelby	9
Fritz	Joanne	6
Gallagher	B. J.	13
Gandhi	Indira	1
García	Juliet V.	9
Gates	Melinda	15
Gawain	Shakti	13
Gersh	Lisa	9
Gifford	Kathie Lee	7, 9
Gilbert	Elizabeth	10
Gocke	Terry Hill	F
Goodman	Ellen	11
Goodrich	Richelle	8
Graham	Bette Nesmith	5
Graham	Katharine	4
Gray	Emma	1, 14
Greer	Germaine	15

Women Referenced by Chapter

Maathai	Wangari	1
Macy	Anne Sullivan	5
Magie	Elizabeth	5
Mansfield	Katherine	3
Mantel	Hilary	11
Marble	Sara	9
Martin	Joel	5
Masters	Sybilla	5
Matz	Allison Adler	9
Mayer	Marissa	9
Mayfield	Karen	9
McBride	Martina	2
McNeill	Ann	7
Mead	Margaret	9
Meir	Golda	6, 9
Mendeloff	Liora	2
Merkel	Angela	9
Mesch	Debra	1
Meynell	Alice	3
Midler	Bette	15
Minden	Eliza Gaynor	14
Mirren	Helen	11
Missett	Judi Sheppard	6
Mitchell	Pat	9
Monnar	Ana	9
Monroe	Marilyn	8, 13
Morrison	Denise	9
Morrissey	Mary Manin	14
Moses	Anna Mary Robertson	3
Muirhead	Lori	9
Napolitano	Janet	9
Nichols	Lisa	11

Sirleaf	Ellen Johnson	9
Sly	Susan	9
Smiley	Monica	9
Smith	Mari	9
Sontag	Susan	15
Spence	Betty	9
Steinem	Gloria	6
Stowe	Harriet Beecher	8
Sue	Marsha Petrie	14
Sullivan	Teresa	4
Sumpter	Shanda	7
Tatum	Beverly Daniel	9
Taylor	Mikki	9
Thatcher	Margaret	1, 4, 9
Tilghman	Shirley	9
Totman	Angela	6, 15
Trigiani	Adriana	F
Trottenberg	Tracey	8
Ulmer	Jackie	9
Van Susteren	Greta	9
Vanderveldt	Ingrid	6
Von Ebner-Eschenbach	Marie	5
Von Tobel	Alexa	9
Wakefield	Ruth	5
Walker	Alice	14
Walters	Barbara	9
Wang	Juno	9
Wang	Vera	15
Warren	Kay	2
Weinstein	Sharon	9
Welch	Florence	11
Weldon	Fay	11

About the Author

Sharon Lechter, CPA, CGMA, is an international expert on money and entrepreneurship as well as a respected author, philanthropist, educator, international speaker, mother, and grandmother. She is the founder and CEO of Pay Your Family First, a financial education organization. President George W. Bush recognized her lifelong passion as an education advocate when he appointed her to the first President's Advisory Council on Financial Literacy. She served both Presidents Bush and Obama in that capacity, advising them on the need for financial literacy education. In 2009, Sharon was appointed to the American Institute of Certified Public Accountants (AICPA) National CPA Financial Literacy Commission as a national spokesperson on the topic of financial literacy. And in 2014, the AICPA designated her as a Financial Literacy Champion. In 2013, she successfully led an initiative to change the laws related to financial literacy education requirements for high school graduation in Arizona.

Sharon is the coauthor of the international bestseller *Rich Dad Poor Dad*, along with fourteen other books in the Rich Dad series.

About the Author

During her ten years as cofounder and CEO of the Rich Dad Company, she led the organization and its brand into an international powerhouse. Her recent best-selling books, *Think and Grow Rich: Three Feet from Gold* and *Outwitting the Devil* were both written in cooperation with the Napoleon Hill Foundation. In 2013, she released *Save Wisely, Spend Happily*, for the AICPA.

A committed philanthropist, Sharon gives back to the world communities as both a volunteer and benefactor. She is a member of the Business Advisory Board for EmpowHer, a company dedicated to women's health issues. Sharon also serves on the national board of Women Presidents Organization, and the national board of Childhelp. She volunteers as an instructor for Thunderbird School of Global Management for both its Artemis Program and its partnership with the U.S. State Department and Goldman Sachs 10,000 Women program.

Sharon has been consistently recognized for her tireless work for women. She was honored in 2012 with the Positively Powerful Women award for Philanthropic Leadership. In 2013, the *Phoenix Business Journal* selected her as of one its 25 Dynamic Women in Business, National Bank of Arizona chose her as its 2013 Woman of the Year, and the *Arizona Business Magazine* highlighted her as one of the 50 Most Influential Women in Arizona Business.

Sharon lives in Paradise Valley, Arizona, with her husband of thirty-three years, Michael, and they enjoy spending time at the Cherry Creek Lodge, on their ranch in Pleasant Valley, Arizona. For more information on Sharon, please visit www.sharonlechter.com.